Cumberland County Pennsylvania

Church Records of the 18th Century

F. Edward Wright

HERITAGE BOOKS
2008

HERITAGE BOOKS
AN IMPRINT OF HERITAGE BOOKS, INC.

Books, CDs, and more—Worldwide

For our listing of thousands of titles see our website
at
www.HeritageBooks.com

Published 2008 by
HERITAGE BOOKS, INC.
Publishing Division
100 Railroad Ave. #104
Westminster, Maryland 21157

Copyright © 1994 F. Edward Wright

All rights reserved. No part of this book may be reproduced or transmitted in any form or by any means, electronic or mechanical, including photocopying, recording or by any information storage and retrieval system without written permission from the author, except for the inclusion of brief quotations in a review.

International Standard Book Numbers
Paperbound: 978-1-58549-279-4
Clothbound: 978-0-7884-7691-4

CONTENTS

Preface v
Introduction vii
Marriage Records of First Presbyterian Church, 1785 - 1800 1
Records of Ziegler's Church 17
Bobenmayer (St. Peter's) Church 19
Poplar (St. John's) Evangelical Lutheran Church 21
Big Spring Presbyterian Church 27
Baptisms of German Reformed Church in Shippenstown 41
First Evangelical Lutheran Church, Carlisle 56
Trindle Spring Lutheran Church 62
St. Stephen's (Longsdorf's) Evangelical Lutheran Church 65
Pastoral Record of the Rev. John Conrad Bucher 71
Session Book of Middle Spring Presbyterian Church 87
Marriages and Baptisms Performed by Rev. Cuthbertson 91
Marriage Licenses Issued by John Agnew, Esq. 95
Tombstone Inscriptions of Meeting-House Springs 98
Marriages by Rev. Robert Cooper 99
Marriage Bonds from the Zeamer Collection 101
Marriage and Deaths from the Carlisle Gazette 103
Baptisms Performed at Carlisle and Recorded in the Register of St. James Episcopal Church, Lancaster, Pennsylvania 120
Index 121

PREFACE

This is a collection of church registers and pastoral records of births, marriages and deaths in Cumberland County of the 18th Century.

Our goal in gathering material for this project was to aid the genealogist by providing a single source of records. We find that many do not know the religious affiliation of their ancestors or the specific church; they do not know if records exist or where to find the records, if they do exist. Hopefully we have made the quest much easier. In looking for the records of a church one is burdened by the variations in church names and townships used by the various repositories. We hope that our approach eliminates all of these stumbling blocks.

Other societies and repositories whose records we researched include the Evangelical and Reformed Historical Society, Lancaster; the Historical Society of Pennsylvania, Philadelphia; the Cumberland County Historical Society, Carlisle; and the A.R. Wentz Library, Theological Seminary, Gettysburg (who permitted us to publish some of their translated records).

Of enormous help in preparing the German church records has been the extensive research performed by Dr. Charles Glatfelter in his published work, *Pastors and People, Volume 1, Pastors and Congregations*. We have referred to it in locating and identifying the German congregations.

F. Edward Wright
Westminster, Maryland 1994

INTRODUCTION

Compared to other early counties of Pennsylvania, Cumberland County had a much greater settlement of Scotch-Irish in its formative years. Hence there were a great number of Presbyterian church founded in the 18th century. Unfortunately only a few of the registers have survived. Churches were established at Silver Springs, Meeting House Springs, Big Spring and Middle Spring. Most of the German (Lutheran and Reformed) records seem to have survived.

PRESBYTERIANS

Middle House Springs

This congregation was formed in 1734. No records of the 18th century have survived for Middle House Springs; we include some tombstone inscriptions of the cemetery of Middle-House Springs, taken from Egle's *Notes and Queries*, Third Series, vol. II, pp. 478-479.

Silvers' Spring

This congregation was also formed in 1734. No records of Silvers' Spring have survived for the 18th century.

Big Spring

The neighborhood of the Big Spring organized a congregation not later than the spring of 1737. Pastors include the following: Thomas Craighead (1738 - 1739); Supplies: James Lyon of Ireland and others; John Blair, D.D. (1742 -ca. 1749 (perhaps 1755 or later)); George Duffield, D.D. (1759 - 1769); William Linn (1777 - 1784); Samuel Wilson (1787 - 1799). Rev. Wilson died March 4, 1799. Supplies following the death of Rev. Samuel Wilson include: Robert Wilson, Thomas Greer, P. Davidson, Matthew Brown, Mr. Burck, William Wilson, Mr. Anderson, Mr. Linn, Mr. Herron, Samuel Waugh, Mr. Kennedy, Dr. Cooper, Mr. Williams and Robert Logan.

In his *History of the Big Spring Presbyterian Church, Newville, PA. 1737-1898*, Gilbert Swope draws upon the papers of Rev. Samuel Wilson, pastor from 1787 to 1799, found in the garret of one of his descendants, along with later papers. About 1789 Rev. Samuel Wilson made lists of members and adherents of the church dividing them into districts, and over each district, an elder was placed. Theses lists give the ages of the persons, and states whether they were in communion, not in communion and whether they were baptized. Swope indicates those communicant members by an asterisk (not shown in our work). Although no year is shown on the original papers, Swope bases the date on known dates of births of persons on the list. Following these "communion lists" are the marriages performed by Rev. Wilson.

Middle Spring

The Middle Spring congregation was formed around 1740. Only the Session Book has survived for the 18th century, and the pastoral records of Rev. Robert Cooper, 1786-1794.

First Presbyterian Church, Carlisle
This church was formed about 1753. Only the marriage records have survived, beginning in 1785; these were originally published in *Pennsylvania Archives*, Second Series, Vol. VIII.

Rev. John Cuthbertson's Diary, 1751-1791
Rev. Cuthbertson was a Reformed Presbyterian minister serving in Adams, York, Cumberland, Lancaster and other counties. Most Presbyterians of this region belonged to the main branch of colonial Presbyterianism as represented by the Synod of Philadelphia, but there was also a congregation of Reformed Presbyterians, or Covenanters. Rev. Cuthbertson was send from Scotland to minister to Scottish Coventers in America in 1751. He kept a diary from 1751 to 1791. From his entries we know he married about 600 persons and baptized over 1800 children. Register of Marriages and Baptisms performed by Rev. John Cuthbertson, 1751-1791, by S. Hellen Fields, was originally printed in 1934, reprinted 1983 by Genealogical Publishing Company, Baltimore. Only those baptisms and marriages which were performed in Cumberland County are included here.

ANGLICAN CHURCH

St. John's Episcopal Church of Carlisle was organized ca. 1754 and the first church built in 1765. The are no known records for the 1700s. In the register of St. James's Episcopal Church of Lancaster County (founded in 1744) are found baptisms performed in 1755 at Carlisle. They are included here.

GERMAN LUTHERAN AND REFORMED

Conrad Bucher organized a German Reformed congregation in Carlisle in 1763. Baptisms and marriages performed in Carlisle are included in this book up through 1769. He died in 1780. Other Reformed minister were William Runkel (1777 - 1784) and Samuel Dubendorff (1790 - 1795). The location of the First Reformed Church today is First United Church of Christ, 30 North Pitt Street, Carlisle.

The first Lutheran minister in Carlisle appears to be Jacob Goering (1776-1783), following by George Butler (ca. 1783 - ca. 1786), Frederick Schaefer (1786 - 1790) and Adam Henry Meyer (1790 - 1793). The location of the Lutheran Church is First Church, East High and South Bedford streets, Carlisle. The register was begun in 1788; records of marriages, burial and baptisms have survived up to 1793. These records have been translated by Mrs. Pearl Reddig Fleck with corrections and additions by the A. R. Wentz Library, Lutheran Theological Seminary, Gettysburg.

Frieden's (Peace) Church
The Reformed congregation was organized in 1793 with the opening a register in 1797. Anthony Hautz was pastor from 1793 to 1804. In 1806 Lutherans joined in a Union Church at Friedens. The Reformed

congregation today is St. Paul's United Church of Christ, 626 Williams Grove Road, Mechanicsburg. The Lutheran Church is St. John's, 5 South Eberly Avenue, Shiremanstown.

Langsdorf Lutheran (St. Stephen's), Silver Spring Township
This congregation was organized ca. 1771. The register was begun in 1789 by Frederick Schaefer which includes records earlier baptisms. Pastors were Jacob Goering (1776 - 1783), probably George Butler (ca. 1783 - ca. 1786), Frederick Schaefer (1786 - 1790) and Adam Henry Meyer (1790 - 1793). Today the church is St. Stephen's Church, located at 30 Carlisle Pike, New Kingston. The records were transcribed and translated at the A.R. Wentz Library under the direction of Pastor Frederick S. Weiser.

Lower Settlement, Trindle Springs, Silver Spring Township
These congregations were organized in the 1770s. Glatfelter assumes that the Lutheran pastors were probably the same as those for Carlisle, beginning with Jacob Goering (1776 - 1783). William Runkel served as the Reformed pastor, 1777 - 1781. According to Glatfelter, the Lutherans began a register in 1789 which was later used by both congregations. The Lutheran records have also been translated and transcribed by the A.R. Wentz Library, under the direction of Pastor Frederick S. Weiser.

Manor Church (Poplar, St. John's)
This is the Lutheran congregation which later formed a Union with the Reformed congregation at Friedens and later separated from the Reformed to become St. John's Evangelical Lutheran Church, Shiermanstown. It began in the 1780s in East Pennsboro Township. The register was begun by Frederick Schaefer in 1787. Frederick D. Schaefer was pastor, 1786 - 1790, followed by Adam Henry Meyer, 1790 - 1793.

Shippensburg
Lutheran and Reformed congregations were organized in Shippensburg in the 1770s. The Lutheran church is Memorial Church, East Orange and South Penn streets, Shippensburg. Lutheran pastors were Jacob Goering (1776 -1783), George Butler (ca. 1783 - ca. 1789) and Anthony Luetge (ca. 1789 - 1794). The Reformed congregation is Grace United Church of Christ, Prince and East Orange streets, Shippensburg. Reformed pastors were Conrad Bucher (1764-1769), William Runkel (1777-1781), Christopher Faber (1781-1786), Cyriacus Spangenberg (1786-1788 and Philip Stock (1792-ca.1798).

St. Peter's Church, Newville [Bloserville]
The congregation was probably established in 1796, the year in which the register was opened. The records were translated by Charles R. Roberts, Allentown, PA, 1935.

Ziegler's Church, Mifflin Township.
These records begin in 1797.

OTHER RECORDS OF MARRIAGES AND DEATHS

Records of marriages and deaths, other than those of churches, have been included in this volume, i.e., marriage licenses issued by John Agnew, county clerk; marriage bonds from the Zeamer Collection; and marriages and deaths published in the Carlisle Gazette.

BIBLIOGRAPHY

Most of the above introduction is based on the following sources.

Egle, William Henry, M.D., M.A. *Notes and Queries Historical, Biographical and Genealogical. Relating Chiefly to Interior Pennsylvania.* Repr. Baltimore: Genealogical Publishing Company, 1970. Originally published Harrisburg, 1901.

Fields, S. Helen. *Register of Marriages and Baptisms Performed by Rev. John Cuthbertson Covenanter Minister 1751 - 1791.* Baltimore: Genealogical Publishing Co., Inc., 1983.

Glatfelter, Charles H. *Pastors and People, Volume 1, Pastors and Congregations.* Breinigsville, PA: The Pennsylvania German Society, 1980.

Pennsylvania German Church Records. From the Pennsylvania German Society Proceedings and Addresses. 3 vols. Baltimore: Genealogical Publications Co., 1983.

Swope, Gilbert Ernest. *History of the Big Spring Presbyterian Church, Newville, PA. 1737-1898.* Newville, PA: Times Steam Printing House, 1898.

Wiley, Samuel T., ed. *Biographical and Portrait Cyclopedia of the Nineteenth Congressional District Pennsylvania ... .* Philadelphia: C.A. Ruoff Company, 1897.

MARRIAGE RECORDS OF THE FIRST PRESBYTERIAN CHURCH, 1785-1800

Taken from "Marriage Record of the First Presbyterian Church at Carlisle, 1785-1812." of the *Pennsylvania Archives*, Second Series, Vol. VIII.
[There are two entries for each marriage, with the bride's surname alphabetically and the other by the groom's surname alphbetically. In some entries we show a slant line is followed by the alternate spelling or information shown in the spouse's other entry. - Ed.]

Adams, Esther and Joseph Neily married April 6, 1792.
Adams, Joseph and ---- ---- married November 12, 1793.
Alcorn, James and Isabella Cochran married May 6, 1793.
Alexander, Isabella and Robert Evans married October 18, 1796.
Alexander, James and Jane Sanderson married April 12, 1798.
Alexander, John and Elizabeth McCleary married October 18, 1792.
Alexander, Joseph and Mary Young married September 25, 1800.
Alexander, Samuel and Isabella Creigh married September 13, 1785.
Alexander, William and Jean Miller married December 18, 1792.
Allen, Agnes and John Day married December 9, 1797.
Allen, Catharine and Samuel Gray married November 14, 1788.
Allen, Elizabeth and Henry Rumble married February 20, 1794.
Allen, Jenny and John Barr married September 16, 1794./Genny
Allen, Margaret and William McAlevy married September 16, 1789.
Allen, W^m and Jenny McCammon married January 4, 1798./McCommon
Anderson, James and Margaret Brownlee married December 11, 1788.
Anderson, James and Margaret Smith married January 5, 1791.
Anderson, James and Mary McQueen married March 22, 1798./McQueon
Anderson, John and Margaret McClure married December 2, 1789.
Anderson, John and Polley Neil married August 8, 1793.
Anderson, Joseph and Betsey Walker married November 22, 1792. /Nov 12
Anderson, Letitia and David Duncan married April 11, 1793.
Anderson, Mary and Alexander Beers married May 14, 1798.
Andrew, Margaret and John Campbell married March 24, 1785.
Armstrong, Dr. James and Polley Stephenson married June 18, 1789.
Armstrong, James and Eleanor Pollock married May 24, 1788.
Armstrong, Robert and Polly Landrum married September 24, 1798. /Laudrum
Armstrong, Thomas and Isabella Stephenson married December 17, 1799.
Arnold, Peter and Susanna Eakard married May 26, 1789.
Arthurs, John and Peggy Smith married October 19, 1792.
Aspell, Margaret and Henry Miller married May 11, 1785./Aspel
Augney, Mary and Robert Mason Uroth married December 27, 1797./Robt
Aull, Jean and Alexander Clinton married June 26, 1792.
Bailey, Elizabeth and Jesse Kennedy married October 27, 1789.
Barker, Martha and Francis White married April 16, 1789.
Barr, John and Genny Allen married September 16, 1794./Jenny
Bayles, Betsey and Wm Cascadon married July 17, 1800./Betsy
Beard, Margaret and David Kilgore married June 26, 1792./1796
Beatty, Samuel and Catharine Caswell married February 10, 1794.
Beckwith, Ann and Joseph Watson married June 21, 1798.
Beers, Alexander and Mary Anderson married May 14, 1798.

Bell, Agness and Joseph Young married July 18, 1788.
Bell, Catharine and John McCune married October 21, 1800.
Bell, James and Jane Milligan married June 10, 1794.
Bell, James and Nancy Haggerty married January 12, 1796.
Bell, Samuel and Eleanor Campbell married May 12, 1796.
Black, Margaret and Gilbert Wade married October 9, 1794.
Blaine, James and Peggy Lyon married January 16, 1795.
Blaine, Jean and John Endsley married November 7, 1797.
Blair, John (son of Randel) and Isabella Hall married May 16, 1795.
Blair, Mary and John Mitchell married June 10, 1794.
Bollinger, Conrad and Sarah Stewart married October 1, 1800.
Bovard, Charles and Rachel Wallace married November 24, 1790.
Bow, Catharine and George Hamilton married May 8, 1793.
Bow, Catharine and John Gaw married July 30, 1788.
Bow, Nancy and Jared Carothers married February 2, 1792.
Boyd, John and Margaret Johnson married July 23, 1793./Johnston
Boyd, Joseph and Elizabeth Jourdan married February 12, 1796.
Boyd, William and Abigail Robeson married March 22, 1792.
Bradley, Margery and Francis McCollum married July 25, 1793. /McCullum
Bradley, Mary and John Glenn married June 7, 1796.
Brandon, Sarah and Robert Moorehead married April 17, 1799.
Brandt, Christopher and Eve Douy married June 8, 1795.
Brice, Mary and Alexander Moore married May 23, 1792.
Briggs, Mary and Jared Pollock married February 13, 1800.
Brisland, Sarah and Lancelot Mollan married November 6, 1788.
Broadley, Daniel and Hannah Jameson married January 1, 1795.
Brooks, James and Rachel McCart married July 11, 1800.
Brown, Alexander and Elizabeth Logue married February 9, 1792.
Brown, Betsey and Henry Wilson married October 31, 1799./1791
Brown, Isabella and Lewis Foulke married January 17, 1788.
Brown, John and Mary Irwin married February 9, 1797.
Brown, Joseph and Polly McFee married October 27, 1789./Polley
Brown, Moses and Jean Donaldson married February 2, 1786.
Brown, Rebecca and Robert Brown married February 23, 1796.
Brown, Robert and Rebecca Brown married February 23, 1796.
Brown, William and Nancy Buchannan married March 15, 1798.
Brown, W^m and Nancy Loughridge married January 12, 1797.
Brownlee, Margaret and James Anderson married December 11, 1788.
Bryan, Patrick and Margery Davis married February 16, 1796.
Buchanan, Robert and Mary McKay married March 1, 1792.
Buchannan, Arthur and Agness Graham married March 5, 1799.
Buchannan, Nancy and William Brown married March 15, 1798.
Burke, Elizabeth and Archibald Cambell married November 16, 1792.
Burkholder, Elizabeth and Peter Latchsha married September 20, 1790.
Burkholder, John and Elizabeth Latchsha married September 20, 1790.
Caldwell, Samuel and Jenny Wilson married December 22, 1796.
Calendar, Pattey and Thomas Duncan married April 28, 1785.
Cambell, Archibald and Elizabeth Burke married November 16, 1792.
Cambell, William and Jenny Grier married March 29, 1796.
Camble, Nancy and John Tongue married March 2, 1789.
Campbell, Eleanor and Samuel Bell married May 12, 1796.
Campbell, John and Margaret Andrew married March 24, 1785.

MARRIAGE RECORDS OF FIRST PRESBYTERIAN CHURCH

Canning, Charles and Jean Huston married June 28, 1793.
Carothers, James, Jun. and Johanna Maria Kline married September 17, 1800.
Carothers, Jared and Nancy Bow married February 2, 1792.
Carothers, John and Polly Holmes married January 10, 1788.
Carothers, Rogers and Sarah Penwell married September 29, 1789.
Cascadon, W^m and Betsy Bayles married July 17, 1800./Betsey
Caswell, Catharine and Samuel Beatty married February 10, 1794.
Chambers, Betsey and William Kelso married November 8, 1792.
Chambers, Margaret and John Logan married April 6, 1797.
Chambers, Mary and John Davidson married May 26, 1789.
Chambers, Polly and Mordecai McKinney married June 17, 1795.
Chapman, James and Nancy Fleming married June 25, 1799.
Christie, Mary and Edward Williams married February 16, 1789.
Clark, Sarah and Thomas White married April 19, 1796.
Clawson, Elsie and Archibald Kelly married May 10, 1793.
Clayton, John and Elizabeth Miller married May 13, 1789.
Clendenan, Isabella and Archibald McCullogh married January 20, 1791.
Clendenan, Jean and Jehu Woodward married May 8, 1794.
Clinton, Alexander and Jean Aull married June 26, 1792.
Cochran, Isabella and James Alcorn married May 6, 1793.
Connelly, Jane and Robert McCormick married May 7, 1799.
Cook, Jacob and Elizabeth Right married October 13, 1795.
Cooper, Adam and Elizabeth Foster married February 13, 1786.
Coots, Margaret and Thomas Ruggles married May 31, 1786.
Coover, Henry and Elizabeth Stair married April 30, 1795.
Copely, Samuel and Jane Sibbet married February 1, 1796.
Coulter, Henry and Amelia Postlethwaite married December 18, 1800.
Cowher, Agness and Samuel Reed married October 21, 1790.
Craft, Gershom and Jean Steel married October 9, 1792.
Craighead, Gilson and Nancy White married September 30, 1790.
Craighead, John and Jean Lamb married March 11, 1788.
Craighead, Rachel and Samuel Lightcap married March 26, 1789.
Craighead, Thomas and Rebecca Weakley married November 15, 1796.
Crane, Richard and Sally Flemming married April 22, 1794.
Crawford, Agnes and Robert Herron married May 29, 1794.
Crawford, Joseph and Ann Davidson married February 11, 1796.
Creigh, Betsey and Samuel Duncan married March 6, 1800.
Creigh, Isabella and Samuel Alexander married September 13, 1785.
Creigh, John and Eleanor Dunbar married May 12, 1796.
Crochet, Elizabeth and David McGowan married March 3, 1791.
Crocket, Elsie and Stephen Keepers married December 18, 1789.
Crocket, James and Sarah Nimmon married January 2, 1798.
Crocket, Sarah and Alexander Trindle married December 19, 1793.
Crocket, Thomas and Esther Johnson married November 16, 1797.
Cromley, John and Mary Robeson married May 17, 1791.
Crosson, Mary and William Douds married May 27, 1793.
Culbertson, Joseph and Polley McCune married April 4, 1793.
Cunningham, Mary and John Urie married September 29, 1792.
Daniel, Thomas and Agnes Dugan married October 25, 1798.
Daugherty, Eleanor and Matthew Hart married May 31, 1785.
Davidson, Ann and Joseph Crawford married February 11, 1796.
Davidson, John and Mary Chambers married May 26, 1789.

4   CUMERLAND COUNTY CHURCH RECORDS OF THE 18TH CENTURY

Davidson, Mary and Samuel Davidson married January 30, 1787.
Davidson, Samuel and Mary Davidson married January 30, 1787.
Davis, Elizabeth and Edwin Putnam, Esq. married June 12, 1800.
Davis, Elizabeth and John Smith married September 7, 1786.
Davis, Elizabeth and John Smith married April 5, 1796.
Davis, Margery and Patrick Bryan married February 16, 1796.
Davis, Polly and Robert Kenny married November 14, 1796.
Davis, Rachel and George Kirkenluber married December 9, 1796.
Day, John and Agnes Allen married December 9, 1797.
Decker, Mary and Sam^1 Galbreath married February 27, 1789.
Dederick, Magdalina and George Swingel married April 23, 1787.
Denney, William and Polley Fleming married May 21, 1789.
Denny, David and Peggy Lyon married July 25, 1793.
Denny, Dennis and Unity McLaughlin married October 2, 1800.
Denny, Peggy and Samuel Simison married April 11, 1793.
Deyrmond, Elizabeth and John Love married February 10, 1796.
Dickson, Andrew and Mary Ramsay married April 2, 1795.
Dimsey, Fergus and Salley Johnson married December 24, 1787. /Johnston
Dimsey, Mary and James Edmiston married September 23, 1795.
Dodds, Thomas and Polley Guthrie married November 24, 1789.
Donaldson, Jean and Moses Brown married February 2, 1786.
Donaldson, John and Rebecca Tremble married June 24, 1794.
Donelly, John and Dorothy Smith married September 6, 1798.
Donnell, Francis and Jean McDonald married July 21, 1791.
Douds, William and Mary Crosson married May 27, 1793.
Douglass, Jane and Alexander Logan married November 6, 1787.
Douglass, John and Margaret Sexton married March 27, 1800.
Douy, Eve and Christopher Brandt married June 8, 1795.
Dowds, Andrew and Sarah Russel married January 24, 1799.
Duffy, Catharine and Hugh Sweney married October 8, 1799./Duffey
Dugan, Agnes and Thomas Daneel married October 25, 1798./Daniel
Dunbar, Eleanor and John Creigh married May 12, 1796.
Dunbar, Elizabeth and Allen Means married September 9, 1790.
Dunbar, Margaret and Thomas Urie married February 7, 1793.
Dunbar, William and Betsey Forbes married April 14, 1796.
Duncan, Anne and Samuel Mahon married June 2, 1792.
Duncan, David and Letitia Anderson married April 11, 1793.
Duncan, James and Margaret Johnson married December 30, 1788. /Johnston
Duncan, Mrs. ---- and Ephraim Polaine married September 20, 1797.
Duncan, Samuel and Betsey Creigh married March 6, 1800.
Duncan, Thomas and Pattey Calendar married April 28, 1785.
Dunlap, Betsey and James Smith married October 26, 1795.
Eagolf, Polly and Thomas Matheson married July 3, 1795.
Eakard, Susanna and Peter Arnold married May 26, 1789.
Eaken, Mary and William Work married March 1, 1785.
Earls, William and Sarah Redman married December 25, 1787.
Eckles, Deborah and James McCullogh married January 26, 1790.
Edmiston, James and Mary Dimsey married September 23, 1795.
Edmiston, Samuel and Jenny Montgomery married November 15, 1787.
Elliott, James and Agnes Gregg married July 14, 1794.
Elliot, Martha and James Giffin married October 7, 1796./Giffen
Elliot, Peggy and Francis McCullogh married November 22, 1796.

MARRIAGE RECORDS OF FIRST PRESBYTERIAN CHURCH

Elliot, Robert and Rebecca Fleming married December 13, 1798.
Endsley, John and Jean Blaine married November 7, 1797.
Evans, Robert and Isabella Alexander married October 18, 1796.
Ewings, Jane and William Lindsey married March 27, 1787.
Fee, Patrick and Margaret McGoldrick married September 12, 1789.
Ferguson, Geo. and Isabella (alias Peggy) Sharon married January 13, 1791.
Ferguson, Margaret and William Hardy married November 18, 1794.
Fields, Rebecca and Benjamin Jones married April 26, 1796.
Fish, Elizabeth and Michael McCall married March 8, 1790.
Fisher, Tobias and Polley Irwin married April 8, 1789.
Fleming, James and Fanny Randolph married May 14, 1793./Tanny
Fleming, Nancy and Charles Gregg married February 24, 1795.
Fleming, Nancy and James Chapman married June 25, 1799.
Fleming, Polley and William Denney married May 21, 1789.
Fleming, Rebecca and Robert Elliot married December 13, 1798.
Fleming, Susanna and Paul Randolph married November 24, 1796.
Flemming, Sally and Richard Crane married April 22, 1794.
Forbes, Betsey and William Dunbar married April 14, 1796.
Forsyth, Isbel and William Webster married August 6, 1788./Isabel
Foster, Elizabeth and Adam Cooper married February 13, 1786.
Foster, James and Elizabeth Hutchison married February 25, 1796.
Foulke, Lewis and Isabella Brown married January 17, 1788.
Frazer, Emelia and John Sterrett married June 9, 1796.
Frazer, Isabella and Samuel Funk married October 19, 1800.
Frazer, Nancy and Robert Hunter married April 9, 1787.
French, Martha and ---- Thompson married October 16, 1790./page said 1700; entry under groom gave 1790, so I made that change here
French, W^m and Jean Gordon married April 26, 1788.
Fullerton, Eliza and Hugh McCormick married April 19, 1793.
Funk, Samuel and Isabella Frazer married October 19, 1800.
Gabby, William and Amelia McCormick married March 27, 1794.
Galbreath, Rebecca and David Herron married July 18, 1793.
Galbreath, Saml and Mary Decker married February 27, 1789.
Galbreath, Samuel and Nancy Moore married January 9, 1798.
Gamble, Elizabeth and Francis Jameson married November 26, 1789.
Gass, James and Rebecca Rowan married April 23, 1793.
Gaw, John and Catherine Bow married July 30, 1788.
Geach, Ann and John Lane married March 2, 1793.
George, Nancy and Samuel Hay married December 1, 1795.
Gest, Anna and Thomas Eliot Kennedy married March 26, 1790. /Kenedy
Gibbon, John and Sarah White married December 25, 1797.
Gibson, Elizabeth and Hugh McCullogh married June 3, 1794.
Gibson, Jane and James Hall married March 22, 1796.
Giffen, Gennet and Wm Hunter married March 9, 1786./Giffin
Giffen, James and Martha Elliot married October 7, 1796./Giffin
Gillespie, George and Sarah Young married March 20, 1788.
Gillmor, Margaret and William Smith married April 4, 1794.
Given, James and Omelia Steel married February 4, 1794.
Gladney, William and Mary Ann Woods married July 7, 1791.
Glenn, John and Genny Hunter married January 9, 1788.
Glenn, John and Mary Bradley married June 7, 1796.
Gold, Joseph and Margaret Rowan married October 23, 1793./Oct 22

CUMERLAND COUNTY CHURCH RECORDS OF THE 18TH CENTURY

Goorley, Sarah and Stephen Ligget married March 6, 1800.
Gordon, Ann and Joseph Hays married July 1, 1788./Hayes
Gordon, Jean and Wm French married April 26, 1788.
Gourley, Samuel and Agnes Sibbet married August 31, 1795.
Graham, Agness and Arthur Buchannan married March 5, 1799.
Graham, Jane and William Greer married August 12, 1800.
Graham, Margaret and Wm Nixon married June 20, 1793.
Gray, Samuel and Catharine Allen married November 14, 1788.
Gray, Samuel and Elizabeth McDowel married February 24, 1791.
Grayson, Jean and Samuel Waugh married July 15, 1791.
Grayson, William and Agness Nimmons married November 16, 1792.
Green, Adam and Jane Moore married May 11, 1795.
Green, Mary and Alexander McBride married September --, 1799.
Greer, Patrick and Elizabeth Wilson married September 22, 1794.
Greer, William and Jane Graham married August 12, 1800.
Gregg, Agnes and James Elliott married July 14, 1794.
Gregg, Charles and Nancy Fleming married February 24, 1795.
Gregg, Elizabeth and George McKee married November 1, 1798.
Gregg, Jane and Francis McEwen married April 19, 1787.
Gregory, Elizabeth and Samuel Lindsey married March 29, 1793.
Grier, Jenny and William Cambell married March 29, 1796.
Grier, Polly and Lieut. David Offly married March 31, 1800.
Griffin, Mary and Charles Sweney married April 13, 1795.
Gustin, Sally and Nathanael Snowden married May 24, 1792.
Guthrie, Polley and Thomas Dodds married November 24, 1789.
Hagerty, Nancy and James Bell married January 12, 1796.
Hague, Elizabeth and Sergt. Benj. Woodward married May 10, 1800.
Hall, Isabella and John (son of Randel) Blair married May 16, 1795.
Hall, James and Jane Gibson married March 22, 1796.
Hamilton, George and Catharine Bow married May 8, 1793.
Hardy, Catharine and Isaac Hoffer married November 22, 1798.
Hardy, William and Margaret Ferguson married November 18, 1794.
Harris, David and Sally Montgomery married November 13, 1798.
Hart, Matthew and Elenor Daugherty married May 31, 1785./Eleanor
Harwick, Elizabeth and John Isset married April 5, 1785.
Hasson, Samuel and Polly Mauson married October 14, 1796.
Hay, Samuel and Nancy George married December 1, 1795.
Hayes, Joseph and Ann Gordon married July 1, 1788./Hays
Hayes, Margaret and ---- ---- married September 16, 1793.
Hayes, Mary and John Rosebury married February 1, 1788.
Hayes, Mary and William Logue married May 11, 1786.
Herren, Reuben and Martha Laird married June 28, 1791.
Herron, David and Rebecca Galbreath married July 18, 1793.
Herron, Robert and Agnes Crawford married May 29, 1794.
Hewes, Caleb and Sarah Magaw married January 31, 1799.
Hoffer, Isaac and Catharine Hardy married November 22, 1798.
Hoffer, Melchor and Matty McClellan married January 27, 1789.
Hoge, James Read and Polley McKinney married March 22, 1791.
Hoge, William and Belle Lyon married April 12, 1798.
Hogg, Martha and John McHaffey married September 22, 1791.
Hogg, Thomas and Betsey Holmes married October 18, 1798.
Holcham, Hannah and Archibald Loudon married November 17, 1796.
Holmes, Abraham and Rebecca Weakley married October 30, 1800.
Holmes, Agness and Robert Wright married November 20, 1798.

Holmes, Betsey and Thomas Hogg married October 18, 1798.
Holmes, Daniel and Peggy Woods married August 23, 1793.
Holmes, Isaac and Jesse Kilgore married March 26, 1789.
Holmes, Jenny and Jesse Kilgore married March 26, 1789.
Holmes, John and Nancy Stephenson married May 31, 1785.
Holmes, Jonathan and Jane Laird married April 19, 1787.
Holmes, Nancy and George Patterson married November 23, 1792.
Holmes, Polly and John Carothers married January 10, 1788.
Holtzoppel, Peggy and James Sloane married December 15, 1794. /Holtzopple
Houk, Adam and Salome Live married May 22, 1793.
Hughes, Betsey and Hugh H. Potts married June 26, 1800.
Hunt, Letitia and Michael Marshall married October 30, 1788.
Hunter, Genny and John Glenn married January 9, 1788.
Hunter, Mary and William Love married August 21, 1791.
Hunter, Robert and Nancy Frazer married April 9, 1787.
Hunter, Thomas and Margaret Mathis married February 1, 1790.
Hunter, W^m and Gennet Giffin married March 9, 1786./Giffen
Huston, Andrew and Elizabeth Simund married May 14, 1793.
Huston, Elizabeth and Andrew Miller married August 16, 1798.
Huston, Jean and Charles Canning married June 28, 1793.
Hutchinson, Francis and Ann Searight married April 26, 1789.
Hutchison, Elizabeth and James Foster married February 25, 1796.
Irwine, Polley and Thomas McCartney married February 16, 1792.
Irwin, Catharine and James Ross married September 23, 1789.
Irwin, Mary and John Brown married February 9, 1797.
Irwin, Polley and Joseph McClellan married June 26, 1788.
Irwin, Polley and Tobias Fisher married April 8, 1789.
Isett, Henry and Lydia Roath married March 15, 1790.
Isset, John and Elizabeth Harwick married April 5, 1785.
Jackson, Samuel and Margaret Ramsey married May 8, 1794.
Jameson, Francis and Elizabeth Gamble married November 26, 1789.
Jameson, Francis and Margaret Melligan married July 27, 1796. /Milligan
Jameson, Hannah and Daniel Broadley married January 1, 1795.
Jameson, Rachel and Morton McDonald married August 1, 1786.
Johnson, Esther and Thomas Crocket married November 16, 1797.
Johnston, Adam and Elizabeth Johnston married February 7, 1787.
Johnston, Elizabeth and Adam Johnston married February 7, 1787.
Johnston, George and Nancy Maxwell married January 24, 1793.
Johnston, Margaret and James Duncan married December 30, 1788. /Johnson
Johnston, Margaret and John Boyd married July 23, 1793./Johnson
Johnston, Rev. John and Jean McBeth married April 1, 1788.
Johnston, Salley and Fergus Dimsey married December 24, 1787. /Johnson
Johnston, Samuel and Rachel Love married December 22, 1795.
Jones, Benjamin and Rebecca Fields married April 26, 1796.
Jourdan, Elizabeth and Joseph Boyd married February 12, 1796.
Jumper, Jean and George Logue married January 15, 1789.
Keepers, Stephen and Elsie Crocket married December 18, 1789.
Kelly, Archibald and Elsie Clawson married May 10, 1793.
Kelly, Grace and Richard Price married November 17, 1793.
Kelly, Patrick and Martha McKinley married October 22, 1795.

CUMERLAND COUNTY CHURCH RECORDS OF THE 18TH CENTURY

Kelly, Samuel and Elizabeth Kilgore married May 9, 1792.
Kelso, William and Betsey Chambers married November 8, 1792.
Kenedy, Thomas Eliot and Anna Gest married March 26, 1790. /Kennedy
Kennedy, Harris and Margaret Mercer married July 26, 1794.
Kennedy, Jesse and Elizabeth Bailey married October 27, 1789.
Kenny, Eleanor and Brice Smith married July 23, 1785.
Kenny, Robert and Polly Davis married November 14, 1796.
Kidd, ---- and ---- Love married December 27, 1787.
Kilgore, David and Margaret Beard married June 26, 1796./1792
Kilgore, Elizabeth and Samuel Kelly married May 9, 1792.
Kilgore, Jesse and Jenny Holmes married March 26, 1789.
Kinkead, John and Mary Lee married April 27, 1796.
Kirk, Mary and Oliver Ramsey married September 13, 1785.
Kirkenluber, George and Rachel Davis married December 9, 1796.
Kline, Johanna Maria and James Carothers, Jun. married September 17, 1800.
Knittle, Henry and Hannah Walker married May 16, 1798.
Lackey, Robert and Mary Shortie married November 25, 1789.
Laird, Jane and Jonathan Holmes married April 19, 1787.
Laird, Martha and Reuben Herren married June 28, 1791.
Lamb, Jane and Stewart Rowan married April 19, 1785.
Lamb, Jean and John Craighead married March 11, 1788.
Lamb, Mary and Samuel Reed married March 1, 1785.
Lane, John and Ann Geach married March 2, 1793.
Latchsha, Elizabeth and John Burkholder married September 20, 1790.
Latchsha, Peter and Elizabeth Burkholder married September 20, 1790.
Latshaw, Joseph and Mary Riddle married November 21, 1799.
Laudrum, Polly and Robert Armstrong married September 24, 1798. /Landrum
Lee, Mary and John Kinkead married April 27, 1796.
Lefevre, Barbara and John Lyne married December 13, 1798.
Lemmon, Jeane and Daniel Morrison married April 23, 1793.
Leviston, William and Nancy Shaw married March 20, 1787.
Ligget, Stephen and Sarah Goorley married March 6, 1800.
Lightcap, Samuel and Rachel Craighead married March 26, 1789.
Linch, Robert and Elizabeth Peeling married June 16, 1800.
Lindsey, Samuel and Elizabeth Gregory married March 29, 1793.
Lindsey, William and Jane Ewings married March 27, 1787.
Little, Eleanor and William Wilson married August 25, 1791.
Live, Salome and Adam Houk married May 22, 1793.
Logan, Alexander and Jane Douglass married November 6, 1787.
Logan, John and Margaret Chambers married April 6, 1797.
Logue, Adam and Nancy Sterrett married June 28, 1792.
Logue, Elizabeth and Alexander Brown married February 9, 1792.
Logue, George and Jean Jumper married January 15, 1789.
Logue, William and Mary Hayes married May 11, 1786.
Loudon, Archibald and Hannah Holcham married November 17, 1796.
Loughridge, Nancy and Wm Brown married January 1, 1797.
Love, ---- and ---- Kidd married December 27, 1787.
Love, James and Mary Passel married December 18, 1789.
Love, John and Elizabeth Deyrmond married February 10, 1796.
Love, Rachel and Samuel Johnston married December 22, 1795.
Love, William and Mary Hunter married August 21, 1791.

MARRIAGE RECORDS OF FIRST PRESBYTERIAN CHURCH

Lutz, Margaret and Samuel Wilson married October 22, 1789.
Lyne, John and Barbara Lefevre married December 13, 1798.
Lyne, Susanna and Robert Smith married May 12, 1791.
Lyon, Belle and William Hoge married April 12, 1798.
Lyon, Peggy and David Denny married July 25, 1793.
Lyon, Peggy and James Blaine married January 16, 1795.
Magaw, Sarah and Caleb Hewes married January 31, 1799.
Magee, George and Elizabeth McElwain married January 3, 1797.
Magee, Polly and John Rhinehart married January 26, 1796.
Mahon, Samuel and Anne Duncan married June 2, 1792.
Marchbanks, James and Ann Ralston married September 28, 1798.
Marshall, Michael and Letitia Hunts married October 30, 1788.
Martin, James and Margaret Walker married August 29, 1798.
Martin, Rosanna and Archibald McKay married June 3, 1789.
Matheson, Thomas and Polly Eagolf married July 3, 1795.
Mathis, Margaret and Thomas Hunter married February 1, 1790.
Matthews, Polley and Roger McGee married June 5, 1793.
Mauson, Polly and Samuel Hasson married October 14, 1796.
Maxwell, Nancy and George Johnston married January 24, 1793.
McAdams, Ann and William Murray married April 9, 1795.
McAfee, Letty and George Sparr married March 18, 1788.
McAlevy, William and Margaret Allen married September 16, 1789.
McAnulty, Hugh and Rachel Spottswood married April 9, 1793.
McBeth, Alex' and Rachel Whitehill married July 8, 1790.
McBeth, Jean and Rev. John Johnston married April 1, 1788.
McBeth, Peggy and James Neely married April 3, 1798.
McBride, Alexander and Mary Green married September --, 1799.
McCabe, Jane and Robert Seetin married August 8, 1798.
McCabe, Patrick and Sarah Power married June 29, 1789.
McCall, Michael and Elizabeth Fish married March 8, 1790.
McCallister, Elizabeth and James Parker married November 6, 1786.
McCallister, Jean and Joseph Pierce married February 26, 1788.
McCart, Rachel and James Brooks married July 11, 1800.
McCartney, John and Elizabeth Wilson married April 20, 1796.
McCartney, Thomas and Polley Irwine married February 16, 1792.
McClain, Dr. James and Patty Sanderson married November 20, 1792.
McCleary, Elizabeth and John Alexander married October 18, 1792.
McCleland, Ann and David Murray married February 17, 1790.
McClellan, Joseph and Polley Irwin married June 26, 1788.
McClellan, Matty and Melchor Hoffer married January 27, 1789.
McClintock, Rachel and Robert Read married March 1, 1792.
McCloud, Kitty and Hercules Murphy married November 3, 1788.
McClure, Charles and Rebecca Parker married March 9, 1797.
McClure, Margaret and John Anderson married December 2, 1789.
McCullum, Francis and Margery Bradley married July 25, 1793.
/McCollum
McCommon, Jenny and William Allen married January 4, 1798.
/McCammon
McCord, Mary and John Scott married February 20, 1792.
McCormick, Amelia and William Gabby married March 27, 1794.
McCormick, Hugh and Eliza Fullerton married April 19, 1793.
McCormick, Robert and Jane Connelly married May 7, 1799.
McCullogh, Archibald and Isabella Clendenan married January 20, 1791.

CUMERLAND COUNTY CHURCH RECORDS OF THE 18TH CENTURY

McCullogh, Francis and Peggy Elliot married November 22, 1796.
McCullogh, George and Elizabeth Thompson married November 29, 1797.
McCullogh, Hugh and Elizabeth Gibson married June 3, 1794.
McCullogh, James and Deborah Eckles married January 26, 1790.
McCullough, John and Polly Williamson married January 11, 1798.
McCune, John and Catharine Bell married October 21, 1800.
McCune, Polley and Joseph Culbertson married April 4, 1793.
McCune, Rosanna and Robert Stewart married April 17, 1793. /McClune
McDaniel, Daniel and Jean Simonds married May 24, 1792.
McDonald, Jean and Francis Donnell married July 21, 1791.
McDonald, Martin and Rachel Jameson married August 1, 1786.
McDowel, Elizabeth and Samuel Gray married February 24, 1791.
McDowel, Lydia and Thomas Parker married May 3, 1786.
McDowel, Nancy and Charles Rainey married April 14, 1796.
McElravy, Mary and Matthew Murdack married October 22, 1795.
McElwain, Elizabeth and George Magee married January 3, 1797.
McEwen, Francis and Jane Gregg married April 19, 1787.
McFarlane, Jean and William Thompson married November 24, 1785.
McFee, Polley and Joseph Brown married October 27, 1789./Polly
McGee, Roger and Polley Matthews married June 5, 1793.
McGoldrick, Margaret and Patrick Fee married September 12, 1789.
McGonagle, Edward and Sally Turner married January 7, 1788.
McGovern, Catharine and John McJunkins married May 3, 1798.
McGowan, David and Elizabeth Crochet married March 3, 1791.
McGranahan, W^m and Mary Roach married May 15, 1789.
McGrew, Archibald and Ruth Miller married September 22, 1786.
McGrew, Elizabeth and Philip Shaw married April 10, 1794.
McHaffey, John and Martha Hogg married September 22, 1791.
McIntyre, Elizabeth and W^m McIntyre married April 17, 1792.
McIntyre, W^m and Elizabeth McIntyre married April 17, 1792.
McJunkins, John and Catharine McGovern married May 3, 1798.
McKay, Archibald and Rosanna Martin married June 3, 1789.
McKay, Mary and Robert Buchanan married March 1, 1792.
McKee, Daniel and Mary Stewart married February 13, 1793.
McKee, George and Elizabeth Gregg married November 1, 1798.
McKimmon, Michael and Mary Patton married November 29, 1791.
McKinley, Daniel and Sarah Smith married January 4, 1791.
McKinley, Henry and Eleanor Stevens married January 3, 1799.
McKinley, James and Margaret Robeson married June 26, 1800.
McKinley, Martha and Patrick Kelly married October 22, 1795.
McKinney, Jean and John Wills married November 28, 1793.
McKinney, Mordecai and Polly Chambers married June 17, 1795.
McKinney, Polley and James Read Hoge married March 22, 1791.
McKnight, John and Grifey Sanderson married November 14, 1787.
McLaughlin, Unity and Dennis Denny married October 2, 1800.
McMichael, Daniel and Jean Orvan married April 28, 1789.
McMullen, William and Mary White married February 27, 1798.
McNealans, William and Polley Reaugh married February 2, 1792.
McQueon, Mary and James Anderson married March 22, 1798. /McQueen
McQueon, Rosanna and Alexander Work married March 21, 1793. /McQueen
Means, Allen and Elizabeth Dunbar married September 9, 1790.
Mehaffy, Bridget and Thomas Mehaffy married February 12, 1798.
Mehaffy, Thomas and Bridget Mehaffy married February 12, 1798.

Mercer, Margaret and Harris Kennedy married July 26, 1794.
Miller, Andrew and Elizabeth Huston married August 16, 1798.
Miller, Elizabeth and John Clayton married May 13, 1789.
Miller, Henry and Margaret Aspel married May 11, 1785./Aspell
Miller, Jean and William Alexander married December 18, 1792.
Miller, John and Jean Temple married April 15, 1794.
Miller, Ruth and Archibald McGrew married Sept 22, 1786.
Miller, William and Eleanor Styles married January 6, 1791.
Milligan, Jane and James Bell married June 10, 1794.
Milligan, Margaret and Francis Jameson married July 27, 1796.
/Melligan
Milligan, W^m and Margaret Sweeney married April 19, 1785.
Mitchell, John and Mary Blair married June 10, 1794.
Mollan, Lancelot and Sarah Brisland married November 6, 1788.
Montgomery, Hetty and John Morrison married September 28, 1791.
Montgomery, Jenny and Saml Edmiston married November 15, 1787.
Montgomery, Sally and David Harris married November 13, 1798.
Montgomery, Samuel and Polley Ramsey married May 1, 1793.
Moore, Alexander and Mary Brice married May 23, 1792.
Moore, Jane and Adam Green married May 11, 1795.
Moore, Nancy and Samuel Galbreath married January 9, 1798.
Moorehead, Robert and Sarah Brandon married April 17, 1799.
Moorhead, Edward and Sarah Passel married March 15, 1796.
Morrison, Daniel and Jeane Lemmon married April 23, 1793.
Morrison, Hans (of Pittsburgh) and Peggy Pollock married November 12, 1795.
Morrison, John and Hetty Montgomery married September 28, 1791.
Murdack, Matthew and Mary McElravy married October 22, 1795.
Murphy, Hercules and Kitty McCloud married November 3, 1788.
Murray, David and Ann McCleland married February 17, 1790.
Murray, William and Ann McAdams married April 9, 1795.
Neely, James and Peggy McBeth married April 3, 1798.
Neil, Polley and John Anderson married August 8, 1793.
Neilson, Polley and William Powers married September 13, 1793.
Neily, Joseph and Esther Adams married April 6, 1792.
Nimmon, Sarah and James Crocket married January 2, 1798.
Nimmons, Agness and William Grayson married November 16, 1792.
Nixon, W^m and Margaret Graham married June 20, 1793.
Norton, Elizabeth and Wm Shields married June 25, 1800.
Officer, David and Elizabeth Walker married October 31, 1793.
Officer, John and Margaret Officer married May 31, 1796.
Officer, Margaret and John Officer married May 31, 1796.
Offly, Lieut. David and Polly Grier married March 31, 1800.
Oliver, Elizabeth and James Thompson married May 4, 1790.
Oliver, Thomas and Isabella Smith married February 14, 1792.
Orr, ---- and Adam Simonton married October 9, 1798.
Orr, David and Rebecca Stephenson married January 31, 1794.
Orr, James and Margaret Thompson married December 1, 1797.
Orvan, Jean and Daniel McMichael married April 28, 1789.
Parker, James and Elizabeth McCallister married November 6, 1786.
Parker, Rebecca and Charles McClure married March 9, 1797.
Parker, Thomas and Lydia McDowel married May 3, 1786.
Parker, William and Elizabeth Templeton married October 28, 1788.
Passel, John and Mary Rowen married May 1, 1793.

CUMERLAND COUNTY CHURCH RECORDS OF THE 18TH CENTURY

Passel, Mary and James Love married December 18, 1789.
Passel, Sarah and Edward Moorhead married March 15, 1796.
Patterson, George and Nancy Holmes married November 23, 1792.
Patterson, Jean and James Walker married April 8, 1794.
Patterson, William and Eva Pense married April 19, 1796.
Patton, Mary and Michael McKimmon married November 29, 1791.
Patton, William and Margaret Silvers married May 30, 1787.
Peeling, Elizabeth and Robert Linch married June 16, 1800.
Pense, Eva and William Patterson married April 19, 1796.
Penwell, Sarah and Rogers Carothers married September 29, 1789.
Pierce, Joseph and Jean McCallister married February 26, 1788.
Polaine, Ephraim and Mrs ---- Duncan married September 20, 1797.
Pollock, Eleanor and James Armstrong married May 24, 1788.
Pollock, Jared and Mary Briggs married February 13, 1800.
Pollock, Peggy and Hans Morrison (of Pittsburg) married November 12, 1795.
Postlethwaite, Amelia and Henry Coulter married December 18, 1800.
Postlethwaite, Dr. James and Elizabeth Smith married April 10, 1799.
Postlethwaite, Joseph and Mary Wilkins married January 3, 1787.
Potts, Hugh H. and Betsey Hughes married June 26, 1800.
Power, Sarah and Patrick McCabe married June 29, 1789.
Powers, William and Polley Nelson married September 13, 1793.
Price, Richard and Grace Kelly married November 17, 1793.
Provens, Charles and Mary Ann Provens married February 13, 1790.
Provens, Mary Ann and Charles Provens married February 13, 1790.
Putman, Edwin, Esq. and Elizabeth Davis married June 12, 1800.
Rainey, Charles and Nancy McDowel married April 14, 1796.
Ralston, Ann and James Marshbanks married September 28, 1798.
Ramsay, Agnes and Richard Weston married April 24, 1798.
Ramsay, Mary and Andrew Dickson married April 2, 1795.
Ramsey, Margaret and Samuel Jackson married May 8, 1794.
Ramsey, Oliver and Mary Kirk married September 13, 1785.
Ramsey, Polley and Samuel Montgomery married May 1, 1793.
Randolph, Paul and Susanna Fleming married November 24, 1796.
Randolph, Rebecca and Wm Sanderson married December 26, 1786.
Randolph, Tanny and James Fleming married May 14, 1793./Fanny
Read, Robert and Rachel McClintock married March 1, 1792.
Reaugh, Polley and William McNealans married February 2, 1792.
Redman, Sarah and William Earls married December 25, 1787.
Reed, Geo. (of N. Castle) and Maria Thompson married October 30, 1786.
Reed, Samuel and Agness Cowher married October 21, 1790.
Reed, Samuel and Mary Lamb married March 1, 1785.
Rhinehart, John and Polly Magee married January 26, 1796.
Riddle, Mary and Joseph Latshaw married November 21, 1799.
Right, Elizabeth and Jacob Cook married October 13, 1795.
Roach, Mary and W^m McGranahan married May 15, 1789.
Roath, Lydia and Henry Isett married March 15, 1790.
Robeson, Abigail and William Boyd married March 22, 1792.
Robeson, Alexander and Jane Sanderson married April 12, 1792.
Robeson, Margaret and James McKinley married June 26, 1800.
Robeson, Mary and John Cromley married May 17, 1791.
Rosebury, John and Mary Hayes married February 1, 1788.

MARRIAGE RECORDS OF FIRST PRESBYTERIAN CHURCH   13

Ross, James and Catharine Irwin married September 23, 1789.
Rowan, Margaret and Joseph Gold married October 22, 1793./Oct 23
Rowan, Peggy and John Stewart married November 14, 1793.
Rowan, Rebecca and James Gass married April 23, 1793.
Rowan, Stewart and Jane Lamb married April 19, 1785.
Rowen, Mary and John Passel married May 1, 1793.
Ruggles, Thomas and Margaret Coots married May 31, 1786.
Rumble, Henry and Elizabeth Allen married February 20, 1794.
Russel, Sarah and Andrew Dowds married January 24, 1799.
Sanderson, Grifey and John McKnight married November 14, 1787.
Sanderson, Jane and Alexander Robeson married April 12, 1792.
Sanderson, Jane and James Alexander married April 12, 1798.
Sanderson, Margaret and Samuel Smiley married June 30, 1789.
Sanderson, Patty and Dr. James McClain married November 20, 1792.
Sanderson, W^m and Rebecca Randolph married December 26, 1786.
Scott, Alexander and Martha Stewart married February 2, 1792.
Scott, John and Mary McCord married February 29, 1792.
Scroggs, Miriam and William Work married April 23, 1792.
Searight, Ann and Francis Hutchinson married April 26, 1789.
Seetin, Robert and Jane McCabe married August 8, 1798.
Semple, Sarah and John Sterrett married February 10, 1791.
Sexton, Margaret and John Douglass married March 27, 1800.
Sharon, Elizabeth and William Steel married November 4, 1788.
Sharon, Isabella (alias Peggy) and Geo. Ferguson married January 13, 1791.
Sharp, Elizabeth and John Smith married October 10, 1792.
Shaw, Nancy and William Leviston married March 20, 1787.
Shaw, Philip and Elizabeth McGrew married April 10, 1794.
Shields, W^m and Elizabeth Norton married June 25, 1800.
Shortie, Mary and Robert Lackey married November 25, 1789.
Sibbet, Agnes and Samuel Gourley married August 31, 1795.
Sibbet, Jane and Samuel Copely married February 1, 1796.
Silvers, Margaret and William Patton married May 30, 1787.
Simison, Samuel and Peggy Denny married April 11, 1793.
Simonds, Jean and Daniel McDaniel married May 24, 1792.
Simonton, Adam and ---- Orr married October 9, 1798.
Simund, Elizabeth and Andrew Huston married May 14, 1793.
Sloane, James and Peggy Holtzopple married December 15, 1794. /Holtzoppel
Smiley, Samuel and Margaret Sanderson married June 30, 1789.
Smiley, Thomas and Genny Sterret married March 23, 1789.
Smith, Brice and Eleanor Kenny married July 23, 1785.
Smith, Dorothy and John Donelly married September 6, 1798.
Smith, Elizabeth and Dr. James Postlethwaite married April 10, 1799.
Smith, George and Isabella Stevens married November 21, 1785.
Smith, Isabella and Thomas Oliver married February 14, 1792.
Smith, James and Betsey Dunlap married October 26, 1795.
Smith, John and Elizabeth Davis married September 7, 1786.
Smith, John and Elizabeth Davis married April 5, 1796.
Smith, John and Elizabeth Sharp married October 10, 1792.
Smith, Margaret and James Anderson married January 5, 1791.
Smith, Peggy and John Arthurs married October 19, 1792.
Smith, Robert and Susanna Lyne married May 12, 1791.

Smith, Sarah and Daniel McKinley married January 4, 1791.
Smith, Thomas and Rebecca Watson married September 10, 1789.
Smith, William and Margaret Gillmor married April 4, 1794.
Snowden, Nathanael and Sally Gustin married May 24, 1792.
Sparr, George and Letty McAfee married March 18, 1788.
Spottswood, Rachel and Hugh McAnulty married April 9, 1793.
Stair, Elizabeth and Henry Coover married April 30, 1795.
Steel, Jean and Gershom Craft married October 9, 1792.
Steel, Omelia and James Given married February 4, 1794.
Steel, William and Elizabeth Sharon married November 4, 1788.
Stephenson, Isabella and Thomas Armstrong married December 17, 1799.
Stephenson, Jean and Edward West married July 5, 1785.
Stephenson, Nancy and John Holmes married May 31, 1785.
Stephenson, Polley and Dr. James Armstrong married June 18, 1789.
Stephenson, Rebecca and David Orr married January 31, 1794.
Sterrett, Genny and Thomas Smiley married March 23, 1789.
Sterrett, John and Emelia Frazer married June 9, 1796.
Sterrett, John and Sarah Semple married February 10, 1791.
Sterrett, Nancy and Adam Logue married June 28, 1792.
Stevens, Eleanor and Henry McKinley married January 3, 1799.
Stevens, Isabella and George Smith married November 21, 1785.
Stewart, John and Peggy Rowan married November 14, 1793.
Stewart, Martha and Alexander Scott married February 2, 1792.
Stewart, Martha and Jacob Walters married November 8, 1791.
Stewart, Mary and Daniel McKee married February 13, 1793.
Stewart, Robert and Roseanna McClune married April 17, 1793. /McCune
Stewart, Sarah and Conrad Bollinger married October 1, 1800.
Stewart, Sarah and John Walker married September 13, 1792.
Stone, Ann and Isaac Williams married October 29, 1793.
Stone, John and Martha Wilson married July 26, 1796.
Styles, Eleanor and William Miller married January 6, 1791.
Sweeney, Margaret and Wm Milligan married April 19, 1785.
Sweiner, Barbara and George Warner married August 3, 1791.
Sweney, Charles and Mary Griffin married April 13, 1795.
Sweney, Hugh and Catharine Duffey married October 8, 1799./Duffy
Swingel, George and Magdalina Dederick married April 23, 1787.
Temple, Jean and John Miller married April 15, 1794.
Templeton, Elizabeth and William Parker married October 28, 1788.
Thompson, Elizabeth and George McCullogh married November 29, 1797.
Thompson, James and Elizabeth Oliver married May 4, 1790.
Thompson, Margaret and James Orr married December 1, 1797.
Thompson, Maria and George Reed (of N. Castle) married October 30, 1786.
Thompson, ---- and Martha French married October 16, 1790.
Thompson, William and Hannah Wallace married June 10, 1788.
Thompson, William and Jean McFarlane married November 24, 1785.
Tongue, John and Nancy Camble married March 2, 1789.
Tremble, Rebecca and John Donaldson married June 24, 1794.
Trimble, George and Martha Waugh married November 4, 1790.
Trindle, Alexander and Sarah Crocket married December 19, 1793.
Trindle, John and Margaret Waddel married April 8, 1795.
Turner, Sally and Edward McGonagle married January 7, 1788.

MARRIAGE RECORDS OF FIRST PRESBYTERIAN CHURCH

Urie, John and Mary Cunningham married September 29, 1792.
Urie, Thomas and Margaret Dunbar married February 7, 1793.
Uruth, Robt. Mason and Mary Augney married December 27, 1797.
/Robert
Waddel, Margaret and John Trindle married April 8, 1795.
Wade, Gilbert and Margaret Black married October 9, 1794.
Walker, Betsey and Joseph Anderson married November 12, 1792. /Nov 22
Walker, Elizabeth and David Officer married October 31, 1793.
Walker, Hannah and Henry Knittle married May 16, 1798.
Walker, James and Jean Patterson married April 8, 1794.
Walker, John and Sarah Stewart married September 13, 1792.
Walker, Margaret and James Martin married August 29, 1798.
Wallace, Hannah and William Thompson married June 10, 1788.
Wallace, Rachel and Charles Bovard married November 24, 1790.
Walters, Jacob and Martha Stewart married November 8, 1791.
Warner, George and Barbara Sweiner married August 3, 1791.
Watson, Joseph and Ann Beckwith married June 21, 1798.
Watson, Rebecca and Thomas Smith married September 10, 1789.
Waugh, Martha and George Trimble married November 4, 1790.
Waugh, Samuel and Jean Grayson married July 15, 1791.
Weakley, Jane and Nathan Woods married May 31, 1796.
Weakley, Rebecca and Abraham Holmes married October 30, 1800.
Weakley, Rebecca and Thomas Craighead married November 15, 1796.
Webster, William and Isabel Forsyth married August 6, 1788./Isbel
West, Edward and Jean Stephenson married July 5, 1785.
Weston, Richard and Agnes Ramsay married April 24, 1798.
White, Francis and Martha Barker married April 16, 1789.
White, Mary and William McMullen married February 27, 1798.
White, Nancy and Gilson Craighead married September 30, 1790.
White, Sarah and John Gibbon married December 25, 1797.
White, Thomas and Sarah Clark married April 19, 1796.
Whitehill, Rachel and Alex^r McBeth married July 8, 1790.
Wilkins, Mary and Joseph Postlethwaite married January 3, 1787.
Williams, Edward and Mary Christie married February 16, 1789.
Williams, Isaac and Ann Stone married October 29, 1793.
Williamson, Polly and John McCullough married January 11, 1798.
Wills, John and Jean McKinney married November 28, 1793.
Wilson, Elizabeth and John McCartney married April 20, 1796.
Wilson, Elizabeth and Patrick Greer married September 22, 1794.
Wilson, Henry and Betsey Brown married October 31, 1791./1799
Wilson, Jenny and Samuel Caldwell married December 22, 1796.
Wilson, Martha and John Stone married July 26, 1796.
Wilson, Samuel and Margaret Lutz married October 22, 1789.
Wilson, William and Eleanor Little married August 25, 1791.
Woods, Mary Ann and William Gladney married July 7, 1791.
Woods, Nathan and Jane Weakley married May 31, 1796.
Woods, Peggy and Daniel Holmes married August 23, 1793.
Woodward, Jehu and Jean Clendenan married May 8, 1794.
Woodward, Sergt. Benj. and Elizabeth Hague married May 10, 1800.
Work, Alexander and Rosanna McQueen married March 21, 1793.
/McQuoen
Work, William and Mary Eaken married March 1, 1785.
Work, William and Miriam Scroggs married April 23, 1792.

Wright, Robert and Agness Holmes married November 20, 1798.
Young, Joseph and Agness Bell married July 18, 1788.
Young, Mary and Joseph Alexander married September 25, 1800.
Young, Sarah and George Gillespie married March 20, 1788.

RECORDS OF ZIEGLER'S CHURCH
Mifflin Township

Fehler, Susanna, daughter of Andrew and Elizabeth Fehler, born February 3, 1797; baptized February 13. Sponsors: Nicholas Fehler and wife.

Jumans, John, son of Joseph Jumans and Sally, born March 2, 1799; baptized March 24 by Rev. John Herbst. Sponsors: John Ziegler and Elizabet.

Dewalt, Tobias, son of John and Mary Dewalt, born April 26, 1799; baptized June 2 by Rev. John Herbst. Sponsors: Henry Ziegler and Jacobina.

Hauser, John, son of John and Eva Hauser, born April 29, 1799; baptized June 2 by Rev. John Herbst. Sponsors: John Hauser, Senior, and Mary Barbara.

Henry, Anna Mary, daughter of John and Eva Henry, born ----; baptized July 21 by Rev. John Herbst. Sponsors: Adam Neidig and Sophia.

Wuest, Alexander, son of Jacob and Elisabeth Wuest, born November 15, (1798); baptized June 25 by Rev. John Herbst. Sponsor: the father Jacob Wuest.

Huber, Daniel, son of Frederick and Anna Elisabeth Huber, born February 15, 1799; baptized March 16 by Rev. John Herbst. Sponsor: John Ziegler.

Huber, Magdelena, daughter of Frederick and Anna Elisabeth Huber, born February 15; baptized March 16. Sponsors: Henry and Molly Wolf.

Bernd, Anna Mary, daughter of John and Anna Mary Bernd, born January 17; baptized March 16, 1800. Sponsors: Henry Ziegler and wife Sabina.

Ziegler, John Philip, son of John and Betsy Ziegler, born January 28; baptized March 16, 1800. Sponsors: Philip Fisher and Catherine.

Beck, George, son of Henry and Catharine Beck, born February 8; baptized March 16, 1800. Sponsors: the parents.

Weber, Jacob, son of Philip and Elisabeth Weber, born October 15, 1799; baptized April 14, 1800. Sponsors: the parents.

Neidig, Magdelena, daughter of Adam and Sophia Neidig, born November 14, 1799; baptized April 14, 1800. Sponsors: John Henrich and w. Eva Maria.

Dui, Margaret, daughter of Adam and Margaret Dui, born February 2; baptized April 14, 1800. Sponsor: Catharine Weiss.

Neustaedter, Conrad, son of Conrad and Catharine Neustaedter, born March 15; baptized April 14, 1800. Sponsors: the parents.

Huhn, Mary, daughter of Christopher and Betty Huhn, born January 11; baptized April 14, 1800 by the Rev. John Herbst. Sponsors: George Knettle and w. Catharine.

Schoenberger, Regina, daughter of Jacob and Mary Schoenberger, born March 27, 1795; baptized May 10, 1800. Sponsors: the parents.

Koken, Elizabeth, daughter of John and Barbara Koken, born

CUMBERLAND COUNTY CHURCH RECORDS OF THE 18TH CENTURY

February 25; baptized May 11, 1800. Sponsors: the parents.
Finkenbeiner, Anna Mary, daughter of John and Elisabeth Finkenbeiner, born February 20; baptized May 15, 1800. Sponsors: Jacob Brauss and w. Anna Mary.
Jacoby, Regina, daughter of Peter and Elisabeth Jacoby, born May 15; baptized July 6, 1800. Sponsors: John Hauser and w. Anna Barbara.
Daelhausen, Daniel, son of Henry Daniel and Anna Catharine Daelhausen, born March 17; baptized July 6, 1800. Sponsor: Daniel Wolf.
Worstin, Samuel, son of John and Julie Worstin, born June 23; baptized August 3, 1800. Sponsors: Simon Essig and wife.
Fehler, Jacob, son of Christian and Christina Fehler, born May 10; baptized July 6. Sponsors: the parents.
Wolf, John, son of Henry and Molly Wolf, born ----; baptized September 6, 1800 by Rev. John Herbst. Sponsors: Felix Weiss and w. Christina.
Leh, John, son of John and Eva Margaret Leh, born ----; baptized January 15, 1801. Sponsors: John Henry and w. Eva Margaret.
Gebford, Mary Catharine, daughter of Abraham and Mary Catharine Gebford, born September 9, 1800; baptized January 15, 1801. Sponsors: Conrad Giess and w. Mary Catharine.
Fehler, Mary Elizabeth, daughter of Andrew and Elisabeth Fehler, born November 26, 1800; baptized March 15, 1801. Sponsors: the parents.
Wagner, Henry, son of John and Anna Mary Wagner, born January 19, 1800; baptized March 15, 1801. Sponsors: the parents.
Henry, Elisabeth, daughter of Abraham and Susanna Henry, born March 5, 1800; baptized March 15, 1801. Sponsors: John Dewalt and w. Polly.

BOBENMAYER (ST. PETER'S) CHURCH

Records of the St. Peter's Church, Upper Frankford Lutheran Charge, Newville, [Bloserville], Cumberland County, PA., originally Bobenmayer's (Union) Church, 1796-1863.

Church Book February 21, 1796
Baptisms

1796
Blaser, Henry, born August 13, 1796; baptized February 12, 1796. Sponsors: Peter Blaser and wife Elizabeth.
Nicholas of Nicholas Hell and Barbara, born February 1, 1797; baptized March 12, [1797]. Sponsors: Bernhard Speck and Magdalena.
John George of John Jacob Wolff and Margaret Elizabeth, born December 10, 1796; baptized March 12, 1797. Sponsors: George Werns and Catharine.
Andrew of John Ernst and Catharine, born January 5, 1797; baptized April 9. Sponsor: Adam Poppenmeyer.
George of Simon Kolb and Margaret, born February 13, 1797; baptized April 14. Sponsors: Bernhart Speck and wife.
John Jacob of Martinus Georg and Barbara, born September 23, 1796; baptized May 7, 1797. Sponsors: John Jacob Wolf and Elizabeth Wolff.
Maria Magdalena of John Philip Heckman and Anna Maria, born April 23, 1797; baptized May 7. Sponsors: Gabriel Pobbenmeyer and Christina.
Peter of Peter Seib and Margaret, born December 29, 1781; baptized April 21, 1797. Sponsor: Martin Bender.
Jacob of Peter Seib and Margaret, born November 3, 1785; baptized April 21, 1797. Sponsors: Gabriel Bobenmeyer and wife.
Michael of Peter Seib and Margaret, born June 16, 1788; baptized April 21, 1797. Sponsors: Martin George and wife.
Henry of Peter Seib and Margaret, born August 17, 1790; baptized April 21, 1797. Sponsor: Simon Kolb.
Anna of Peter Seib and Margaret, born September 7, 1792; baptized April 21, 1797. Sponsors: John Ernst and wife.
Elizabeth of Conrad Rufner and Eva, born October 18, 1796; baptized June 18. Sponsors: father and mother.
Catharine of Henry Albert and Catharine, born September 23, 1796; baptized August 13, 1797. Sponsors: Gabriel Bobinmeier and Catharine.
George of Jacob Heraug and Catharine, born July 30; baptized August 13. Sponsors: Conrad Klein and Magdalena Seib.
William of John Lieberd and Julia, born April 12; baptized ----. Sponsors: John Steitz and Elizabeth Lieberd.
Leah of Martin Marzzall and Susanna, born July 31; baptized September 10. Sponsors: ----.
Magdalena of Adam Mell and wife, born September 12; baptized ---- by John Herbst. Sponsor: Jacob Heraff ?

CUMBERLAND COUNTY CHURCH RECORDS OF THE 18TH CENTURY

1798

George of John Gensmer and wife, born August 4; baptized ---- by John Herbst. Sponsors: Peter Blaser and Elizabeth.
---- of Henry Rein and Anna Maria, born January 16; baptized ---- by John Herbst. Sponsors: John Mitz and wife.
Julyeriel ? of George Werns and Catharine, born January 10; baptized ---- by John Herbst. Sponsors: ----.
John Martin of Jacob Wolff and wife, born June 22; baptized July 8 by John Herbst. Sponsors: Martin Bender and wife.
Samuel of ---- Blaser, born April 28; baptized November 8 by John Herbst. Sponsors: Martin George and wife.
---- of Philip Shmid and wife, born June 15; baptized September 8 by John Herbst. Sponsors: Michael Lein and wife.
Samuel of John Koenig and wife, born March 28; baptized April 21 by John Herbst. Sponsor: Gabriel Bobmeier.
Maria of Henry Albert and wife, born November 13, 1797; baptized April 21 by John Herbst.

1799

Maria Catharine of ---- Bruckmann, born December 15, 1798; baptized June 2. Sponsors: John Ernst and Catharine.
John George of Philip Heckman, born ----; baptized August 18 by John Herbst.
Philip of Valentine Hon, born ----; baptized August 18 by John Herbst.
Maria of William Sturt, born ----; baptized August 18 by John Herbst.

1800

Susanna of Philip Schneyder and wife, born April 11; baptized ----. Sponsors: the parents.
William of ---- Eiler, born November 27, 1799; baptized ---- by John Herbst. Sponsors: Martin George and wife.

1801

Fiana of ---- Kolb, born September 9; baptized September 9 by John Herbst. Sponsor: Margaret Der.
Magdalena of ---- Bender, born ----; baptized August 28. Sponsors: Martin Bender and wife.
Maria Charlotta of John Koenig, born October 20; baptized December 20 by John Herbst. Sponsors: Josefus Saddorius and Maria Charlotta Bobenmeier.
Anna of John Holl, born October 5; baptized December 20 by John Herbst. Sponsors: the parents.
Daniel of John Ernst and wife, born September 6, 1799 (at three o'clock in the sign of the marksman); baptized September 29 by John Herbst. Sponsors: Henry Kern and Anna Maria.
Elizabeth of Henry Kern and wife, born March 28, 1795; baptized ---- by John Herbst. Sponsors: Peter Blaser and wife.
Salome of Henry Kern and wife, born February 12, 1797; baptized ---- by John Herbst. Sponsors: Henry Blaser and wife.

POPLAR CHURCH

Poplar, or St. John's Evangelical Lutheran Church, Shiremanstown, Cumberland Co, PA.

Baptisms by Rev. F. D. Schaeffer

Johannes of Johannes Wormle and Anna Maria, born ----; baptized June 21. Sponsors: the parents.
Georg of Johannes Wormle and Anna Maria, born ----; baptized February 3. Sponsors: the parents.
Elisabeth of J. Georg Wormle and Elisabeth, born ----; baptized - ----. Sponsors: the parents.
Johan Jacob of Conrad Schmid and Margaretha, born ----; baptized September 21, 1788. Sponsors: George Wild and Catharina his wife.
Elisabeth of Georg Zuber and Elisabeth, born June 7, 1787; baptized September 21, 1789. Sponsors: Anna Maria and Emmerich Wilz.
Andreas of Georg Zuber and Elisabeth his wife, born June 22, 1788; baptized September 21, 1788. Sponsors: Johannes Albert and Maria Barbara.
Anna Maria of Marthin Thomas and his wife Ursala, born April 2, 1788; baptized October 5, 1788. Sponsor: Elisabeth Miphin.
Johannes of Phillip Hoch and Elisabeth, born May 23, 1788; baptized October 19, 1788. Sponsors: Johannes Albert and Maria Barbara.
Magdelena of Friedrich Gramlich and Eva his wife, born December 7, 1788; baptized March 25, 1789. Sponsor: Elisabeth Gramlich, spinster.
Johann Georg of Daniel Frank and Dorothea his wife, born 1st Advent 1788; baptized May 17, 1789. Sponsors: Johannes Georg Wormle and Elisabeth his wife.
Anna Catharina of Johan Georg Mild [Wild] and Anna Catharina, born November 17, 1788; baptized May 17, 1789. Sponsors: Conrad Schmid and Margaretha his wife.
Johannes of Johannes Huephler and his wife, born November 21, 1788; baptized May 24, 1789. Sponsors: Johannes Wormle and his wife.
Johan Cassber of Cassber Hob and his wife, born December 18, 1788; baptized May 24, 1789. Sponsors: Marthin Domma and his wife.
Michael of Michael Ruble and his wife, born December 18, 1788; baptized May 24, 1789. Sponsors: Jacob Ruble and his wife.
Johann Georg of Johann Georg Pannestache and his wife, born November 15, 1788; baptized May 24, 1789. Sponsors: Engehart Wurmle and his wife.
Johannes of Henrich Steinbrindt and Eleonora his wife, born June 2, 1789; baptized June 12, 1789. Sponsors: Georg Sehner and Madlena his wife.
Maria Machthalena of Thomas Muller and Maria (?), born June 7, 1789; baptized October 15. Sponsor: Henrich Rothreft(?).
Maria Catharina of Georg Wormle and Elisabeth, born September 24, 1789; baptized December 25, 1789. Sponsors: the parents.

22 CUMBERLAND COUNTY CHURCH RECORDS OF THE 18TH CENTURY

1790 Baptisms by Rev. Adam Henry Meyer

Jacob of Maj. Tiwitte and his lawful wife Elizabeth born Lochman; baptized November 12, 1790, aged 3 years. Sponsors: his father and his mother.

Barbara of Maj. Tiwitte and his lawful wife Elizabeth born Lochman; baptized November 12, 1790, aged one and a half years. Sponsors: father and mother.

Baptized November 15, 1790. Advertised. Barbara of Mr. Conrad Rupple and his lawful wife Veronica born Wittmer, born November 3, 1780; baptized June 4, 1787. (She confessed herself at the baptism as belonging to the true Evangelical Lutheran Religion.) Sponsor: Magdalena Rupple.

Baptized November 15, 1790. Advertised. Maria of Mr. Conrad Rupple and his lawful wife Veronica born Wittmer, born February 12, 1785, and baptized. Sponsor: Maria Rupple.

Elizabeth of Mr. Isaac Kuntze and his lawful wife Margarita born Schwartz, born ----; baptized November 14, 1790, at her father's house. Sponsors: Elizabeth Schwartz and Mr. Johan Schwartz.

Johanne of Jacob Eichelberger and his lawful wife Margaret born Rupple, born ----; baptized April 12, 1790. Sponsors: Christoph Eichelberger and his wife Margaret.

Catharin Elizabet of Nicolaus Schlichter and his lawful wife Catharina born Felten, born July 22; baptized April 20, 1790, before confirmation. Sponsors: Mrs. Elizabeth Kreitzer and Mr. Nicolas Kreitzer.

Baptisms, 1791

Mary of Mr. Abraham Adams, residing over the Connigogussne(?), and his lawful wife Elizabeth, born McGuire; baptized May 28, 1791, aged 4 and a half years old. Sponsors: the parents.

Isaac of Mr. Abraham Adams, residing over the Connigogussne(?), and his lawful wife Elizabeth born McGuire; baptized May 28, 1791, aged 2-3/4 years. Sponsors: the parents.

Johan Wilhelm of John Henrich Steinbring and his lawful wife Eleanor born Lehner, born January 1 of this year; baptized June 20, 1791. Sponsors: Georg Lehner and the mother.

Maria Elizabeth of Mr. Jacob Freidrich Velde and his lawful wife Catharina born Gruenewalter, born ----; baptized August 21, 1791. Sponsors: Maria Gruenewalter and the father and mother.

Catharina of Johan Nicolaus Kreitzer and his lawful wife Elizabeth born Kiemmel, born ----; baptized August 21, 1791. Sponsors: Mr. Adam Kreitzer and his wife and the father and mother.

Juliana of Mr. Adam Kreitzer and his lawful wife Elizabeth, born ----; baptized September 1, 1791. Sponsors: the mother, Mr. Adam Kreitzer and the minister, Mr. A. H. Meyer.

Susanna of Mr. Jean Schwanfeld and his lawful wife Barbara, born ----; baptized October 29, 1791. Sponsors: Mr. Jacob Rupple and his wife.

Henry of Molle Leime, daughter of Michel Leime, and Henry Foree born out of wedlock; baptized November 27, 1791, aged 3 years old. Witnesses: mother and the schoolmaster.

POPLAR (ST. JOHN'S) CHURCH   23

Baptisms, 1792

Anna Maria of Johannes Weiser and his lawful wife Justina, born November 3, 1791; baptized February 19, 1792. Sponsors: Elizabeth Rubble and the parents.
Anna Catharina (a twin) of Mr. Freidrich Bretz and his lawful wife Magdalena, born ----; baptized May 26, 1792.
Elizabeth (a twin) of Mr. Freidrich Bretz and his lawful wife Magdalena, born ----; baptized May 26, 1792.
Susanna of Mr. Wilhelm Mokhel and Salome, born ----; baptized May 26, 1792. Sponsors: Jacob Friedrich Velde, Catarina Velder, Abraham Bretz, Hinr. Cretzberger.
Sophia of Jac. Ruple junior and Anna Maria, born ----; baptized September 9, 1792. Sponsor: Anna Ruple.
Charles of Mr. Henry Stuart and his wife Isabella, born ----; baptized September 9, 1792. Sponsors: godfather and the father.
William of Mr. Henry Stuart and his wife Isabella, born September 9, 1792 ; baptized same day at Mr. Conrad Rupple's. Sponsors: godfather and the father.
Anna Eva of Mr. Johan Bauer and his wife Catharina; baptized September 9, 1792, aged 2 years old. Sponsors: father and mother.
Johannes of Joh. Bauer and his wife Catharina, born ----; baptized same day in his parents' house. Sponsors: Mr. Dewald Erfurt and his wife Magdalena.
Christina of ? and Maria, born ----; baptized October 1, 1792. Sponsor: Eva ?.
Elisabeth of Jacob ? and ?, born ----; baptized September 25, 1793. Sponsors: Joh. Nicolaus and Elisabeth Kreitzer.
Susana of Joseph Koch(?) and Anna Maria, born ----; baptized September 19, 1794. Sponsors: Nicolaus Schaefter(?) and Susana.
Joh. Georg of Conrath Weber and Catherina, born ----; baptized May 13, 179(4)(?). Sponsors: the parents.
Maria of Jacob Heit(?) and Maria Barbara (?), born ----; baptized December 10, 1794. Sponsor: Maria ?
Sarah of Christoph Eichenberger and Barbara, born ----; baptized November 24, 1793. Sponsors: Jacob Wormle and Elisabeth his wife.
Johannes of Abraham Pratz and Maria, born ----; baptized May 9, 1794. Sponsors: Christopher Eichenberger and Barbara his wife.
Maria of Johannes Wormly, born ----; baptized July 19, 1794. Sponsors: the parents.
Maria of Jacob Rupply and Maria, born ----; baptized February 29, 1794. Sponsors: the parents.
Susana of Henrich S. MannesSchmidt and Eva, born ----; baptized May 31, 1794. Sponsors: Christian LaubenSchweiler and Susana.
Anna Elisabeth of Casper Treiber and Elisabeth, born ----; baptized March 5, 1794. Sponsors: Valentine Bruchman and Anna Elisabeth.
Joh. Georg. of Thomas Minsch and Magdalena, born ----; baptized November 2, 1794. Sponsor. Joh: Georg Minsch.
Friedreich of Friedreich Lang and Christina, born ----; baptized September 21, 1794. Sponsors: Jonas Rupp and Catharina.

Georg Elter of Engelhart Wormly and Elisabeth, born ----;
baptized December 7, 1794. Sponsors: Georg Wormly and
Elisabeth.
Jacob of Georg Eble and Anna, born March 18; baptized May 17,
1795. Sponsor: Englehardt Wormly.
Georg of Georg Eble and Anna, born February 21, 1786; baptized
May 17, 1795. Sponsor: isdem.
Samuel of Georg Eble and Anna, born November 10, 1787; baptized
May 17, 1795.
A. Maria of Georg Eble and Anna, born November 3, 1790; baptized
May 17, 1795.
Anna of Georg Eble and Anna, born beginning of December 1794;
baptized May 17, 1795.
Elisabeth of Emrick John and Mary, born ----; baptized April 12,
1795. Sponsors: Jacob Rupply and Maria.
Maria of Jacob Caszler and Catharina, born ----; baptized April
28, 1795. Sponsors: Georg Brentz and Catharina.
Samuel of Georg Lutz and Catharina, born ----; baptized January
15, 1796. Sponsor: Abraham Wolf.
Ana Cathar. of Henrich Jungst, born ----; baptized November --,
1765.
Catharina of Henrich Jungst and Christina, born ----; baptized
November 22, 1795. Sponsor: Peter Jungst.
Greth of Alexander Weyth, born ----; baptized October 2, 1789.
Sponsors: Johanes Jaig and Magdalena.
Eva of Johanes Jaig and Magdalena, born ----; baptized March 17,
1795. Sponsors: Magdalena Weygand.
Joh. Jacob of Georg Wormly, born ----; baptized May 22, 1796.
Sponsors: Jacob Wormly and Elisabeth.
Susana of Georg Wormly, born ----; baptized May 22, 1796.
Sponsor: Susana Lutzin.
Sara of Georg Wild and Catharina, born ----; baptized January 12,
1796. Sponsor: Maria Albert.
Engelhardt of Engelhard Wormly and Elisabeth, born January 19,
1797; baptized 29th of the same. Sponsors: Jacob Feger and his
wife Elisabeth.
Henrich of Jacob Rubly and Anna Maria, born July 28, 1795;
baptized September 4. Sponsors: the parents.
Abraham of Abraham Pretz and Anna Maria, born February 12, 1797;
baptized April 30. Sponsors: Simon Pretz and Catharina.
Johannes of Georg Man and A. Maria, born July 1; baptized
September 31, 1797. Sponsors: Jacob Wormly and Elisabeth.
Johan Georg of Arnold Hofelmann and Eva, born October 20, 1797;
baptized January 6, 1798. Sponsors: the parents.
Veronica of Conrad Rubly and Veronica, born October 11, 1797;
baptized March 20, 1798. Sponsors: Jacob Rubly and A. Maria.
Benjamin of Martin Muller and Sally, born January 30; baptized
March 20, 1798. Sponsors: Frid. Schultz and A. Maria.
Joseph of Francis Strong and Jenny, born March 2; baptized May 9.
Sponsors: the parents.
Johannes of Adam Hertz and Maria, born June 11; baptized August
5. Sponsors: Engelhardt Wormly and Elisabeth.
Johannes Georg of Joh. Georg Wormly and Catharina his wife, born
August 15; baptized October 7, 1798. Sponsors: Johannes Wormly

POPLAR (ST. JOHN'S) CHURCH 25

and Maria.
David of Joh. Wormly and Maria his wife, born December 25, 1798; baptized January 7, 1799. Sponsors: the parents.
Abraham of Engelhardt Wormly and Elisabeth, born February 24; baptized April 7, 1799. Sponsors: Johannes Rubly and Barbara.
Georg of Joh. Rubly and Barbara, born December 14, 1798; baptized January 13, 1799. Sponsors: Jacob Rubly and Maria.
Johannes of Johannes Heck and Elisabeth Kisecker (unmarried), born February 8. Sponsors: Nicolaus Kisecker and Anna Margaretha.
Anna of Henrich Ernstberger and Anna, born January 16; baptized June 16, 1799. Sponsors: the parents.
Benjamin of Geo. Werftel(?) and Maria, born November 2, 1798; baptized June 23, 1799. Sponsors: the parents.
Anna Maria of Joh. Schafer and Christina, born March 29; baptized August 4, 1799. Sponsors: Christoph Eichelberger and Barbara.
Susanna of Thomas Wharton and Susanna, born September 29, 1796; baptized September 15, 1799. Sponsors: Valentine Stegmuller and A. Elisabeth.
Johannes of Nicolaus Schamburg and Barbara, born February 26; baptized January 1, 1800. Sponsor: the mother.
Barbara of Hanna Ily (in celebacy), born December 20, 1799; baptized March 2, 1800. Sponsor: Elisabeth Koch.
Johannes of Philip Koch and Elisabeth, born November 17, 1799; baptized March 8, 1800. Sponsors: Joh. Emerich and Cath. Kiesecker.
Philip of Philip Koch and Elisabett, born ----; baptized January 10, 1798. Sponsors: Phil. Hickernel(?) and Cath. Thomas.
Elisabeth of Geo. Wolf and Elisabeth, born March 13, 1797; baptized April 12, 1800. Sponsor: the mother.
Johannes of Georg Kober and Eva, born August 15, 1799; baptized July 29, 1801. Sponsors: Christoph Eichelberger and Barbara.
Sarah of Georg Kober and Eva, born March 8; baptized as above [July 29, 1801]. Sponsor: Elis. Schafer.
Maria of Georg Wormle and Catharina, born August 29, 1800; baptized 5 weeks afterwards. Sponsor: Elis. Wormle.
Johannes of Henr. Trabinger and Eva, born August 30, 1800; baptized September 27, 1801. Sponsors: the parents.
David of Henrich John and Anna Maria, born March 3, 1795; baptized May 29, 1802. Sponsor: Dewald Erfurt.
Margaretha of Henrich John and Anna Maria, born September 18, 1797; baptized on the same day. Sponsors: Jacob Eichelberger and Maria.
Willhelm of Henrich John and Anna Maria, born October 21, 1800; baptized on the same day. Sponsors: Daniel Humeldorf and Eva.
Elisabet of Adam Thomas, born September 22, 1777; baptized October 28, 1808. Sponsors: ----.

Confirmations, during the year 1790-1791
Sunday after Easter, 1790, Catechumens

Jacob Haas, 26 years
Conrad Bretz, 18 years
Jacob Dewald, 17 years

Erf. Dewald, 14 years
J. Adam Harris, 22 years
Conr. Renninger, 19 years
Adam Bretz, 28 (23?) years
Johan Bennitsch, 17 years
Jac. (Behr ?), 19 years
Johannes Bauer, 35 years
Joh. Pater, 18 years
Elisabeth Rupple
Anna Rupple
Elis. Eichelberg
Anna Mar. Renninger
Elis. Bennitsch
Cathar. Schlichter
Cathar. Fischer
Cathar. Adiben
Anna Mar. Muller
Mar. Magd. Dorren

        2nd lecture 17th Sunday after Trinity

Christ. Eichelberger and his wife
Joh. Jac. Eichelberger and his wife Margr. Wolff

BIG SPRING PRESBYTERIAN CHURCH

Taken from *Big Spring Presbyterian Church, Newville, PA, 1737-1898*, by Gilbert Ernest Swope, Newville, PA. James Steam Printing House, 1898.

Communion Lists

Communion Lists 1789
John Carson's District

Robert Mickie, 68
Agnes Mickie, 64
David Mickie, 22
Elenor Mickie, 20
Hannah Mickie, 18
Phillis, a negro.
Thomas E. Fullerton, 21
Isabel Fullerton, 18
John Ackman, 30
Mary Ackman, 28
Elenor Laughlin, 70
Matthew Laughlin, 30
Paul Laughlin, 27
Doctor Laughlin, 24
Peggy McCune, 17
Samuel McCune, 16
John McCune, 12
Lillian M. Flin, 7
Isabel McCune, 50
Robert McCune, 17
Rebecca Parks, 13
William Parks, 11
David Parks, 9
Priscilla Carson, 35
Elisha Carson, 20
John Carson, 18
Hannah Carson, 16
Joseph McGuffine, 32
Jane McGuffine, 27
William McGuffine, 9
Mary McGuffine, 7
Robert McGuffine, 4
William Leman, --
Samuel Leman, 7
Martha Leman, 29
William Leman, 5
James Johnston, 23
Margaret Johnson, 22
Robert Johnson, 20
William Auld, 30
Christiana Auld, 25
Mary Auld, 7
Martha Ewing, 70
Samuel Findlay, 35

James Denny, 21
William McCracken, 35
Elizabeth McCracken, --
Betsy Peoples, 16
Robert Peoples, 14
Martha McCracken, 9
Jenny McCracken, 7
Jonathan, a Negro.
Prudence Farhner, 19
Robert Mickie, 45
Isamiah Mickie, 35
Andrew Mickie, 12
Mary Mickie, 10
Thomas Mickie, 7
John Smith, 20
Jonathan Kilgore, 27
Ruth Kilgore, 22
John Caldwell, a member of session, --
Anne Caldwell, 45
James Caldwell, --
John Caldwell, 20
Elizabeth and Samuel Caldwell, 14
Ann Caldwell, 12

William Lindsay's District

William Hunter, 60
Jane Hunter, 60
John McIntire, --
Sally McIntire, 18
Joseph McIntire, 14
David Shannon, 55
Sarah Shannon, 47
Lenard Shannon, 21
Samuel Shannon, 19
Patty Cowly, 8
William Warrington, 9
William Walker, 50
Jane Walker, 50
Elizabeth Walker, 25
James Walker, 19
William Walker, 18
Rachel Walker, 16

28 CUMBERLAND COUNTY CHURCH RECORDS OF THE 18TH CENTURY

Jane Walker, 15
Samuel Walker, 10
Joseph Walker, 45
Rachel Walker, 40
Mary Walker, 18
Elizabeth Walker, 16
Jane Walker, 12
Isabel Walker, 9
Hannah Walker, 7
James Walker, 6
Andrew Walker, 40
Mary Walker, 38
James Walker, 18
Joseph Walker, 11
Jane Walker, 9
Betsy Walker, 7
Robert Walker, 56
Margaret Walker, 50
Mary Walker, 19
John Walker, 17
Elizabeth Walker, 14
Margaret Walker, 8
Robert Walker, 6
Gabriel Glen, 55
Jane Glen, 40
Rachel Mills, 24
Gabriel Glen, 50
William Glen, 9
Jenny Glen, 7
Jared Graham, 24
Jenny Graham, 20
John Brown, 55
Martha Brown, 50
Mary Brown, 20
John Brown, 18
William Brown, 15
Agnes Brown, 16
James Brown, 11
James McGovern, 35
Ann McGovern, 20
Mary McGovern, 8
Francis Donnel
George Lightel
Sarah Lightel
William Hunter, 50
Jane Hunter, 50
James Hunter, 17
Agnes Hunter, 17
William Hunter, 15
Lathie Hunter, 13
Jane Hunter, 11
Lathie Wilson
John McTeer, 23
Agnes McTeer, 20

Adam Brattan, 35
Martha Brattan, 9
John Gilmore
William Wilson, 60
Mary Wilson, 59
Samuel Wilson, 25
Mary Wilson, 20
Margaret Sayers, 17
James Wilson, 27
Margaret Wilson, 22
William Giffin, 35
Elenor Giffin, 30
Betsy Giffin, 11
Sally Giffin, 5
Joseph Pollock, 30
Mary Pollock, 28
Thomas Jacob, 30
Elizabeth Jacob, 27
Elenor Jacob, 12
Mary Jacob, 9
William Patton, 25
Mary Patton, 25
William Ferguson
James Marshbank, 25
William Patton, 80
Janet Patton, 78
John Patton, 30
William Patton, 27
Margaret Patton, 25
William Devinport, 23
Robert Patton, 12
Samuel Bayle, 30
Martha Bayle, 25
Horace Brattan, 17
Anne Brattan, 15
David Ewing, 24
Elizabeth Ewing, 22
James Graham, 60
Susannah Graham, 45
Thomas Graham, 21
Arthur Graham, 19
Isaiah Graham, 18
James Graham, 14
Elizabeth Moor, 18
Margaret Moor, 12
Robert Boyd, 16
Margaret McFarlane, 55
Robert McFarlane, 22
Ann McFarlane, 19
Mary McFarlane, 16
Elizabeth McFarlane, 13
Hannah McFarlane, 10
William Brisby, 40
Sarah Brisby, 35

Nancy Brisby, 13
Betsy Brisby, 12
William Brisby, 10
John Brisby, 8
Elizabeth Wilson, 70
Matthew Wilson, 28
Prudence Penwell, 16
Joseph Edmonston, 25
Agnes Edmonston, 22
Adam Conelly, 17
James McFarlane, 27
Elizabeth McFarlane, 23
Ceasar and Dick
James Johnson, 30
Martha Johnson, 28
Peggy Johnson, 10
Jenny Johnson, 6
Samuel Lindsy, 60
Nancy Lindsy, 55
Samuel Lindsy
Robert Lindsy
Jenny Lindsy, 20
Nancy Lindsy, 16
William Lindsy, 27
Jane Lindsy
Robert Huston, 50
Martha Huston, 50
Nancy Huston, 20
Peggy Huston, 18
John Espy, 20
William Clark, 24
John Love, 27
Margaret Love, 25
James Love, 25
Thomas Love, 22
William Clark, 67
Agnes Clark
John Clark, 13
John Woods, 80
Jane Woods, 80
Richard Woods, 27
Isabel Woods, 35
Robert Woods, 25
Polly Woods, 18
Joseph Woods, 14
Adam Hays, 86
Joseph Hays, 23
Anne Hays, 18
John Green 16
Nancy Allen, 13
Patrick Gibson
Martha Gibson
James Connelly, 22
William Connelly, 20

Elizabeth Connelly, 18
Charity Connelly, 17
Joseph Means, 26
Nancy Means, 24
John McFarlane, 60
Elizabeth McFarlane, 50
Sarah McFarlane, 20
James McFarlane, 16
Robert McFarlane, 14
Andrew McFarlane, 14
Thomas Buchanan, 30
Agnes Buchanan, 28
Robert Buchanan, 8
William Buchannan, 6
Jenny McClellan, 14
William McFarlane, 56
Elizabeth McFarlane, 50
David Murray, 22
Anne McClellan, 16
James Hall, 9

John Bell's District

Elleanor Gillespie, 67
Geo. Gillespie (absent), 25
James Gorly, 7
Sal, a negro.
James Gillespie, 38
Jane Gillespie, 30
William Gillespie, 7
Mat. M. Gillespie, 5
John Talbart, 10
Rebecca Armstrong, 50
James Johnston, 78
James Johnston, 38
Alexander Johnston, 16
Mary Johnston, 14
John Johnston, 10
Jane Johnston, 8
James Johnston, 5
Robert Dunbar
Samuel Wilson, 26
Samuel Hawthorn, 32
Margaret Hawthorn, 28
James Hawthorn, 9
George Kelsy, 60
Elizabeth Kelsy, 28
Jane Kelsy, 20
George Kelsy, 22
Elizabeth Bell, 52
Katharine Brown, 50
Robert Bell, 24

Jane Bell, 22
William Bell, 24
Joseph Bell, 17
George Bell, 15
John Bell, 13
Thomas Bell, 12
Katharine Bell, 10
Alexander Officer, 60
Mary Officer, 67
James Officer, 36
Mary Officer, 30
Jane Gordon, 19
Katharine Gray, 20
Samuel Miller, 17
William Douglas, 47
Mary Douglas, 41
Margaret Douglas, 16
Agnes Douglas, 14
John Douglas, 12
Mary Douglas, 10
William Douglas, 7
Margaret McClure, 55
Jennet McClure, 25
Hannah Anderson, 23
Margaret McClure, 19
Andrew McClure, 21
James Laird, 34
Jane Laird, 24
Joseph Halbert, 20
John O'Neil, 40
Thomas Espey, 50
Ann Espey, 42
Margaret Espey, 20
William Espey, 18
Rachel Espey, 16
Ann Espey, 13
Robert Espey, 11
Elizabeth Espey, 9
James Espey, 7
Robert McClure, 55
Margaret McClure, 20
Nancy McClure, 16
Robert McClure, 14
Mary McClure, 12
Betsy McClure, 7
Alexander Leckey, 26
Elizabeth Leckey, 29

Robert Patterson's District

Thomas Glen, 60
Elizabeth Glen, 54
Thomas Glen, 21

Alexander Glen, 19
John Glen, 17
Sarah Patterson, 60
Obediah Patterson, 25
Zacheus Patterson, 20
Deborah Patterson, 18
Daniel Kelly, 30
Elizabeth Kelly, 36
Christian Kelly, 50
William Kelly, 16
Ann Kelly, 14
Richard Kelly, 12
James Houston, 70
John Huston, 24
Andrew Huston, 22
Sarah Huston, 26
Jane Huston, 18
Thomas Norton, -0 [? year]
Sarah Norton, 36
Betsy Norton, 9
Thomas Norton, 7
Elizabeth McCulloch, 56
James McCulloch, 20
Robert McCulloch, 12
Rosian Adair, 8
William Wagstas [Wagstaf], 30
Charity Wagstas [Wagstaf], 19
Agnes Irwin, 70
Thomas Grier, 35
Jane Grier, 25
Ann Browster, 60
William Browster, 25
Alexander Browster, 22
Mary Carithers, 28
Charles McConel, 56
Isabel McConel, 46
Eleanor McConel, 17
Martha McConel, 16
Mary McConel, 13
Jenny McConel, 10
John McConel, 7
William Woods, 60
Samuel Woods, 26
Jenny Woods, 24
John Woods, 22
Mary Woods, 20
Mat, a negro.
William Woods, 25
Jane Woods, 22
Nathan Woods, 8
Samuel Goodling, 15
John Mitchel, 10
Janet Ramsey, 60
Nathan Ramsey, 25

Mary Ramsey, 13
Agnes Ramsey, 17
Elizabeth Ramsey, 16
Margaret Ramsey, 14
Alexander McBride, 26
Tabitha McBride, 24
Mary Patterson, 60
Esther Patterson, 20
Ann Patterson, 18
Sarah Patterson, 16
Elizabeth Patterson, 14
Thomas Patterson, 12
Robert Johnston, 30
Ann Johnston, 35
Margaret Harper, 28
John Lemon, 45
Elizabeth Lemon, 35
Jane Lemon, 14
Nancy Lemon, 12
Polly Lemon, 10
Robert Fowler, 30
Elizabeth Fowler, 19
John Fowler, 23
William Ewing, 40
Jane Ewing, 35
Nancy Ewing, 14
Robert Ewing, 9
William Ewing, 7
Alexander Ewing, 5
Katharine Crawford, 12
Thomas Ewing, 45
Mariana Ewing, 40
John Ewing, 15
Rebecca Ewing, 6
Alexander Clark, 12
Elenor Reigh, 60
Samuel Reigh
Mary Reigh, 16
Joseph Gourd, 25
Margaret Gourd, 24
Nancy Homes
John McCurdy, 20
Elizabeth McCurdy, 24
Joseph Van Horn, 30
Annie Van Horn, 25
John Ewing, 50
Sarah Ewing, 48
Jane Ewing, 22
William Ewing, 20
Martha Ewing, 16
Matthew Ewing, 16
Mary Ewing, 12
James Ewing, 10
Rebecca Ewing, 8

James Ewing, 52
Jane Ewing, 44
Thomas Ewing, 16
Rebecca Ewing, 14
Anna Ewing, 11
James Ewing, 7
Thomas Adams, 30
Agnes Adams, 28
Jenny Adams, 14
Samuel Adams, 10
Richard Adams, 7
David McCurdy, 60
Mrs. McCurdy, 57
James McCurdy, 25
Mary Morris
David McCurdy, 20
Janet McCurdy, 19
Nancy Lowry, 18
Adam Clelland, 35
Jane Clelland, 45
John Calvert, 20
Eleo Galbraith, 9
William Appleby, 35
Nancy Appleby, 28
Eliza Appleby, 14
J. Appleby, 12
Jane Appleby, 10
John Appleby, 9
James Leeper, 45
Mary Leeper, 40
Allen Leeper, 16
Martha Leeper, 13
James Leeper, 11
Sally Leeper, 9
Jack, a mulatto.
William Hunter, 23
Elizabeth Hunter, 21

Robert Lusk's District

Robert Lusk was one of five brothers who emigrated from Ireland at an early date and settled in this vicinity. He bought a farm in Mifflin township, known as the "Fountain of Health Farm," which had been warranted to Andrew McElwain, about 1730. Robert Lusk married Martha McClure of Adams County.

Mary Sterret, 80

CUMBERLAND COUNTY CHURCH RECORDS OF THE 18TH CENTURY

David Sterret, 50
Rachel Sterret, 48
Robert Sterret, 24
Bryce I. Sterret, 22
David Sterret, 20
Elizabeth Sterret, 18
John Sterret, 16
William Sterret, 10
Elizabeth McMullan, 8
Sandon, a negro.
Ned, a negro.
Andrew Patterson, 35
Mary Patterson
Jane Patterson, 15
Nathan Patterson, 13
Samuel Patterson, 11
James Patterson, 9
Sarah Patterson, 8
William Stephenson, 40
Jane Stephenson, 33
Elizabeth Stephenson, 12
James Stevenson, 10
James McElwain, 37
Mary McElwain, 12
John McElwain, 10
Ruth McElwain, 7
Andrew McElwain, 33
Elizabeth McElwain, 30
Elizabeth Mason, 17
Mary McElwain, 8
Robert McElwain, 7
Jane McElwain, 5
Mary McElwain, 70
Robert McElwain, 22
Elizabeth McElwain, 20
John Paten, 50
Francis Paten
William Paten, 20
James Paten, 18
John Paten, 16
Joseph Paten, 14
Mary Paten, 12
Thomas Paten, 9
Robert Paten, 7
Fanny Paten, 7
Joseph Shannon, 25
Mary Shannon, 26
John Morrow, 30
Hannah Morrow, 29
Mary Morrow, 8
David Ramsey, 110
Sarah Ramsey, 13
Anne Ramsey, 11
Margaret Ramsey, 9

Mary Ramsey, 7
David Ramsey, 5
Robert Lusk, 27
Martha Lusk, 21
Jane Lusk, 4
Thomas Martin
Mary Martin, 25
Rosanna Martin, 18
John Martin, 16
Jane Martin, 14
James Hamilton
George Hamilton
Ruth Hamilton
Andrew Bell, 40
Betsy Bell, 13
Samuel Bell, 10
Matty Bell, 7
John Bell, 17
John McClure, 17
Betsy Johnson
Robert Bell, 48
Jane Bell, 49
Walter Bell, 16
William Bell, 15
David Bell, 13
Peggy Bell, 11

Samuel M'Cormick's District

Samuel M'Cormick was born 1726 and died September 4th, 1803. He married Eliza Bowman, who was born 1727, and died October 7, 1811. He settled in Mifflin Township, prior to 1781. He first purchased the farm, now known as the Asper farm. This he sold and bought from William McFarlane, the farm below Doubling Gap, on which he died, now owned by W. H. McCrea. That he was greatly concerned for his own, and the spiritual welfare of the people over which he had charged, is evinced by his many letters to his pastor, on these subjects.

Isabella Hall, 67
Ruth Cook, 14
John Reed, 50
Sarah Reed, 34
Elizabeth Long, 10

BIG SPRING PRESBYTERIAN CHURCH 33

Samuel Lowry, 9
John Montroe, 62
Mary Ann Montroe, 31
Margaret Montroe, 14
William Montroe, 9
Reuben Montroe, 6
Sarah Denison, 84
Martha French, 45
Thomas Mathers, 54
Mary Mathers, 50
Margaret Mathers, 20
William Mathers, 18
Jane Mathers, 16
Mary Fenton, 80
Samuel Fenton, 40
Ann Fenton, 30
James Fenton, 13
Robert Fenton, 11
Samuel Fenton, 9
John Fenton, 7
Andrew Thompson, 40
Mary Thompson, 40
Mary Ann Thompson, 18
Hugh Thompson, 16
Samuel Thompson, 14
Hannah Thompson, 12
Andrew Thompson, 10
James W. Thompson, 8
James Walker, 26
Jane Walker, 25
George Taylor, 60
Elenor Taylor, 55
George Taylor, 24
Nancy Taylor, 20
James Patterson, 40
Mary Patterson, 38
Nancy Patterson, 15
Thomas Patterson, 12
Robert Patterson, 10
Isaac Durbara, 50
Jane Durbara, 20
Reuben Durbara, 20
John Durbara, 18
Alexander McClintock, 40
Sarah McClintock, 39
David Dougherty, 19
John Stars, 19
Elizabeth Palm, 11
James Brannan, 40
Mary Brannan, 19
John Brannan, 16
Thomas Brannan, 12
William Brannan, 9
John McFarlane, 50

Mary McFarlane, 50
James McFarlane, 26
Margaret McFarlane, 24
Elizabeth McFarlane, 15
John McFarlane, 13
Alexander McFarlane, 11
Ann McFarlane, 10
William McFarlane, 8
John Shannon, 33
Agnes Shannon, 30
Mary Shannon, 12
Ann Shannon, 11
Andrew Shannon, 9
Sarah Shannon, 7
John Wallace, 32
Elizabeth Wallace, 30
William Mophet, 36
Rebecca Mophet, 38
Jane Mophet, 12
Phoebe Mophet, 10
Thomas Barnes, 70
Grizel Barnes, 55
Margaret Barnes, 27
David Barnes, 20
Robert Barnes, 17
Elizabeth McCormick, wife of
   the elder, 60
Joseph McCormick, 23
Thomas McCormick, 21
Ann McCormick, 18
Jane McCormick, 16
John Purdie, 40
Margaret Purdie, 40
Thomas Purdie, 18
James Purdie, 14
Rachel Purdie, 12
Mary Purdie, 10
John Purdie, 8
Robert Gallespie, 45
Elizabeth Gallespie, 40
William Gallespie, 19
Samuel Gallespie, 14
Nancy Gallespie, 12
Nelly Gallespie, 10
Grace, a negro.
Nathaniel Gallespie, 33
Martha Gallespie, 32
Millie Gallespie, 10
Mary Gallespie, 8
Ann Gallespie, 6
Thomas Pennel, 16
Sarah Majoirs, 45
Elizabeth Majoirs, 21
Isaac Majoirs, 11

CUMBERLAND COUNTY CHURCH RECORDS OF THE 18TH CENTURY

Nancy Majoirs, 9
Hugh Ramsey, 30
Margaret Ramsey, 25
John Mitchel, 25
Margaret Mitchel
Samuel Mitchel, 35
Mary Mitchel, 34
John Mitchel, 14
Ezekiel Mitchel, 11
James Mitchel, 7
Alexander Elliott, 35
Agnes Elliott, 35
Jannet Elliott, 13
Mary Elliott, 10
Catharine Elliott, 8

David Ralston's District

David Ralston, was a son of Andrew Ralston, who settled, 1728, on the farm now owned by Mrs. Parker, opposite the Newville station. David was one of five children, and came into possession of his father's farm, where he lived until 1806, when he moved to Westmoreland County, and died near Greensburg, 1810. He was twice married, first to a Miss Scott, second to Miss Elizabeth McClintock. Both wives died at Big Spring. By his first wife, David Ralston had issue: Elizabeth married Thomas Jacob; Jane married, first, a Mr. McDonald, and secondly, a Mr. Taylor; Elenor married a Mr. Miller; James married Ruth Carson; Andrew married Miss Kirkpatrick. By his second wife David Ralston had issue: Agnes married a Mr. Allsworth; Margaret married a Mr. Moorhead; Ann married Mr. Banks; Mary unmarried; Sarah unmarried; David married Lacy McAllister.

John Brown, 40
Elizabeth Brown, 38
Adam Brown, 18
Mary Brown, 16
Margaret Brown, 14
Elizabeth Brown, 12
Hannah Brown, 10
Joseph Brown, 8
Ann Brown, 6
William Smith, 32
Sarah Smith, 30
Robert Smith
John Smith
Elizabeth Smith
Mary Smith
John Turner, 60
Mary Turner, 56
Joseph Turner, 20
Sally Turner, 6
Thomas Moore, 60
Saml. Moore
John Mitchel
Lacy Mitchel
Jennet Mathers, 50
Samuel Mathers, 35
Isabella Mathers, 33
John Mathers, 12
Thomas Mathers, 10
Joseph Mathers, 25
Eleanor Mathers, 23
Robert Hutchison, 50
Mary Hutchison, 48
Nancy Hutchison, 14
Robert Hutchison, 12
Mary Hutchison, 10
Walter, a negro.
John Adams, 27
Jenny Adams, 20
Elizabeth Ralston, wife of the elder, 45
Nancy Ralston, 14
Margaret Ralston, 12
Amy Ralston, 10
Mary Ralston, 8
Sally Ralston, 7
David Ralston, 5
John Reed, 20
Eleanor Reed, 25
Sally Reed, 7
Grant, a negro.
John Hodge, 81
Agnes Hodge, 60
William Laughlin, 69
Mary Laughlin, 48
James Laughlin, 17
John Laughlin, 15
William Laughlin, 9
Rachel, a negro.
Catherine Atchison

BIG SPRING PRESBYTERIAN CHURCH 35

Atchison Laughlin
Rosannah Hutchison, 18
Martha Hutchison, 16
Mary Laughlin
Margaret McKein, 35
William McKein, 19
Mary McKein, 17
Elizabeth McKein, 14
Mary Patton, 30
Elizabeth McEntire, 28
James Mitchel, 50
Mary Mitchel, 48
Eve Mitchel
Elizabeth Mitchel
Rebecca Mitchel, 13
James Mitchel, 9
Mary Mitchel, 7
William Duncan, 26
Margaret Duncan, 23
Charity Davis, 12
James Irwin
Isabel Irwin
John Irwin
Mary Irwin
Mary Irwin
Eleanor Irwin
Caleb Ardiler, 30
Jane Ardiler, 28
Francis Morris, 9
Garman Jacobs, 29
Katherine Jacobs, 24

Hugh Lauglin's District

Jane Laughlin, 34
Buhard Brines, 12
David, a negro, 25
Alexander Laughlin, 52
Charity Laughlin, 37
Susana Laughlin, 15
Ann Laughlin, 10
John Laughlin, 8
Eve, a negro.
Jack, a negro.
Hall, a negro.
Robert McCormick, 30
Esther McCormick, 38
Wm. Nisbit (absent) 28
Esther Nisbit, 19
James Stewart (absent), 28
Thomas Martin
Eleanor Stewart, 22
Thomas Montgomery, 20

Rebecca McMullin, 13
John Allen, 26
Isabella Allen, 20
Hugh Allen, 57
Jennet Allen, 50
Elizabeth Allen, 18
Alexander Allen, 19
Jenny Allen, 14
David Allen, 13
David Williamson, 35
Samuel Williamson, 13
Hugh McElhenny, 30
Margaret McElhenny, 33
Hugh Kirkpatrick, 13
Richard Nicholdson, 73
Mary Nicholdson, 77
James Nicholdson, 33
Mary Nicholdson, 33
Isaac Shannon, 18
James Steen, 13
Sal, a negro.
Pomp, a negro.
Robert Shannon, 64
Jane Shannon, 63
Sarah Shannon, 30
John Shannon, 33
Mary Shannon, 20
Mary McGuffin, 5
Robert Morrison, 56
Elizabeth Morrison, 58
Robert Morrison, 20
Mary Morrison, 16
William Morrison, 13
Samuel McElhenny, 40
Mary McElhenny, 38
George Sully, 16
Rebecca McElhenny, 66
Martha McCasland, 47
William Montgomery, 14
Sarah McGlaughlin and family
Robert Barr and family
John Gorrel, 47
Isabella Gorrel, 50
Isabel Moor, 9
Joseph Shannon and family
John McGuffine, 30
William Hanna, 60
Samuel Morrow, 60
Jane Morrow, 50
William McGuffine, 20
John Bell, 45
Martha Bell, 38
Walter McClure, 16
Jenny Bell, 8

William Bryson, 60
Margaret Bryson, 53
Rebecca Bryson, 26
Samuel Bryson, 19
Hugh Bryson, 15
Ellenor Donoway, 10
Allen Means, 24
Alexander Wier, 24
William Carnahan, 77
Martha Carnahan, 66
Joseph Carnahan, 29
Robert Carnahan, 25
Judith Carnahan, 24
Rob't Mathers and family
John Wright, 30
Jennet Wright, 30
Margaret Wright, 18
William Thompson, 81
Ellenor Thompson, 71
Aaron Hains, 12
Tom, a negro.
Hannah, a negro.
Matthew Thompson, 30
Ann Thompson, 23
Mary Allison, 9

John Robinson's District

James Laughlin, 68
Mary Laughlin, 30
Robert Laughlin, 24
Hugh Laughlin, 18
William Laughlin, 20
Elizabeth Laughlin, 15
Robert M. Gopock, 8
Esther Robinson, 50
Mary Robinson, 10
Esther Robinson, 7
John Robinson, 5
William Thompson, 25
Jane Thompson, 24
Sally Chapman, 8
Susanna Thompson, 56
Alexander Thompson, 28
Leacy Thompson, 24
Peggy Thompson, 22
Hugh Thompson, 20
Sally Grier, 10
Adam Carnahan, 50
Agnes Carnahan, 36
James Carnahan, 17
Agnes Carnahan, 14
Adam Carnahan, 20

Elizabeth Carnahan, 8
Joseph Wilson, 82
Mary Wilson, 66
Joseph Wilson, 28
William Wilson, 23
Ann Wilson, 21
Ann Kennedy, 10
Jane Jack, 60
James Jack, 25
Cynthia Jack, 23
Andrew Jack, 21
Hannah Jack, 17
John Wilt and family
Agnes McGoffine, 60
James McGoffine, 35
John McGoffine, 33
S. Work, 53
Sal, a Negro.
William Work, 25
Elizabeth Work, 23
Alexander Work, 20
James Work, 18
Susanna Work, 16
S. Work, 14
John Work, 27
Mary Work, 23
James Carson, 39
Mary Carson, 31
Janet Carson, 9
Solomon Lightcap, 60
Mary Lightcap, 55
Samuel Lightcap, 25
Solomon Lightcap, 24
Levi Lightcap, 22
Nancy Lightcap, 21
Elizabeth Lightcap, 20
William Lightcap, 18
Godfrey Lightcap, 16
Thomas Lightcap, 14
John Morain, 65
Sarah Morain, 76
John Morain, 30
John Laughlin, 30
Margaret Laughlin, 28
James Carithers, 8
Jeremiah McKibben, 31
Mary McKibben, 29
Fan, a Negro.

John McKeehan's District

John McKeehan was one of four
brothers who settled in West

Pennsboro township at an early date. His brothers were Benjamin, James and Alexander. He died March 7, 1813, aged 75 years. His wife Elizabeth died June 20, 1822, aged 77 years.

James Turner, 29
Mary Turner, 29
James Walker (absent), 30
---- Johnson, 43
Thomas Johnson, 57
Mary Johnson, 21
Jean Johnson, 17
Margaret Johnson, 13
---- Johnson, 8
William Miller, 21
John Miller, 20
James Houston, 33
Isabel Houston, 25
Robert Houston, 6
John Davidson, 42
Leacy Davidson, 38
John Davidson, 16
James Davidson, 14
Ann Davidson, 9
Bill, a negro.
David Glen, 36
Mary Glen, 26
William Hanna, 11
John Rippet, 40
Elizabeth Rippet, 34
Rebecca Rippet, 10
Mary Rippet, 8
Matthew Davidson and family
George McKeehan, 40
Mary McKeehan, 30
Mary McKeehan, 6

Jenny McKeehan, 7
Randle Blair, 40
Charity Blair, 38
John Blair, 16
Daniel Blair, 13
Jenny Blair, 9
Elizabeth McKeehan, 45
George McKeehan, 18
James McKeehan, 16
John McKeehan, 14
Samuel McKeehan, 11
Alexander McKeehan, 9
Mary Ann McKeehan
James Atchison, 68
Elizabeth Atchison, 66
Jacob Atchison, 23
Benjamin Atchison, 20
Deborah Boyd, 45
John Boyd, 19
George Boyd, 15
James Boyd, 13
Eleanor Boyd, 10
Benjamin McKeehan, 30
Margaret McKeehan, 27
Elizabeth McKeehan, 25
James McKeehan, 35
Mary McKeehan, 30
Nancy McKeehan, 16
Peggy McKeehan, 14
John McKeehan, 13
Betsy McKeehan, 10
Margaret Eager
Robert Beard
Elizabeth Beard, 35
Margaret Beard, 17
James Beard, 12
Anne Beard, 10

Marriages by Rev. Samuel Wilson

Appleby, William and Agnes McCurdy, February 7, 1787.
Atchison, Joseph and Elizabeth Moor, March 26, 1789.
Alexander, James and Margaret Harper, October 25, 1792.
Armstrong, James and Nancy Lemond, April 8, 1794.
Armstrong, James and ---- Liggat, November 4, 1794.
Armstrong, Robert and Mary McDowell, April 30, 1795.
Anderson, James and Eleanor Crow, June 27, 1797.
Barr, Robert and Elizabeth Allen, May 27, 1788.
Bell, Robert and Rachel Espey, May 29, 1788.
Browster, William and Margaret Robison, March 1, 1790.
Blair, ---- and ---- Hunter, October 23, 1792.
Blain, Robert and Mary Craig, February 17, 1795.
Bell, Joseph and Elizabeth Sharp, April 30, 1795.

Barr, John and Sarah Gailly, (?) May 5, 1795.
Brown, Alexander and Mary Jacob, December 8, 1795.
Brown, William and Rachel Walker, July 28, 1796.
Bell, William and Elizabeth Stephenson, September 15, 1796.
Boyd, George and Elizabeth Brown, March 2, 1797.
Brandon, Thomas and Mary Fertig, January 9, 1798.
Clark, Henry and Mary Lowry, October 25, 1788.
Crowel, ---- and ---- Walker, July 24, 1789.
Carson, Elisha and Margaret Eager, March 29, 1791.
Carnahan, Robert and Agnes Wallace, (?) October 10, 1791.
Cowden, William and Eliza Whitelock, April 29, 1793.
Crowel, Samuel and Mary Walker, May 26, 1795.
Carnahan, James and Katharine Drugon, (?) January 20, 1797.
Crow, George and Margaret McElwain, August 17, 1797.
Culver, Levi and Nancy Agnew, December 22, 1796.
Durbarrow, ---- and ---- Martin, May 13, 1793.
Duncan, William and Nancy McKeehan, May 31, 1792.
Davidson, John and Betsy Young, September 30, 1794.
Davidson, Francis and Elizabeth Myler, April 30, 1795.
Douglas, John and Nancy McDowell, March 1, 1798.
Duncan, James and Mary Ewing, June 5, 1798.
Emmett, Samuel and Rebecca Bryson, June 19, 1788.
Espey, John and Margaret Huston, November 10, 1789.
Elder, John and ---- Monemy, (?) August 15, 1793.
Fullerton, Thomas Elder and Isabella McCune, March 27, 1788.
Fowler, John and Eleanor Mickie, February 19, 1789.
Finley, Samuel and Polly Brown, May 5, 1789.
Fox, John and Rachel Crowell, November 22, 1796.
Fleming, James and Jenny Cloyd, July 17, 1798.
Frother, Joseph and Nancy Liggate, November 20, 1798.
Graham, Francis and Margaret Randles, May 22, 1788.
Graham, Isaiah and Nancy Lindsay, February 12, 1793.
Geddes, Dr. John and Elizabeth Peebles, June 17, 1794.
Green, John and Barbara Ridsbaugh, February 24, 1794.
Glenn, Alexander and Susanna McKinstre, June 11, 1795.
Geddes, James and Margaret Douglass, March 1, 1796.
Graham, Arthur and Nancy McClure, February 14, 1797.
Gillespie, David and Rebecca Rippet, March 8, 1798.
Glendenning, James and Rebecca Armstrong, June 12, 1798.
Huston, John and Deborah Patterson, December 15, 1789.
Huston, Robert and Agnes Bell, September 2, 1793.
Harper, William and Esther Patterson, April 1, 1794.
Hughs, Thomas and Nancy Crawford, May 1, 1794.
Hanna, James and ---- Reed, June 10, 1794.
Hemphill, James and Cynthia Jack, September 3, 1795.
Hawkes, John and Christian Espey, August 16, 1796.
Hadden, (?) Thomas and Mary Dridge, March 14, 1797.
Holmes, George and Sarah Armstrong, August 14, 1798.
Jones, Hugh and Anne Gamble, June 21, 1787.
Johnson, Andrew and Elizabeth Johnson, December 18, 1788.
Jones, James and Betsy Bell, June 10, 1794.
Johnston, Alexander and Mary Armstrong, December 30, 1794.
Kennedy, John and Martha Graham, April 22, 1787.
Ker, William and Mary Woods, May 12, 1789.

Kilgore, Robert and Margaret Kelly, January 20, 1791.
Kirkpatrick, James and Margaret McKeehan, April 7, 1791.
Kerr, Matthew and Elizabeth Work, January 1, 1793.
Kelly, James and Sarah Lauderdale, July 15, 1794.
Laughlin, Dr. Thomas and Betsy Laughlin, January 24, 1791.
Leecock, William and Margaret Falkner, May 30, 1793.
Laughlin, Matthew and Phebe Piper, April 29, 1794.
Lightcap, William and Mary McElwain, February 23, 1796.
Lindsy, Robert and Betsy Connelly, February 21, 1797.
Laughlin, Dr. Thomas and Nancy Piper, July 18, 1797.
McCleary, John and Elizabeth Ewing, July 5, 1787.
McRory, Samuel and Anne Spence, December 4, 1788.
McGlaughlin, Daniel and Elizabeth Lightcap, February 5, 1789.
McCurdy, David and ---- Appelby, August 25, 1789.
McElwain, R. and ---- McGlaughlin, October 7, 1789.
Mayes, Samuel and Barbara Harper, December 17, 1789.
McCormick, Joseph and Leacy Thompson, January 19, 1790.
McElwain, Andrew and Margaret Bell, August 26, 1790.
McGuffine, William and Elizabeth Porter, January 25, 1791.
McCausland, Mark and Sally Hunter. [no date listed]
Morrison, Robert and Susanna Work, October 11, 1791.
McClaran, Thomas and Hannah Mickey, October 20, 1791.
Moor, Samuel and ---- McConnel, January 7, 1792.
Mason, Isaac and Elizabeth Kirkpatrick, June 7, 1792.
Martin, Thomas and Widow Stewart, August 16, 1792.
McCune, Samuel and Hannah Brady, December 26, 1793.
McFaden, John and Nancy Harper, June 10, 1794.
Michal, John and Katharine Carrick, June 10, 1794.
Murdock, Robert and Elizabeth Cummins, November 18, 1794.
McCormick, Robert and Elizabeth McCullough, November 27, 1794.
Marshall, John and Jane Leacock, April 21, 1795.
McGoffine, ---- and Sarah Crair, May 4, 1795.
Martin, John and Hannah Thompson, January 14, 1796.
McKean, William and Sarah Auld, June 30, 1796.
McKeehan, John and Betsy McKeehan, October 25, 1796.
Murphy, Philip and Jane ----, April 21, 1797.
McCormick, Joseph and Charity Connelly, April 27, 1797.
Mathers, Robert and Nancy Carnahan, February 8, 1798.
McLandburg, John and Margaret Young, February 5, 1799.
Mitchel, Andrew and Mary Ann McKeehan, February 13, 1799.
Nicholdson, John and Mary McElwain, July 29, 1794.
Patton, John and Elizabeth McEntire, August 18, 1789.
Patterson, Obediah and Anne Patterson, May 5, 1791.
Porterfield, William and Mary Shannon, April 21, 1795.
Patton, John and Sarah Shannon, May 14, 1795.
Pennwell, Thomas and Rachel Rodman, April 19, 1796.
Plunkett, Isaac and Lydia Hanna, May 24, 1796.
Peebles, Robert and Jane Kennedy, June 21, 1796.
Patton, Andrew and Mary Patton, October 18, 1796.
Patterson, Nathan and Nancy Laughlin, December 13, 1798.
Patterson, Robert and ---- Armstrong, September 27, 1792.
Patterson, John and Jenny Neal, October 11, 1792.
Quigley, James and Grizelda McKinney, March 31, 1795.
Rainey, James and Elizabeth Brownfield, April 23, 1795.

Roberts, John and Nancy Gillespie, May 12, 1795.
Smith, Archibald and Mary Anderson, August 24, 1789.
Shannon, Isaac and Jane Porter, February 1, 1791.
Seelly, William and ---- Morrow, October 31, 1791.
Shannon, Leonard and Jane Walker, January 3, 1793.
Sterrett, James and Margaret McClure, December 9, 1793.
Sterrett, Benjamin and Peggy Bell, March 27, 1794.
Scroggs, Allan and Peggy Craig, September 22, 1795.
Steel, Robert and Letty Work, October 27, 1795.
Scott, John and Mary McFarlane, April 5, 1796.
Stephenson, James and Elizabeth Sterrett, May 10, 1796.
Shannon, James and Elizabeth Gees, March 16, 1797.
Sharp, David and Isabella Orr, August 14, 1798.
Thompson, Matthew and Ruth Robinson, June 16, 1796.
Taylor, Andrew and Mary Lightcap, February 6, 1798.
Vanhorn, Joseph and Martha Ewing, November 22, 1792.
Vanderbelt, Cornelius and Mary Steel. [No date listed.]
Woodburn, Matthew and Katharine Fulton, February 12, 1799.
Wilson, Samuel and Peggy Espey, June 11, 1789.
Wallace, Patrick and Sally Officer, September 20, 1791.
Wallace, Hugh and Margaret Dearmon, July 2, 1792.
Woodburn, James and Nancy Martin, February 14, 1793.
Woodruff, Anthony and Mary Chapman, March 5, 1793.
Young, John and Sarah McCann, September 18, 1798.

- - - - -

In the appendix of Swope's *History of the Big Spring Presbyterian Church* ... he gives previously omitted names of persons who were "adherents of the Big Spring Church in John Carson's district on page 30 ..." This is in error in that page 30 lists those of another district. The names are listed here with the caution that they probably were either in John Carson's District or William Lindsay's District.

Samuel McCune, 14
Hugh McCune, 12
John McCune, 60
Mary McCune, 40
Adam Fullerton, 16
James Fullerton, 14
Alexander Fullerton, 11
John McCune, 9
Robert McCune, 7
Samuel Weir, 66
Jane Weir, 30
George Weir, 30
Margaret Weir, 25
Agnes Marten
George, a Negro
Elizabeth Kilgore, 70
Jesse Kilgore, 22
Robert Kilgore, 19
William Kilgore
Isabel Kilgore, 21

Mary Hawks, 12
James Mickey, 24
Agnes Mickey, 19
Joseph Parks, 55
Rebecca Parks, 50
Thomas Parks, 20
Joseph Parks, 18
Anna Parks, 16
John C. Parks, 14

BAPTISM BOOK FOR THE CHURCH IN SHIPPENSTOWN, PA.

Translated from photostats found in the Pennsylvania State Museum by Harold K. Trout, and brought to Lancaster for translation, by Elizabeth C. Kieffer, Archivist of the Historical Society of the Evengelical and Reformed Church. 1962.

[Dates of births and baptisms sometimes seem reversed.]

Johannes Kaufman was born October 13, 1770.
Catharina Kaufman was born August 25, 1773.
Elizabetha Kaufman was born April 5, 1775.
Jacob Kaufman was born December 4, 1776.
Salomea Kaufman was born December 16, 1778.
Margaretha Kaufman was born December 6, 1780.
Friedrich Kaufman was born January 25, 1783.
Isaac Kaufman was born August 18, 1784.
Magdalena Kaufman was born October 9, 1786.

p.10
Johann Heinrich of Johann Benjamin Cuhn and Maria Barbara, born ----; baptized March 25, 1771. Sponsors: Heinrich Decker and Anna Maria Brumbach.
Johann Peter of Johann Benjamin Cuhn and Maria Barbara, born November 6, 1772; baptized ----. Sponsors: Peter Brumbach and Catharina.
Maria Elisabetha of Johann Benjamin Kuhun and Maria Barbara, born June 18, 1774; baptized ----; died January 28, 1786. Sponsors: Jacob Schoost(?) and Elisabeth Brumbach.
Catharina of Johann Benjamin Kuhun and Maria Barbara, born May 12, 1788; baptized ----. Sponsors: Michael Miller and Catharina Brumbach.
William of Michael Widtringer(?) and Christina, born February 15, 1776; baptized ----. Sponsors: Peter Stambach and Catharina Stambach.
Wilhelm of Friedrich Beymer and Christina, born June 1776; baptized July 1776. Sponsors: Caspar Salzgeber and wife.
Anna of David Altich and wife, born April 10, 1776; baptized July 30, 1776. Sponsors: parents.
Johannes of Johannes Pedi and wife Magdalene, born March 25, 1782(sic); baptized ----. Sponsors: Johannes Dietrich and Margaretha.
Jacob of Conrad Böhmer and Julianna, born August 23; baptized August 23, 1778. Sponsors: Georg Spielman and Anna Maria.
Johannes of Christian Erdinger and Anna Maria, born October 8, 1778(sic); baptized September 13, 1778. Sponsor: Johannes Pehst(?), single.
Johannes of Michael Dreckstler, born December 7, 1779; baptized ----. Sponsors: Johannes Engel and Eleanora.
Johann Georg of George Heilman and Binna Maria, born September 18, 1779; baptized October 3, 1779. Sponsors: parents.
Anna Maria of Nicolaus Evert and Catharina, born April 15, 1779; baptized October 3, 1779. Sponsors: parents.

Johannes of Christian Miller and Feronica, born January 19, 1779; baptized October 3, 1779. Sponsors: Johannes Kaiser and Barbara.
Johannes of Johannes Reinhard and Salome, born May 22, 1779; baptized October 3, 1779. Sponsors: Johannes Peht(?), single.
Jacob of Michael Wint and Margaretha, born May 4, 1779; baptized October 3, 1779. Sponsors: Nicholas Wint and Margaretha.
Susanna of Johannes Schneider and Barbara, born November 26, 1778; baptized October 3, 1779. Sponsors: Easker Linch and Sophia.
Peter of Samuel Brendel and Elisabetha, born August 17, 1779; baptized October 3, 1779. Sponsors: Peter Stambaugh and Catharina.
Henrich of Georg Strigleder and Elisabetha, born April 10, 1779; baptized October 3, 1779. Sponsors: parents.
Maria Sarah of Jacob Mühleisen and Susanna, born August 7, 1779; baptized October 3, 1780. Sponsors: Cristoff Mühleisen and Maria Sarah.
Peter of James Stambach, born March 18; baptized May 3, 1781. Sponsor: James Schaaf.
Johannes Hertiner, born August 23, 1780; baptized May 3, 1781. Sponsors: Benjamin Kuhn and wife.
Fallentin Weirich(?), born August 6, 1780; baptized May 3, 1781. Sponsors: Benjamin Kuhn and wife.
Peter Schaast, born January 28, 1778; baptized May 3, 1781. Sponsors: Peter Schaast and Magdalene Stambach.
Maria Elisabeth Schaast, born ---- 23, 1780; baptized May 3, 1781. Sponsor: Maria Catharina Stambach.
Johannes Schëbel, born November 23, 1780; baptized May 3, 1781. Sponsors: Johannes Dietrich and Margaretha.
Maria Magdalena Müller, born March 13, 1781; baptized June 10. Sponsors: Johannes Leg and Magdalena.
Maria Susanna Leister, born April 22, 1781; baptized May 3, 1781. Sponsor: Susanna Stambach.
Maria Reider, born July 10, 1781; baptized September 9, 1781. Sponsors: parents.
Anna Hag of Johannes Haug and Anna Margaretha, born August 24, 1781; baptized December 7. Sponsors: parents.
Jacob Weiss, born October 13, 1781; baptized ----. Sponsors: parents.
Maria Sarah Bernhart, born March 22, 1781; baptized ----. Sponsors: Johannes Keiller(?) and wife.
Catharina of Bas Doet(?) and Christina, born October 26, 1781; baptized 25 hujus ani. Sponsors: parents.
Anna Elisabetha of Jacob Stambach and Margaretha, born December 13, 1781 (80); baptized 25 hujus mensis. Sponsors: Peter Schaaf and his young daughter Catharina.
Georg of Schnurat Reiner and Margaret, born November 18, 1781; baptized January 20, 1782. Sponsor: Lorentz Stambach.
Joh. Peter of Christian Reidinger and Anna Maria, born September 22; baptized October 13. Sponsors: Peter Stambach and wife.
Daniel of Michael Deiseler and Elisabeth, born April 8; baptized October 13, 1782. Sponsors: Daniel Altig and Elisabeth.

GERMAN REFORMED CHURCH, SHIPPENSBURG 43

Elisabetha of Robert Deel and Cristina, born December 5, 1782; baptized January 9, 1783. Sponsors: Shims Shaft and Elisabetha.
David of Elias Lauer and Elisabetha, born February 20, 1782; baptized January 2, 1785. Sponsor: Adam Bender.
Maria Magdalena of Christian Erdinger and Anna Maria, born January 27, 1785; baptized February 11, 1785. Sponsors: Johannes Peg and Maria Magdalena.
Bernhard of Bernhard Sauer and Barbara, born November 28, 1784; baptized April 10, 1785. Sponsors: parents.
Johannes of Jacob Witmer and Anna Maria, born January 2, 1785; baptized May 15, 1785. Sponsors: Michael Dressler and Elisabeth.
Johannes of Phillip Stambach and Elisabeth, born February 12, 1785; baptized May 15, 1785. Sponsors: Conrad Reiners and Margaretha.
Jacob of Jacob Stambach and Gertraut, born March 28; baptized May 15, 1785. Sponsors: Johannes Dietrich and Margaretha.
Johan Peter of Conrad Böhmer and Juliana, born May 18; baptized June 12, 1785. Sponsors: Peter Stambach and Catharina.
Maria Elisabetha of Johannes Wilt and Anna Maria, born March 11; baptized July 10, 1785. Sponsors: Johannes Sailer and Catharina.
Johann Adam of Adam Siebert and Elisabetha, born April 17; baptized July 10, 1785. Sponsors: Jacob Kintzle and Elisabetha.
Johann Peter of Johannes Kerbach and Anna Dorothea, born June 14; baptized July 10, 1785. Sponsor: Johann Peter Scaaf alone.
Wilhelm of Ludwig Miller and Barbara, born June 22; baptized August 7, 1785. Sponsors: Wändel Wäber and Elisabetha.
Friedrich of Caspar Saltzgeber and Catharina, born June 2; baptized August 7, 1785. Sponsors: parents.
Sara of Johannes Behr and M. Magdalena, born June 30, 1785; baptized August 14, 1785. Sponsors: parents.
Elisabeth of Michael Trexler and Elisabetha, born August 2, 1784; baptized November 3, 1784. Sponsors: Jacob Helm and Christina.
Jacob of Michael Trexler and Elisabetha, born August 8, 1786; baptized 1786. Sponsors: Christian Weiser and Susanna.
Maria Susanna of Johannes Luck and Magdalena, born October 16, 1785; baptized December 25. Sponsors: John Friedrich Schoepflein and Susanna.
Jacob of Robert Sheedt and Christina, born November 29; baptized January 1. Sponsors: Jacob Kaiser and Catharina.
Johannes of Elias Lauer and Elisabetha, born November 2; baptized January 29, 1786. Sponsors: Conrath Lind and Anna Maria.
Johann Peter of John Friedrich Shepfley and Susanna, born September 9; baptized November 19, 1786. Sponsors: Peter Stambach and Catharina.
Magdalena, an illegitmate child of Magdalena Schmidt who says the father was Johannes Ooster of Hagerstown, born June 16, 1786; baptized February 25, 1787. Sponsor: the mother.
Benjamin of Wendel Weber and Elizabeth (born Kowel), born February 18, [1787]; baptized February 26. Sponsors: Lorentz Houtz and Anna Catharina.

Johann Wilhelm of Lorentz Houtz and Anna Catharina, born October 17, 1786; baptized February 26, 1787. Sponsors: Wendel Weber and Elizabeth.
Johann Georg of Jacob Küntzler, widower, born January 3, 1786; baptized February 26, 1787. Sponsor: the father.
Johannes of Georg Giesemann and Catharina (born Schopp), born July 6, 1786; baptized February 26, 1787. Sponsor: Joh. Nicolaus Schopp, "juv. patris consobrinus". [Children of two sisters i.e. he and the father were cousins.]
Johann Wilhelm of William Baak and Margaretha (born Schoop), born September 8, 1786; baptized February 26, 1787. Sponsors: Georg. Giesemann and Catharina (born Schoop).
Anna Maria of Michael Müller and Elisabeth (born Beiter), born February 13, 1787; baptized March 25. Sponsor: Anna Maria married name Haupt.
Christina of Johann Weber and Elisabeth, born January 2, 1787; baptized March 25, 1787. Sponsor: Christina Ihly.
Elisabeth, an illegitimate child of Anna Maria Franklin and the father declared to be Wilhelm Ried, down in the country, born January 7; baptized March 27, 1787. Sponsors: the grandparents, Johann Weber and Elisabeth.
Johann Heinrich of Johann Heinrich Engell and Anna Elisabeth (born Hild), born April 17, 1787; baptized 22 of same. Sponsors: Deacon of the Reformed congregation Johannes Baak and wife Magdalena (born Stampach).
Johannes of Adam Sieber and Elisabeth, born November 18, 1786; baptized March 22, 1787. Sponsors: Deacon of our congregation, Johannes Sayler and wife Catharina (born Grein).
James of William Armstrong and Elisabeth, born March 19, 1787; baptized same day. Sponsors: Michael Dressler and Elisabeth.
Margaretha of Elias Meyler and Margaretha, born October 11, 1783; baptized April 22, 1787. Sponsors: parents.
Joseph of Elias Meyler and Margaretha, born December 24, 1786; baptized April 22, 1787. Sponsors: parents.
Samuel Füllsen of Jacob Mühleysen and Susanna, dates not given. Sponsors: Valentin Haupt and Anna Maria.
Anna Margaretha of Jacob Stampach and Anna Gertraut (born Schaaf), born April 4, 1787; baptized May 27, 1787. Sponsors: Peter Stampach and Elisabeth (born Schaaf).
Anna Catharina of Michael Kärcher, born January 27, 1787; baptized May 27. Sponsors: Peter Stampach and Elisabeth.
Anna Catharina of Christian Weiser, Lutheran deacon, and Susanna (born Kunckel), born January 27, 1787; baptized (May?) 27. Sponsors: Michael Drechsler and Elisabeth (born Krauss).
Anna Maria of Peter Mukerspach(?) and Elisabeth, nee Frey, born May 4; baptized June 17. Sponsors: Johann Frey and Anna Maria Ziegler, single.
Anna Dorothea of Johannes Herpouch and Anna Dorothea (born Schaaf), born ----; baptized June 17. Sponsors: James Schaaf and Elisabeth (born Stampach).
Jacob of Jacob Käyser and Catharina (born Stampach), born June 4, 1787; baptized August 12, ej.a. Sponsors: James Schaaf and Elisabeth (born Stampach).

GERMAN REFORMED CHURCH, SHIPPENSBURG   45

David of Christian Müller and Veronica (born Rucker), born July 8, 1787; baptized August 12. Sponsors: parents.
Eva, illegitimate child of Rosina Römer and father said to be Samuel Gordrick, born September 27, 1783; baptized August 12, 1787. Sponsors: Elder of the Church, Johannes Dietrich, and Anna Margaretha.
Georg of Michael Fritz and Louisa, born October 3, 1787; baptized October 14. Sponsors: Georg Frey and Margaretha.
Samuel of Christoph Beitel and Anna Maria, born July 3; baptized October 21. Sponsors: Georg Anstadt and Magdalena.
Friedrich of schoolmaster Friedrich Schöpfler and Susanna, born November 9; baptized November 15 in the school. Sponsors: parents.
Philip of Conrad Böhmer and Juliana, born November 9; baptized December 2, 1787. Sponsor: Phillip Jung, Jr.
David of Church elder Johannes Böher (or Böcher) and Magdalena, born January 15, (1788); baptized January 29 at home. Sponsors: parents.
Johann Philip of Deacon Johannes Baak and Maria Magdalena, born January 9, (1788); baptized January 9 at home. Sponsors: parents.
Christian of Heinrich Lind and Catharina, born January 15; baptized February 17, 1788. Sponsor: Christian Lind, Jr.
Anna Christina of Abraham Frey and Susanna, born January 13; baptized May 9, 1788. Sponsors: Jacob Helm, Sr., and Christina.
James of James Stahl and Anna Maria, born October 6, 1787; baptized March 30, 1788. Sponsors: James Schaaf and Elisabeth (born Stampach).
Elisabeth of Heinrich Grünewald, resident of Chambersburg, and wife Eva, born November 14, 1787; baptized March 25, 1788 at the father's house at Chambersburg. Sponsors: parents.
Peter, 30 years old, married; baptized March 29, 1788 in the church at Shippensburg. Sponsors: the two deacons of the said congregation, Mister Johannes Peck and Mister Johann Seyler.
Elisabeth married name Schmidt, 22 years old; baptized March 29, 1788 in the church at Shippensburg.
Heinrich, born (date left blank); baptized March 29, 1788 in the church at Shippensburg.
Susanna of Johannes Höhn, Elder of the Church, and wife Susanna, born December 20, 1787; baptized April 27, 1788. Sponsors: Heinrich Huneberger and Catharina.
Susanna of Michael Trexler and Elisabeth, born October 10; baptized December 9, 1788. Sponsors: Christian Weiser and Susanna.
Magdalena of Fredrich Shepfley and Susanna, born January 9; baptized April 5, 1789. Sponsors: parents.
Christian of James Shoapf and Elisabetha, born January 9; baptized April 5, 1788(sic). Sponsors: Christian Erdinger and wife.
Jacob of Jacob Kayser and Catharina, born February 24; baptized April 5, 1789. Sponsors: parents.
Susanna of Andreas Probst and Susanna, born and baptized November 8, 1789. Sponsors: Jacobus Schaf and Elisabeth.

Catharina of Adam Rehner and Maria, born January 13; baptized March 17, 1790. Sponsors: Michael Kircher and Eva.
Jacob of Jacob Preiss and Catarina, born August 21, 1789; baptized ----. Sponsors: Christian Ertinger and Anna Mary.
Catharina of Wendel Martin and Elizabetha, born February 27, 1787; baptized ---- [1790]. Sponsors: Peter Stambach and Elisabeth.
Elisabetha of Wendel Martin and Elizabetha, born November 25, 1788; baptized ---- [1790]. Sponsors: the parents.
Johannes of Georg Ihle and Barbara, born April 4, 1790; baptized June 8, 1790. Sponsors: Johannes Moll and Maria.
Anna Maria of Michael Friederich and Loweina, born ----; baptized August 8, 1790. Sponsors: Christian Erdinger and Anna Maria.
Johann Jacob of Georg Zuber and Elisabeth, born April 20, 1790; baptized September 5, 1790. Sponsors: Peter Katz and Margaretha.
Daniel of Philip Christ and Christina, born August 7; baptized September 12, 1790. Sponsors: parents.
Samuel of Johannes Säler and Catharina, born August 11, 1789; baptized August 16, 1789. Sponsors: Johann Adam and wife and grandparents.
Anna Margaretha of Martin Harman and Margaretha, born March 18; baptized April 22, 1791. Sponsors: Johannes Kleppinger and Anna Margaretha.
Philip of Christian Erlanger and Anna Maria, born April 15, 1791; baptized May 8, 1791. Sponsors: Philip and Anna Maria Lauffman.
Magdalena of Michael Trexler and Elisabet, born December 10, 1790; baptized December 10, 1790. Sponsors: Peter Kramer and Magdalena.
Johannes of Adam Kayser and Sara, born February 7, 1791; baptized May 22, 1791. Sponsors: Johannes Behl(?) and Magdalena.
Jacobus of Jacobus Schaff and Elisabet, born May 3, 1791; baptized July 24. Sponsors: Peter Stambach and Catharina.
Johannes of Christian Miller and Veronica, born May 30, 1791; baptized July 24. Sponsor: self.
Maria of Conrad Böhmer and Julianna, born June 19, 1791; baptized July 10. Sponsor: self.
Johannes of Abraham Beitelmann and Gertraut, born July 11, 1791; baptized August 14. Sponsors: Johannes Haun and Anna.
Catharina of Benjamin Loggenhader(?) and Elisabeth, born July 22, 1791; baptized August 28. Sponsor: Georg Schaller.
Catharina of Adam Blum and Margaretha, born August 15, 1791; baptized September 25. Sponsors: Johannes Kroll and Catharina.
Johannes of Jacob Frey and Susanna, born (no date); baptized September 25, (1790). Sponsors: Jacob Widmer and Margaretha.
Adam of Michael Fritz and Lowisa, born August 26; baptized September 25. Sponsors: Adam Blum and Margaretha.
Elisabet of Jacob Albrecht and Catharina, born April 7. Sponsors: Christian Erlinger and Anna Maria.
Catharina of Jacob Kaiser and Catharina, born (no date); baptized November 9. Sponsors: Peter Stambach and Catharina.

GERMAN REFORMED CHURCH, SHIPPENSBURG 47

Catharina of Thomas Hold and Elizabeth, born September 4, 1791; baptized November 9, (1790).
Johannes of Friedrich Schindel and Margaretha, born ----; baptized November 9, (1790). Sponsor: George Böhmer.
Johannes of Georg. Züber and Elizabeth, born August 19; baptized November 20. Sponsors: Johannes Höhn and Anna.
Wilhelm of Philip Christ and Christina, born March 29; baptized May 2, (1791). Sponsor: self.
Elisabet of Heinrich Aune, born (no date); baptized May 17. Sponsors: Conrad Böhmer and Julia.
Georg of Ludwig Riggel and Margaretha, born November 12; baptized May 17. Sponsor: self.
Peter of Peter Huffman and Christina, born (no date); baptized May 17. Sponsors: Peter Palmer and Magdalena.
Anna Margaretha of Joseph Stahl and Elisabet, born May 4; baptized May 28. Sponsors: Johannes Kleppinger and Anna Margaretha.
Jacobus of Johannes Fried(?) and wife, born July 8, 1792; baptized July 29. Sponsors: Jacobus Shofe and wife.
David of David Heckedorn and Elisabeth, born April 6, 1792; baptized August 5.
Jacob of Adam Rehmer(?) and Maria, born June 20, 1792; baptized August 5. Sponsors: Peter Stambach and Elisabeth.
Michael of Michael Windt and Margaretha, born October 19, 1792(?), baptized August 19.
Johannes of Leonhart Hammschier and Maria Catharina, born August 2, 1792; baptized September 9. Sponsors: Johannes Kleppinger and Margaretha.
Johann Georg Gell of Johannes Hirschman and Elijah(sic), born August 5; baptized September 16. Sponsor: Lorentz Brandtlein.
Catharina of Adam Rehrer(?) and Sara, born August 16; baptized September 16. Sponsors: Johannes Kraft and Catharina.
Julianna of Georg Bähmer and Christina, born July 29, 1792; baptized September 30, 1792. Sponsors: Conrad Böhmer and Julianna.
Magdalena of Andreas Stahl and Magdalena, born September 16, 1792; baptized September 30. Sponsors: Johannes Kehrbach and Anna Dorothea.
George of Andreas Zubber and Maria, born -- 1764(!); baptized October 29, 1792. Sponsors: Conrad Boemer and John Redid.
Johannes of Andreas Zubber and Maria, born August 1, 1766; baptized October 29, 1792. Sponsors: Conrad Boemer and John Redid.
Simon of Benjamin Holtzinger(?) and Elisabeth, born November 4, 1792; baptized December 23, 1792. Sponsors: Valentin Hauzzert(?) and Anna Maria.
Anna Margaretha of Michael Trexler and Elisabeth, born March 1, 1773; baptized May 12, (1793). Sponsors: Adam Blum and Margaretha.
Joseph of Jacob Philips and Catharina, born July 3, 1793; baptized July 28. Sponsors: parents.
Ephraim of Johannes Moll and Maria, born July 31, 1793; baptized August 11. Sponsors: Jacob Rahm and Barbara.

48 CUMBERLAND COUNTY CHURCH RECORDS OF THE 18TH CENTURY

Jakobus of Johannes Freak(?) and Magdalena, born July 8, 1792; baptized July 28. Sponsors: Jakobus Schaaf and Elisabeth.
Elisabeth of George Reith and Greta, born June 10, 1793; baptized September 15. Sponsors: ----.
Johannes of Peter Muttersprach and Elisabetha, born July 4; baptized September 22. Sponsors: Jacob Frey and Susanna.
Elisabetha of Abraham Frey and Susanna, born August 15; baptized September 22. Sponsors: Johannes Park (Burk?) and Magdalena.
Elisabetha of George Frey and Elisabetha, born September 3; baptized September 22. Sponsors: Valentin Hauzer and Anna Maria.
Elisabeth of Philip Brustman and Maria, born December 15, 1791; baptized February --, 1792(?). Sponsors: Jacob Gräber and Anna Maria.
Jacob of Philip Brustmann and Maria, born October 16, 1793; baptized November 10, 1793. Sponsors: parents.
Anna Maria of Elias Ritter and Margaretha, born October 30, 1793; baptized November 10, 1793. Sponsors: Conrad Bömer and Juliann.
Susanna of Georg Trissler and Catharina, born September 6, 1793; baptized November 10, 1793. Sponsors: Johannes Höhn and Juliann.
Sara of Abr. Beutel and Gertrud, born September 25; baptized November 10, 1793. Sponsors: Peter Krämer and Maria.
Thomas of Thomas Hold and Elisabet, born February 9, 1794; baptized March 30, (1794). Sponsors: ----.
Elisabet of Philip Christ and Christina, born January 26, 1794.
Catharina of Johannes Hirschmann and Elisabet, January 23 [born/bapt.?].
Johannes of Philip Christ and Christina, born July 19, 1785. Sponsors: Peter Frey and wife.
Jacob of Philip Christ and Christina, born April 6; baptized May 6, 1788. Sponsors: Valentin Haupt and wife.
Adam of Philip Christ and Christina, born December -, 1788; baptized May 6, 1788. Sponsors: ----.
Johannes of Johannes Kapp (Rapp?) and Elisabet, born ----; baptized April 27, (1794). Sponsors: Conrad Kapp and Catharina.
Elisabet of David Heckedorn and Elisabet, born February 9, 1794; baptized April 27. Sponsor: self.
Peter of Jacob Treisch and Catharina, born December 2, 1793; baptized April 27. Sponsors: Peter Treisch and Elisabeth.
Anna Maria of Jacob Treisch and Catharina, born August 20, 1791; baptized April 27. Sponsors: parents.
Johannes of Peter Krämer and Maria, born February 23, 1794; baptized April 27. Sponsors: Peter Trexler and Veronica Vogt.
Johannes Wilhelm of George Zuber and Elisabetha, born October 28, 1794. Sponsors: Wilhelm Giesener and wife.
Elisabet of Ludwig Rippel and Margaretha, born January 7, 1794; baptized May 26, (1794). Sponsors: ----.
Christian of Jacob Voltz and Stina, born March 16, 1793; baptized August 17, 1794. Sponsors: ----.
Samuel of Christian Meiser and Susanna, born March 19, 1794; baptized August 17. Sponsors: ----.

GERMAN REFORMED CHURCH, SHIPPENSBURG 49

Susanna of Jacob Helm and Rosina, born February 9, 1794; baptized August 17. Sponsor: Peter Treisch.
Catharina of Jacob Frey and Susanna, born May 14, 1794; baptized September 14. Sponsors: Conrad Lind and Catharina.
Johannes of Jacob Walter and Magdalena, born July 15. Sponsor: Johannes Palmer; baptized September 14.
Jakob of Jacobus Schaaf and Elisabetha, born June 9, 1794; baptized September 14. Sponsors: Jakob Rahm and Barbara.
Catharina of Leonhardt Hamshier and Maria Catharina, born August 20, 1794; baptized September 28. Sponsors: Johannes Schneider and Catharina.
Peter of Peter Stambach and Elisabetha, born June 14, 1794; baptized September 28. Sponsors: Friederich Stambach and Elisabetha Balmer.
Samuel of Friederich Schiebel and Margaretha, born October 28, 1794; baptized December 25. Sponsors: Friedrich Bainer and Christina.
Johann Jacob of Martin Haman and Elisabeth, born December 28, 1794; baptized March 1, (1795). Sponsors: parents.
Samuel of Johannes Freck and Magdalena, born January 13, 1795; baptized April 12, 1795. Sponsors: parents.
Henrich of Andreas Meyl(?) and Magdalena, born February 23, 1795; baptized May 24. Sponsor: Henrich Kaufman.
Salome of Wilhelm Gelten(?) and Catharina, born October 15, 1794; baptized May 24, [1795]. Sponsors: Conrad Kopt(?) and Catharina.
Elisabeth of George Trissler and Catharina, born February 20, 1795; baptized May 24, [1795]. Sponsors: Friedrich ---- and Barbara.
Elisabeth of Jacob Leitner and Elisabeth, born January 12, 1795; baptized June 28, (1795). Sponsors: Peter Kramer and Maria.
Adam of George Reith and Maria Catharina, born April 12, 1795; baptized July 21. Sponsor: self.
Johannes of Johannes Hatten and Juliann, born June 21, 1795; baptized August 16. Sponsors: Benjamin Kappenheimer and Elisabeth.
Johann Georg of Michael Müller and Elisabetha, born ---- 1795; baptized September 14. Sponsors: Michael Meng(?) and Charlotta.
Maria Magdalena of Joseph Nagl and Elisabeth, born August 12, 1795; baptized October 11. Sponsors: George Ley and Anna Maria.
Jacob of Jacob Winterbald and Elisabeth, born August 10, 1795; baptized October 11. Sponsors: Abraham Breitelman? and Gertrud.
Samuel of Johannes Schneider and Catharina, born December 28, 1795; baptized March 13, (1796). Sponsors: John Redett and Catharina.
Jakob of Johan Freisch and Maria, born February 10, 1796; baptized April 10. Sponsors: parents.
Johannes of Jakob Treisch and Catharina, born December 6, 1795; baptized April 10. Sponsors: Peter Bremer and Anna Maria.
Catharina of Philipp Christ and Catharina, born March 9, 1796; baptized April 10. Sponsors: parents.

50   CUMBERLAND COUNTY CHURCH RECORDS OF THE 18TH CENTURY

Johann Peter of Peter Kircher and Magdalena, born October 15, 1795; baptized May 8, 1796. Sponsors: Jacob Vogelgesang and Catharina.
Anna Margaret of Georg Frey and wife, born February 15; baptized 30. Sponsors: Adam Blum and wife.
Anna Margaret and Bernhart Hamscher and Catharina, born July 17, 1796; baptized August 28, 1796. Sponsors: Johannes Lay and wife.
Lorentz of Martin Haman and Margaretha, born October 2, 1796; baptized February 19, 1797. Sponsors: parents.
Susanna of Jacob Sthorminger(?) and Barbara, born September 21, 1796; baptized February 26, 1797. Sponsors: Abr. Beitelman and wife.
Wilhelm of Jacob Beidtener and wife Lydia, born and baptized March 26, 1797. Sponsors: Philip Faust and wife.
Elisabeth of Joseph Stahl and Elisabeth, born April 16; baptized March 26, 1797. Sponsors: parents.
Annamari of Benjamin Koppenhäffer and Elisabeth, born September 17, 1794; baptized by Herr Litza. Sponsors: Caspar Lee and Sophia.
Elisabeth of Benjamin Koppenhäffer and Elisabeth, born February 28, 1796; baptized by Herr Litza. Sponsors: parents.
Daniel of Johannes Luhtz and Elizabeth, born July 19, 1796; baptized May 6. Sponsors: Daniel Sansebey(?) and Elizabeth Luhtz.
Anna Margaretha of Adam Linter and Catharina, born ---- 1796; baptized April 17, 1797. Sponsors: Johannes Dietrich and wife.
Andreas of Jacob Walter and Magdalena, born --- 1795; baptized May 20, 1797. Sponsors: parents.
Johannes of Jacob Vogelsang and Magdalena, born April 15, 1796; baptized May 21. Sponsors: Peter Kiefer and Magdalena.
Sophia of Wendel Mailen and Elisabeth, born May 27; baptized July 2. Sponsors: parents.
Susanna Elisabetha of Johann Kukken(?) and Julianna, born June 21; baptized July 30. Sponsor: Margaretha Beitzel.
Maria Magdalena of Johann Georg Kuhn and Maria Katharin, born February --, 1797; baptized August 13. Sponsors: Bernhard Momsher and Maria Katharin.
Elisabeth of Andreas Ihle and Elisabeth, born August 27, 1796; baptized August 26, 1797. Sponsor: Maria Ihle.
Anna Maria of Conrad Drechsler and Pfronica, born July 11, (1797); baptized August 27. Sponsors: Peter Krämer and Maria.
Anna Maria of Jacob Frey and Susanna, born June 23; baptized September 24. Sponsors: parents.
Anna of Johannes Herb and Ana Maria, born October 10; baptized October 28. Sponsor: Anna Weary.
Magdalena of Johann Meier and Catharina, born November 1; baptized December 30. Sponsors: parents.
Wilhelm of Elisabeth Spielman and Johann Gebser, born March 2, 1796; baptized December 30. Sponsor: mother.
Samuel of Philip Truung, born ----; baptized December 31. Sponsors: ----.
David of Johannes Greist and Catharina, born December 29, 1797; baptized January 21, 1798. Sponsors: parents.

Elisabeth of Johannes Herschman and Elisabetha, born October 1, 1797; baptized --- 21, 1798. Sponsors: Samuel Brendel and Elisabetha.
Sara of Philip Christ and Christina, born December 6, 1798; baptized February 11, 1798. Sponsors: parents.
Anna Maria of George Unger and Anna Maria, born January 9; baptized February 18, 1798. Sponsors: Peter Kiefer and Magdalena.
Maria Elisabeth of Christoph Beitel and Margareth, born January 15, 1788; baptized February 18. Sponsors: Peter Ralz(?) and Maria Elisabeth.
Magdalena of Friedrich Böhman and Christina, born January 17, 1798; baptized February 18. Sponsors: Caspar Salzgeber and wife.
Jacob of Michael Miller and wife, born December 6; baptized April 11. Sponsors: parents.
Susanna of Peter Diessler and Maria, born ----; baptized January 17, (1798). Sponsors: Christian Dreiser and Christina.
Rachel of Mary Lutlow and Paul M. Clothlan English Presbyterian, born February 25, 1797; baptized February 26, 1798. Sponsor: Susanna Scharlotta mark.
Maria Magdalena of Martin Claddy and Catharina, born December 17, 1797; baptized April 1. Sponsors: Johan Leu(?) and Maria.
Johann Jacob of Johann Garroll(?) and Catharina, born ----; baptized April 1. Sponsors: Jacob Witmer and Maria.
Anna Maria of Anton Klippenger (or Dissinger) and Anna Margaretha, born February 18; baptized April 15. Sponsors: Georg Kressler and Susanna.
Jacob of Benjamin Koppenheffer and Elisabeth, born ----; baptized April 15. Sponsors: parents.
Bernhart (or Lenhart) of Jacob Winterbald and Elisabeth, born September 7, 1797; baptized April 15. Sponsors: Abraham Beitelman and Gertraut.
Jacob of Huyses(?) Arndt and Catharina, born May 13; baptized June 25. Sponsors: John Muller and Catharina.
Catharina of Andreas and Elisabeth Ihle, born October 15, 1797; baptized March 13, 1798. Sponsors: Johann Heil and Anna Maria.
Maria of John Treiser and Maria, born March 19; baptized May 13.
Johann Adam of Christian Hoch and Maria, born May 4; baptized May 28.
Peter Rüger, June 24. [uncertain as to meaning of dates]
Peter Kiefer, June 24. [uncertain as to meaning of dates]
Johann of Jacob Spielmann and Eva, born July 20, bapt. July 29. Sponsors: Jacob Spielman and Catharina Schultz.
Samuel of Nicolas Krahl and Catharina, born June 13; baptized August 12, (1798). Sponsors: parents.
Elisabeth of Bernhart Ferber(?) and Maria Elisabeth, born ----; baptized September 10, 1798. Sponsors: Johann Weiser and Anna Maria.
Conrad of Jacob Zettel and Catharina, born ----; baptized October 24, 1798. Sponsors: parents.
Susanna Charlotta of Michael Mark and Margaretha, born ----; baptized March 29, 1799. Sponsors: Michael Mark and Susan Charlotta.

Jacobus of John Hern and Anna Maria, born ----; baptized May 17, 1799. Sponsors: parents.
Susanna of David Treisch and Maria, born ----; baptized August 13, 1798. Sponsors: parents.
Jacobus of Joseph Stahl and Elisabeth, born ----; baptized May 26, 1799. Sponsors: John Lie and Margaretha.
Philipp of Philipp Christ and Christina, born ----; baptized April 18. Sponsors: parents.
Sarah of Georg Carl and Catharina, born April 6, 1799; baptized ----. Sponsor: the mother.
Anna Catharina of Andres Berchtel and Barbara, born ----; baptized March 6, 1799. Sponsors: parents.
Michael of Johannes Hirschman and Elizabeth, born March 9, 1799; baptized ----. Sponsors: Micha Hartel and Susanna.
Maria Catharina of Heinrich Albrecht and Barbara, born ----; baptized June 21, 1799. Sponsor: Jacob ----.
Margaretha of ---- Oberlin and Maria, born ----; baptized July 14, 1799. Sponsor: Adam Oberlin.
Susanna Charlot of Peter ---- and Susanna Charlotte, born ----; baptized July 3, 1799. Sponsors: Micha Mark and Sus. Charlot.
Johann of Georg Krafft and Catharina, born ----; baptized July 9. Sponsors: John Krafft and Esther.
Anna Maria of John Bauer and Catha, born ----; baptized May 7. Sponsors: Christian Meisser and Susanna.
Jacob of Johannes Fenck(?) and Magdalena, born ----; baptized November 28, 1799. Sponsors: parents.
Susanna of John Weiser and Maria, born ----; baptized October 8, 1799. Sponsors: Bernhard Rebbert and Elisabeth.
Samuel of Micha Miller and Elisabeth, born ----; baptized March 24, 1800. Sponsors: parents.
Chatharina of Stephen Aei(?) and Magdalena, born ----; baptized May 19, (1800). Sponsors: Philip Fischer and Catharina.
Sara of Peter Krämer and Maria, born ----; baptized April 13. Sponsors: Peter Grüber and Susanna.
Barbara of Wendel Marte and Elisabeth, born ----; baptized May 30. Sponsors: parents.
Wilhelm of Jacob Zettel and Catharina, born ----; baptized October 22, 1800. Sponsors: parents.
Elisabeth of Michael Mauck and Margareth, born ----; baptized October 30, 1800. Sponsors: Michael Müller and Elisabeth.
Margareth of Johni Vatten and Juliana, born ----; baptized October 1, 1800. Sponsors: John Kleppinger and Marga.
Alena of Johi Drecksler and Schimine, born ----; baptized October 20. Sponsors: Conrad Drecksler and Fronica.

Catechumens, Admitted for the first time to the Holy Communion

Confirmed May 26, 1787,
Pentecost Eve
James Schaaf, 36 years old, married
Conrad Lind, 21
Christian Lind, 18
Heinrich Cone, 16

Heinrich Liehr, 15
Martin H̶a̶m̶m̶o̶n̶, 18
Christoph Leonard, 18
Phillip Hammon, 16
Johannes Kerpach, 23, married
Peter Stampach, 25, married
Adam Leonard, 16
Friedrich Stampach, 18

GERMAN REFORMED CHURCH, SHIPPENSBURG

Adam Römer, 18
Susanna Liehr, 17
Anna Maria Liehr, 16
Elisabeth Stampach, 16
Elisabeth (married) Stampach, 25
Magdalena Schumacher, 17
Margaretha Schumacher, 15
Maria Leonhard, 14

Confirmed March 29, 1788
Johannes Giese, 15
Johannes Lind, 17
Johannes Umberger, 17-1/2
Peter Brücker, 30, baptised before confirmation
Georg Böhmer, 19
Friedrich Böhmer, 17
Johannes Böhmer, 15
Heinrich Werner, 16
Susanna (married) Bocker, 19
Magdalena Hausknecht, 17
Susanna Umbergerin, 16
Elisabeth (married) Schmidt, 22, baptised before confirmation

Communicants, May 27, 1787 at Pentecost
Johannes Liehr, elder
Johannes Hehn, elder
Johannes Seÿler, deacon
Johannes Beeck, deacon
Johann Friedrich Stampach
Johann Peter Schaaf
Johann Reddet
Johann Jacob Hammon
Johann Benjamin Cone
Rudolph Frey
Michael Müller
Conrad Lind
Heinrich Lind
Christoph Leonhard
Peter Hehn, Jr.
George Thiel
Adam Sievert
Conrad Wern
and 13 male catechumens
Maria Madgalena, wife of deacon Beeck
Susanna, wife of Schöpfle
Elisabeth, wife of Schaaf
Anna Gertrud, wife of Stampach
Elisabeth, wife of Engell
Margaretha, wife of Dietrich
Maria, wife of Lind
Sophia, wife of Siess
Catharina, wife of Lind
Elisabeth, wife of Sievert
Sophia Ehrhart, widow from Chambersburg
Eva Liehr
Maria Catharina Liehr
Anna Margaretha Liehr
Rosina Römerin
and seven female catechumens

Communicants, October 14, 1787
Elder Johannes Liehr
Deacon Johannes Beeck
Peter Stampach
Daniel Altig
Jacob Käyser
James Schaaf
Conrad Lind, Sr.
Heinrich Lind
Johann Brücker
Conrad Werner
Christian Müller
Christoph Leonhard, Sr.
Johannes Kerpach
Conrad Lind, Jr., single
Christian Lind, single
Friederich Dewain, single
Christoph Leonhard, single
Johan Adam Leonhard, single
Adam Römer, single
Martin Hammon, single
Phillip Hammon, single
Heinrich Liehr, single
Friedrich Stampach, single
Anna Margaretha Beeck
Margareth Dietrich
Elisabeth Altig
Maria Margaretha Kaÿser
Elisabeth Schaaf
Anna Maria Lind
Sophia Siess
Elisabeth Brücker
Catharina Lind
Elisabeth Engel
Catharina Bernhard
Veronica Müller
Anna Dorothea Kerpach
Eva Liehr, single
Catharina Liehr, single
Anna Margaret Liehr, single
Magdalena Schumacher, single

54 CUMBERLAND COUNTY CHURCH RECORDS OF THE 18TH CENTURY

Margaretha Schumacher, single
Elisabeth Stampach, single
Maria Leonhard, single
Rosina Römer, single

Communicants, March 30, 8 days
after Easter
Deacon, Mr. Johannes Beeck
Peter Stampach
Conrad Lind
Peter Schaaf
James Schaaf
Heinrich Lind
Johannes Boocher
Jacob Hammon
Johann Reddet
Johannes Kerpach
Martin Hammon, single
Phillip Hammon, single
Adam Leonhard, single
Adam Römer, single
Friedrich Dewein, single
eight male catechumens, 29
March 1788
Magdalena Beeck
Margaretha Dietrich
Susanna Schoepfle
Elisabeth Schaaf
Anna Maria Lind
Sophia Siess
Elisabeth Brücker
Catharina Brücker, Conrad
Lind's daughter
Catharina Brücker, Peter
Brücker's wife
Catharina Lind
Maria Leonhard

four female catechumens, March 29, 1788

Communicants, May 10,
Pentecost, 1799
Peter Miller and wife
Catharina
Christian Meiser and wife
Susanna
Jacob Vogelgesanger and
Elisabeth
Heinrich Engel
Ludwig Dippel and Margaretha
Johann Dietrich
Philip Kressner and Christina

Michael Kirchertner(?) and Eva
Jacob Kreischner(?) and
Catharina
Herman (????) (could be
Richert?)
Jacob Kreisch
Johann Derringer
Adam Wolssner and Eva
Joh. Derringer
Barbara Derringer
Jacob Spielmann and wife Eva
Bernhard Sauer and wife
Barbara
Conrad Leinert
Conrad Drecksler and wife
Fronica
Elisabeth Bauer
Heinrich Vogt
Catharina Carll
Magdal. Vogt
Susanna Catharina Redett
Elisabeth Vogt
Elisab. Katz
Cath. Glateiss
Marga Beistel
Anna Maria Spilman
Maria Widmer
Elisabeth Handels
George Landi
George Kressler and wife
Catharina
Antony Kleppinger and wife
Anna Margaretha
Henrich Kleppinger
Jacob Krämer
Peter Rieger
Nelle Treisch

Communicants 8 days before
Pentecost, May 24, 1800
Friedrich Oberlin, Jun.
Reichert Treisch and wife
Nelle
Jacob Stahl and wife Elisabeth
Jacob Moor
Maria Elisabeth Saur
Cathar. Saur
Jacob Treischt
Johann Purmann
Maria Wittmer, old
Elisabeth Wittmer
Elisabeth Vogt
Fronica Trecksler
Elisabeth Stahl

Antonio Kleppinger and wife
  Anna Margaretha
Christian Lieh
Barbara Stambach
Conrad Dreichsler
Anna Maria Steck
Michael Maack and wife Susanna
  Charlotte
Catharine Carelson
Michael Mayer
Catherine Mayer
Michael Müller and wife
  Elisabeth
Margareth Rippel
Eva Maurer
John Rippel
Peter Krämer
John McKay
Georg Krämer
Maria Müller
John Bauer and wife Catharina

September 22, (1800?)
John Dietrich and wife
  Elisabeth
Jacob Vogelgesang and wife
  Elisabeth
Maria Margar. Vogelgesang
Adam Mayer and wife Margareth
Catharina Stambacher
Elisabeth Ebert
Maria Ebert
Wendel Martin and wife
  Elisabeth
Peter Salzgeber

Marriages

Johannes Boocker, bachelor, skindresser of Shippensburg, to Susanna Mühleysen, virgin, on February 26, 1787.
Jacob Frey, bachelor, to Susanna Treysch, virgo, on August 27.
Abraham Höbling, bachelor, to Margaretha Schnierle, virgo, on June 22, 1788.

FIRST EVANGELICAL LUTHERAN CHURCH, CARLISLE,
Cumberland Co, PA
Parish Registers, 1788-1923

Baptisms

Anna Judith of John Jacob Geigle and Catharina, born August 29, 1788; baptized September 14, 1788. Sponsors: Georg Jacob Geigle and wife.
Anna Maria of Jacob Kraus, born ----; baptized ----. Sponsors: parents.
Joseph of Jacob Weber and Catharina, born July 24, 1788; baptized September 17, 1788. Sponsors: parents.
Friedrich David of Friedrich David Schäfer and Rosina, born July 22, 1787; baptized July 28, 1787. Sponsor: Ludwig Rosenmiller.
Johan Georg Friedrich of Gottfried Lus and Elisabeth, born September 29, 1788; baptized October 26, 1788. Sponsors: Conrad Schumpber and wife Iva.
Christina of Christian Ceferry(?) and Justina, born August 26, 1788; baptized September 18, 1788. Sponsor: Anna Margretta Buschin.
Catharina Elisabeth of Jacob Herrauf and Catrina, born December 12, 1788; baptized January 18, 1789. Sponsors: Georg Klein and Catharina.
Johan Georg of John Peter Draher and Anna Elisabeth, born February 11, 1789; baptized April 21, 1789. Sponsors: parents.
Johannes of Georg Kübler and Maria, born February 15, 1789; baptized April 26, 1789. Sponsors: parents.
Catharina of Jacob Boos and Maria Barbara, born December 21, 1788; baptized April 26, 1789. Sponsors: Georg Müller and Catharina.
Johannes of Philip Pheffer and Anna Maria, born April 26, 1789; baptized July 31, 1789. Sponsors: John George Lautermilch and Catharina.
Elisabeth of John Sensebach and Regina, born May 30, 1789; baptized July 5, 1789. Sponsors: Conrad Zumber and Eva.
Anna Maria of Joseph Schramm and Barbara, born September 11, 1789; baptized November 8, 1789. Sponsors: Jacob Kräber and Anna Maria.
Johannes of Georg Feile and Sara, born May 28, 1789; baptized November 19, 1789. Sponsor: Johannes Feile.
Christian of Christian Höck and Barbara, born November 13, 1789; baptized January 17, 1790. Sponsors: Johannes Kräber and Eva.
Lydia of Adam Holzapfel and Margretha, born October 14, 1789; baptized January 17, 1790. Sponsors: Jacob Kräber and Maria.
Sara of John Jacob Geigle and Catharina, born December 23, 1789; baptized January 20, 1790. Sponsors: parents.
Jacob of Leon Keller and Catharina, born April 27, 1788; baptized May --, 1788. Sponsors: parents.
Anna Maria of Bernhard Keller and Catherina, born November 16, 1789; baptized December 6, 1789. Sponsors: parents.
Georg Christian of Thomas Wilson Bradle and Maria Catharina Tummler at Bannibrok, 1-1/2 miles from Carlisle, born (not

given); baptized September 11, 1790. Sponsor: Christian Demann.
Catharina of John Appell and Magdalena Weissen, born May 11, 1790; baptized September 12, 1790 in the parsonage. Sponsors: parents and Cath. Weissen.
Catharina Dorothea of Bernhard Lehar and Louise Haberlander of Homburg, (birth not given); baptized September 28, 1790, about 3 years old. Sponsors: the parents and Fredr. Ru--- and wife, in Carlisle.
Mar. Magdalena of Hinrich Stöfer and Magdalena Spengler residing near Bermudian Creek, born August 24, 1790; baptized October 7, 1790 in the church there. Sponsors: Peter Spengler and Anne Mar. Spengler.
Anna Maria of William Kaup and Maria, nee Rentzheimer, in Westberry Twp., born November 5, 1789; baptized October 25, 1790. Sponsors: Maria Holtzapfeln and parents.
Susanna of George Ottenberger and Cathrina, nee Steiffeson, (birth not given); baptized March 7, 1791. Sponsors: Anna Maria Steifesohn and mother.
Prudentia Ellis of Jean Gotthrie and Sarah, nee Dewis, born March 1, 1779; baptized March 30, 1791. Sponsors: Prudentia Praun and parents.
Samuel of Adam Ebbrich and ----, nee La Ferre, born January 23, 1791; baptized April 9, 1791. Sponsors: parents.
Susanna of Jeremias Miller and Maria, nee Schade, born January 11, 1791; baptized April 9, 1791. Sponsors: parents.
Gottfried of Gottfried Lutz and Elisabeth, nee Wilmsen, born March 17, 1791; baptized April 9, 1791. Sponsors: parents.
Anna Henrica of Louis Morgan and Elisabeth, married to Jacob Schaefer, residing on the Tusquerorah, born December 17, 1768; baptized April 16, 1791 at the pastor's house. Sponsors: Pastor Ad. Hinrich Mejer, her husband, and his brother.
Anna Maria, widow of Michael Wagener, Middletown Township, born November 15, 1768; baptized April 19, 1791 in the pastor's house. Sponsors: Elisabeth Wagner, the sister, Mrs. Catharina Schäfer, and Pastor Ad. Hinrich Mejer.
Johannes of Jo. Joap and Magdalena, nee Richtson, born February 16, 1791; baptized April 24, 1791. Sponsors: parents.
Elisabeth of Stephen Merten and Elisabeth, nee Paff, born May 6, 1791; baptized June 6, 1791. Sponsors: George Paff and Cathar. Warms.
Anna Maria of Georg Kiebler and Anna Maria, nee Kiefer, born April 11, 1791; baptized June 6, 1791. Sponsors: Greta Kiefer and father.
Mary of Sam. Hunter and wife Rattschen Schoeps in Carlisle, born May 6, 1791; baptized June 24, 1791. Sponsors: parents.
Mary of Jonathan Bailey and Sarah Stopelse, (birth not given); baptized July 17, 1791. Sponsor: Mrs. Polle Pegge Crodders.
Mary of Jacob Miller and Elisabeth, nee Kaket, baptized August 3, 1791, now 18 months. Sponsors: parents.
Elisabeth of Jacob Edelblat and Elisabeth, nee Strubelin, both of Ege Furnace, birth not given; baptized August 3, 1791. Sponsors: mother and Mrs. Jacob Müller.
Samuel Hunter's wife, Mrs. Röttschel, nee Schelps, married March 15, 1791, dau of ---- and Anna ----, baptized August 3, 1791.

Sponsors: her husband and Mrs. Elisabeth Schaefer from Longdorf.
Maria Murrai of Thomas Murrai and Elisabeth, nee Seufer(?), born August 6, 1789; baptized August 3, 1791. Sponsors: parents and Mr. Fridrich Stucki(?) from Carlisle.
Elisabeth of Bille Kerle and Elisabeth Pauhe [of?] Trenton, born September 10, 1790; baptized April 12, 1791. Sponsor: mother.
Catharina of Johannes Richter and Magdalena, nee Hemken, born July 22, 1791; baptized September 17, 1791. Sponsors: parents and grandparents.
Catharina of Jo. Christian Golander and Anna Maria, nee Zimmer, baptized September 17, 1791, age 1 year old. Sponsors: parents, Nic. Lange and Anna Christina Lange.
Johannes of Johannes Sensebach and Regina, nee Feininger, (birth not given); baptized October 9, 1791. Sponsors: grandmother and parents.
Apollonia of Jacob Stumm and Catarina, nee Geristen, (birth not given); baptized October 9, 1791. Sponsors: parents.
Aisett of Aisett Corry and Barbara, baptized November 17, 1791, age 8 months. Sponsors: parents.
Nancy of Aiset Corry and Barbara, baptized November 17, 1791, age 3 years. Sponsors: parents.
Maria Magdalena of Henry Egolff and Maria Magdalena Hoop, born September 1, 1791; baptized December 4, 1791, at Mr. George Cainer's house. Sponsors: mother and Elisabeth Schäfers.
Jacob of John Cräber and wife, (birth not given); baptized December 4, 1791. Sponsors: Jacob Craber and wife and parents.
Rosina Elisabeth of Jacob Fretzeninger and Magdalena, nee Wolff, baptized December 21, 1791, age 4 months. Sponsors: Mr. ----'s wife [blurred].
Elisabeth of William Schmidt and Anna Maria, nee Knuppel, (birth not given); baptized January 2, 1792. Sponsor: Elisabeth Schäfer.
Anna Mar. Rosina of Christian Gottfried Mariel and Margreth, nee Hamuth, baptized January 28, 1792, age 11 months. Sponsors: grandmother, mother, Jacob Hamuth, father, Christian Gottfried Mareil.
Johannes of Mr. Holzapfel and wife, nee Cräber, born ----; baptized May 20, 1793. Sponsors: John Cräber and wife, together with the parents.
Johann George of Adam Kiefer and Elisabeth, nee Fahclern [sic], across the creek in Middletown Twp., born ----; baptized May 28, 1793. Sponsors: daughter Marg. Kiefer and parents.
Elisabeth of Jacob Fetter and Catharina in Carlisle, born ----; baptized May 30, 1793. Sponsors: parents.
Jean of Dewalt Rollstieg and Ruffi near Carlisle, Pa., born ----; baptized August 19, 1793. Sponsors: parents.

Burials

Jacob Holtzapfel, son of Adam Holtzapfel, residing 3-1/2 miles from Carlisle, died August 13, 1790 (age 20 years, 9 months) of a consumptive disease, buried August 15, 1790.

Magdalena Boger, the late Christian Boger's surviving daughter in the "Klets," died February 5, 1791 (age 12 years), buried the 6th.
Johannes Selander, son of Christian Selander, from Middletown Township, died at age 11-3/4 years, buried September 17, 1791.
---- Schelli, son of ---- Schelle, in Carlisle, died age -- years, buried ---- 1791. With a funeral sermon.
George Christle [sic] Richter, son of Jo. Richter, in Middletown Township, died age 2 years 1 month, buried October 13, 1791. With a funeral sermon.
Anna Stukki, wife of Mr. Friedrich Stucki, died age 54 years, buried October 31, 1791. With a funeral sermon.
Mrs. Rosina Coinern, nee Faselern, wife of George Coiner, died age 23 years and [some or 2] months, buried November 27, 1791, with a funeral sermon the 28th.
Polle Hubern, born April 25, 1789, died February 19 from whooping cough; buried February 20, 1792, with a sermon on the cemetery.

Marriages

Mr. Freiderich Brets, son of Simon Bretz, Isberger Twp., Cumberland County, married Miss Magdalene Harten, daughter of John Hart, on October 26, 1790 - near the Dunckers Cloister, Lancaster Co"
Dewald Rellsing from Ireland married Elizabeth Edebach of German background (her father residing on Connegene Creek) on November 11, 1790 in the minister's house [Adam Henr. Mejer].
George Michael Wolff, widower, residing on Mistress Faseler's plantation, married widow Sophia Margaretha Schwartz on November 11, 1790 in Sheriff Buchanan's house.
Mr. Gottfried Stahl, son of George Stahl of Monnachen Twp., (York County), married Miss Elizabeth Kowel, daughter of Benj. Kowel, on November 16, 1790 in the minister's house [Adam Henr. Mejer].
Jean Mehonig married Cathrine Jenan Bail on November 21, 1790, in the minister's house [Adam Henr. Mejer]. Witness: Fried. Wickey.
Hinrich Walte, son of Casp. Walte, Ober Sollford Twp., married Miss Cathrina Wittmeijer, child of the late Stoffel Wittmeier, near Langstaff, on November 23, 1790, in Mr. Gräber's house.
Christofer David Wörle, born across the mountains, married Gertrut Weyermann, child of Henry Weyermann of Folk's Mill, Jorcks Twp., on November 21, 1790, in Carlisle.
Mr. Thomas George married Mrs. Polle Widdain of Big Spring on January 6, 1791, in the minister's house [Adam Henr. Mejer].
William Rogliff married Margreth Kohlmann on February 1, 1791, in the minister's house [Adam Henr. Mejer].
Jean Miller married Lisabeth Goddrie on February 11, 1791, in the minister's house [Adam Henr. Mejer].
William Galaspe married Elisabeth Dunne on February 24, 1791, in the minister's house [Adam Henr. Mejer].
Samuel Hunter married Rottschen Schulpe on March 15, 1791, in the minister's house [Adam Henr. Mejer].
Anthony McKerbes married Sarah McKean on March 17, 1791, in the minister's house [Adam Henr. Mejer].

Jumuk Mollen married Mrs. Martha McKeslin on March 22, 1791, in the minister's house [Adam Henr. Mejer].
Patrik McFerlan married Polle Garner of York Twp. on April 27, 1791, in Mr. Craber's house.
Samuel Schleiffer married Rebecca Delong of Big Spring on May 6, 1791, in Mrs. S. Hoekin's house.
Hugh Stephens married Mary Kraft of Carlisle on May 6, 1791, in the minister's house [Adam Henr. Mejer].
Andrew Karr married Elisabeth Philips on May 9, 1791, in the minister's house [Adam Henr. Mejer].
Robert Wilson of Carlisle married Elisabeth Henry on May 25, 1791, in the house of the father of the bride.
Janne K'Nusen [sic] married Nancy Wilson on May 26, 1791, by Mr. Henry.
William Weyermann married Mrs. Mary Anderwood on June 2, 1791, in the Black Horse ("Schw. Ross").
Andrew Morrphe married Cathrin McClaud, widow of Wm. McClaud, on June 25, 1791, in her house.
Joseph Hedson married Sarah Welsch, daughter of Dan Welsch, on October 4, 1791, in Carlisle.
John Jotti, son of Hinr. Jotti, near Lisbon, married Anna Maria Gehr, daughter of Joseph Gehr, near Lisbon, on November 28, 1791, in Mr. Welsch's house.
John McCartney, a formerly married man, married Barbara Naas, daughter of N. H. Hass, by license, on November 29, 1791, 7 miles from Carlisle.
Mr. William Klindenner married Nancy O. Harri on February 25, 1792, in the minister's house [Adam Henr. Mejer].
Mr. Ebenezer Harbrid, 12 miles from Carlisle on Balt: road married Magdalena Wallick, of the same place, on March 6, 1792, in the minister's house [Adam Henr. Mejer] in the presence of the bride's father.
Mr. Christopher Jist, widower of Lancaster County, married Maria Wagnern, widow of Mich. Wagner, 3 miles from Carlisle, on March 20, 1792, in Mrs. Hock's house.
Mr. Samuel Schäfer, son of Abraham Schäfer, near Langstaff, married Maria Elisabeth Reichwein, daughter of Christopher Reichwein across the "Connego-queen" Creek, on March 20, 1792, in the minister's house [Adam Henr. Mejer].
Jo. Mich. Cast, son of Mr. Cast near Carlisle, married Syb. Margr. Lain, daughter of Mr. Lain of Schermann's Valley, on March 27, 1792, in the house of Mr. McLain.
Martin Diller, widower, 3 miles from Carlisle, married Miss Magdalena Jungen, daughter of Mr. Junge who lives 3 miles from Carlisle, on April 11, 1792, in the minister's house [Adam Henr. Mejer].
James Clerk, not far from Carlisle, married to Jean Beatty, whose parents are in Virginia, on April 13, 1792. in the minister's house [Adam Henr. Mejer].
James Harwich, a discharged soldier, married Cathr. French, widow, of Chester Co.,on April 16, 1792, in the minister's house [Adam Henr. Mejer].
Jean Kerren married Nancy Wilson on April 29, 1792, in the minister's house [Adam Henr. Mejer].

Georg Wilson of Upper Bermuthian married Miss Cathrin Ziegler of the same place on May 15, 1792, at Mr. Jacob Craber's.
Adam Reisinger of York County married Miss Elisabeth Penn, daughter of Philip Penn, on August 21, 1792, at Mr. Jacob Kräber's.
Mr. Jacob Vogelsgesang married Margaretha Kiefer on September 16, 1792, in the minister's house [Adam Henr. Mejer].
William Dewer, 3 miles above Shippensburg, married Rebecca Carr from Tuscarora (Tuskerora) on September 18, 1792, in the minister's house [Adam Henr. Mejer].
George Faseler, near Carlisle, married Molle Diller, child of Casper Diller, near Carlisle, on October 2, 1792, in Mr. C. Diller's house.
Ephraim Reuter, "Bermutschen," York County, married July Diller, daughter of Casper Diller, on October 2, 1792, in Mr. C. Diller's house.
Mr. George Fechert of Hagerstown married Mrs. Cathrina Fischbach Faust on October 3, 1792, in the minister's house [Adam Henr. Mejer].
Carl Ludwig Hachmeister married Elisabeth Shäfers of Langstaff on October 7, 1792, in the minister's house [Adam Henr. Mejer].

TRINDLE SPRING LUTHERAN CHURCH

1792

William of Mr. Henry Stuart and his wife Isabella, born ----; baptized at Mr. Conrad Rupple's. Sponsors: godfather, the father himself.
Anna Eva of Mr. Johan Bauer and his wife Catharina, baptized September 9, 1792, age 2 years old. Sponsors: father and mother.
Johannes of Joh. Bauer and his wife Catharina, born ----; baptized eodem [September 9, 1792] in his parents' house. Sponsors: Mr. Dewald Erfurt and his wife Magdalena.

1794
(Children baptized by Rev. John Herbst)

Christina of Smick Tschan and Maria, born October 1, 1792; baptized ----. Sponsor: Eva Wummeldorf.
Elisabeth of Jacob Losler and Cathar., born September 25, 1793; baptized ----. Sponsors: Joh. Nicolaus and Elisabeth Kreitzer.
Susana of Joseph Koch and Anna Maria, born September 19, 1794; baptized ----. Sponsors: Nicolaus Schäffer and Susana.
Joh. Georg of Conrath Weber and Catherina, born May 13, 179(4)?; baptized ----. Sponsors: the parents.
Maria of Jacob Heck and Maria Barbara, born December 10, 1794; baptized ----. Sponsor: Maria Emrichen.
Sara of Christoph Eichenberger and Barbara, born November 24, 1793; baptized ----. Sponsors: Jacob Wörmle and Elisabeth his wife.
Johannes of Abraham Pretz and Maria, born May 9, 1794; baptized ----. Sponsors: Christopher Eichenberger and Barbara his wife.
Maria of Johannes Wormlÿ, born July 19, 1794; baptized ----. Sponsors: the parents.
Maria of Jacob Rupply and Maria, born February 27, 1794; baptized ----. Sponsors: the parents.
Susana of Henrich S. Manneschmidt and Eva, born May 31, 1794; baptized ----. Sponsors: Christian Laubenschweiler and Susana.
Anna Elisabeth of Casper Treiber and Elisabeth, born March 5, 1794; baptized ----. Sponsors: Valentine Bruchman and Anna Elisabeth.
Joh. Georg. of Hannos Miesch and Magdalena, born November 2, 1794; baptized ----. Sponsor: Joh. Georg Miesch.
Friedreich of Friedreich Lang and Christina, born September 21, 1794; baptized ----. Sponsors: Jonas Rupp and Catharina.
Georg Elter of Englehart Wörmly and Elisabeth, born December 7, 1784; baptized ----. Sponsors: Georg Wörmly and Elisabeth Wörmly.
Jacob of Georg Eble and Anna, born March 13; baptized May 17, 1795. Sponsor: Engelhardt Wormly.
Georg of Georg Eble and Anna, born February 21, 1786; baptized as above [May 17, 1795]. Sponsors: isdem [Engelhardt Wormly].
Samuel of Georg Eble and Anna, born November 10, 1787; baptized as above [May 17, 1795]. Sponsors: name not given.
A. Maria ----, born November 3, 1790; baptized as above [May 17, 1795]. Sponsors: name not given.

TRINDLE SPRING LUTHERAN CHURCH 63

Anna ----, born Beginning of December 1794; baptized as above [May 17, 1795]. Sponsors: name not given.
Elisabeth of Enick John and Mary, born April 12, 1795; baptized ----. Sponsors: Jacob Rupplÿ and Maria.
Maria of Jacob Fessler and Catharina, born April 22, 1795; baptized ----. Sponsors: Georg Bennetsch and Catharina.
Samuel of Georg Lutz and Catharina, born January 15, 1796; baptized ----. Sponsor: Abraham Wolf.
Ana Cathar. of Henrich Jüngst, born November --, 1765; baptized ----.
Catharina of Henrich Jüngst and Christina, born November 22, 1795. Sponsors: Peter Jüngst and Catharina.
Greth of Alexander Weÿth, born October 2, 1789; baptized ----. Sponsors: Johanes Jaig and Magdalena.
Eva of Johanes Jaig and Magdalena, born March 17, 1795; baptized ----. Sponsor: Magdalena Weÿgand.
Joh. Jacob of Georg Wörmly, born May 22, 1796; baptized ----. Sponsors: Jacob Wormly and Elisabeth.
Susana of Georg Wörmly, born May 22, 1796; baptized ----. Sponsor: Susana Lutzin.
Sara of Georg Wild and Catharina, born January 12, 1796; baptized ----. Sponsor: Maria Albert.
Engelhardt of Engelhard Wörmly and Elisabeth, born January 19, 1797; baptized 29 of the same. Sponsors: Jacob Feger and his wife Elisabeth.
Henrich of Jacob Rubly and Anna Maria, born July 28, 1796; baptized September 4. Sponsors: the parents.
Abraham of Abraham Pretz and Anna Maria, born February 12, 1797; baptized April 30. Sponsors: Simon Pretz and Catharina.
Johannes of Georg Man and A. Maria, born July 1; baptized September 30, 1797. Sponsors: Jacob Wörmly and Elisabeth.
Johann Georg of Arnold Höfelmann and Eva, born October 20, 1797; baptized January 6, 1798. Sponsors: the parents.
Veronica of Conrad Rubly and Veronica, born October 11, 1797; baptized March 20, 1798. Sponsors: Jacob Rubly and A. Maria.
Benjamin of Martin Müller and Sally, born January 30; baptized March 20, 1798. Sponsors: Frid. Schultz and A. Maria.
Joseph of Francis Strong and Jenny, born March 2; baptized May 9. Sponsors: the parents.
Johannes of Adam Hertz and Maria, born June 11; baptized August 5. Sponsors: Engelhardt Wörmly and Elisabeth.
Johannes Georg of Joh. Georg Wörmly and Catharina his wife, born August 15; baptized October 7, 1798. Sponsors: Johannes Wörmly and Maria.
David of Joh. Wörmly and Maria his wife, born December 25, 1798; baptized January 7, 1799. Sponsors: the parents.
Abraham of Engelhardt Wörmly and Elisabeth, born February 24; baptized April 7, 1799. Sponsors: Johannes Rubly and Barbara.
Georg of Joh. Rubly and Barbara, born December 14, 1798; baptized January 13, 1799. Sponsors: Jacob Rubly and Maria.

64 CUMBERLAND COUNTY CHURCH RECORDS OF THE 18TH CENTURY

Johannes of Johannes Heck and Elisabeth Kisecker (unmarried), born February 8; baptized ----. Sponsor: Nicolaus Kisecker.
Anna of Henrich Ernstberger and Anna, born January 16; baptized June 16, 1799. Sponsors: the parents.
Benjamin of Geo. Werffel and Maria, born November 2, 1798; baptized June 23, 1799. Sponsors: the parents.
Anna Maria of Joh. Schäfer and Christina, born March 29; baptized August 4, 1799. Sponsors: Christoph Eichelberger and Barbara.
Susanna of Thomas Wharton and Susanna, born September 29, 1798; baptized September 15, 1799. Sponsors: Valentine Stegmüller and A. Elisabeth.
Johannes of Nicolaus Schamburg and Barbara, born February 26; baptized January 1, 1800. Sponsor: the mother.
Barbara of Hanna Ily (in celebacy), born December 30, 1799; baptized March 2, 1800. Sponsor: Elisabeth Koch.
Johannes of Philip Koch and Elisabeth, born November 17, 1799; baptized March 2, 1800. Sponsors: Joh. Emmerich and Cath. Kiesecker.
Philip of Philip Koch and Elisabeth, born ----; baptized January 10, 1798. Sponsors: Phil. Hickernel and Cath. Thomas.
Elisabeth of Geo. Wolf and Elisabeth, born March 13, 1797; baptized April 12, 1800. Sponsor: the mother.
Johannes of Georg Kober and Eva, born August 15, 1799; baptized July 29, 1801. Sponsors: Christoph Eichelberger and Barbara.
Sarah of iidem [Georg Kober and Eva], born March 8; baptized as above [July 29, 1801]. Sponsor: Elis. Schäfer.
Maria of Georg Wörmle and Catharina, born August 29, 1800; baptized 5 weeks afterwards. Sponsor: Elis. Wörmle.
Johannes of Henr. Trabinger and Eva, born August 30, 1800; baptized September 27, 1801. Sponsors: the parents.
Polly of Willh. Stegmüller and Elis., born April 3; baptized as above [September 27, 1801]. Sponsors: Valentine Stegmüller and Elis.

(Children baptized by Rev. F. D. Sanno)

David of Henrich John and Anna Maria, born March 3, 1795; baptized May 29, 1802. Sponsor: Dewald Erfurt.
Margaretha of Henrich John and Anna Maria, born September 18, 1797; baptized on same day [May 29, 1802]. Sponsors: Jacob Eichelberger and Maria.
Willhelm of Henrich John and Anna Maria, born October 21, 1800; baptized on same day [May 29, 1802].
Elisabet of Adam Thomas, born September 22, 1777; baptized October 28, 1808. Sponsors: name not given.

ST. STEPHEN'S (LONGSDORF'S) EVANGELICAL LUTHERAN CHURCH
New Kingston, Silver Spring Township, Cumberland Co., PA.

Maria Magdalena of Phillip Bauer and Elisabeth, born March 6, 1789; baptised March 15, 1789. Sponsor: Maria Magdalena Steern, widow.
Maria of Nicolaus Bobb and Catharina, born November 21, 1788; baptized May 9, 1789. Sponsors: parents.
Johan Phillipp of Phillip Lansdorf and Anna, his wife, born January 3, 1784; baptized January 11, 1784. Sponsors: Michael Hack and Apollonia.
Johan Michael of Phillip Lansdorf and Anna, his wife, born August 10, 1785; baptized August 30, 1785. Sponsors: parents.
Maria Elisabeth of Phillip Lansdorf and Anna, his wife, born September 20, 1787; baptized October 14, 1787. Sponsors: parents.
Elisabeth of Martin Langsdorf and Anna Margretha, born January 14, 1778; baptized January 18, 1778. Sponsors: Henrich Langsdorf and Elisabeth.
Anna Margretha of Martin Langsdorf and Anna Margretha, born November 30, 1779; baptized December 1779. Sponsors: Michel Bohr and Anna Margretha.
Henrich of Martin Langsdorf and Anna Margretha, born November 26, 1781; baptized September 1782. Sponsors: Henrich Langsdorf, widower, and Anna Margaretha Langsdorfin.
Anna Maria of Martin Langsdorf and Anna Margretha, born May 15, 1785; baptized June 1785. Sponsors: the parents.
Johann Martin of Martin Langsdorf and Anna Margretha, born March 25, 1788; baptized March 30, 1788. Sponsors: the parents.
Phillipp of Phillip Schneider and Barbara, born December 1774; baptized January 1775. Sponsors: Phillip Langsdorf, single, and Susanna Emminger, single.
Johannes of Phillip Schneider and Barbara, born June 28, 1778; baptized July 1778. Sponsors: Balthaser Schneider and Susanna Schneidern.
Maria Magdalena of Phillip Schneider and Barbara, born September 16, 1784; baptized October 1784. Sponsors: Wilhelm Bohr, Maria Magdalena and the parents.
Margretha of Phillip Schneider and Barbara, born September 16, 1784; baptized October 1784. Sponsors: Wilhelm Bohr, Maria Magdalena and the parents.
Sara of Philip Ebert and Elisabetha, [born or baptized] May 22, 1790. Sponsors: Johann Christoph Albert and Barbar Albert.
Reinick of Isaac Engeni [?] and Barbaras, born September 18, 1789; baptized December 20, 1789. Sponsors: Johannes Reinick and the child's mother.
Johannes of Martin Härman and Catharina, born October 18, 1789; baptized December 20, 1789. Sponsors: Michael Hag and Apelonia.
Christina of Johannes Griel and Maria Elisabetha, born November 6, 1785; baptized April 14, 1786. Sponsors: Michael Hack and Apelonia.

Maria Elisabeth of Jacob Roth and Catharina, born October 18, 1789; baptized May 16, 1790. Sponsors: Johannes Gunckel and Elisabeth.
Elisabeth of Henrich Schmith and his wife, born December 9, 1782; baptized 1783. Sponsors: Michael Hack and Apelonia.
Johan Phillip of Henrich Schmith and his wife, born May 25, 1784; baptized May 30, 1784. Sponsors: Phillip Langsdorf and Anna.
Catharina of Henrich Schmith and his wife, born June 17, 1786; baptized June 29, 1786. Sponsors: the parents.
Anna Barbara of Henrich Schmith and his wife, born May 5, 1788; baptized June 1788. Sponsors: Phillip Bauer and Elisabeth.
Catharina of Martin Langsdorff and Margaretha, born May 29, 1790; baptized June 1, 1790. Sponsors: parents.
Anna Maria of Henrich Schmidd and Dorothea, born July 17, 1790; baptized July 26, 1790. Sponsors: Jacob Kast and Anna Catharina.
Johannes of Jacob Lahmert and Cathrina (nee Opach), born ----; baptized August 8, 1790. Sponsors: the parents.
Salomon of Caspar Dieler and Christina (nee Wolffen), in Allen Township, born ----; baptized October 10, 1790. Sponsors: the parents
Johann Adam of Peter Schäfer and Susanna (nee Wenrich), born September 23, 1790; baptized November 6, 1790. Sponsors: the parents.
Chatharina of Adam Langsdorff and Elisabeth (nee Schöfferen), born June 19, 1790; baptized June 26, 1790. Sponsors: Andreas Bob and his wife Susana.
Wilhelm of Wilhelm Bohr and Maria Elisabeth, born ----; baptized November 21, 1790. Sponsor: Lucas Schalle near Stestz.
Johann of Johann Besahard and Catharina Elisabeth (nee Schalle), born ----; baptized November 21, 1790. Sponsors: grandfather, Mr. Schalle, and father.
Anna Catharina of Abraham Krieger and Maria Judith (nee Geigeson), [born or baptized] January 6, 1791. Sponsor: Anna Catharina Stect.
Johannes of Daniel Sallathe and Maria (nee West), born ----; baptized March 12, 1791. Sponsors: Andreas Popp and Susanna Popp.
Salome of Davis Schmidt and Anna Margreth (nee Killinger), born ----; baptized March 27, 1791. Sponsors: Jacob Cost and Anna Cath. Kast [sic].
Elisabeth of Jean Guerie and Maria (nee Ewers), born ----; baptized April 22, 1791. Sponsors: the mother, grandmother and grandfather.
Philip of Phil. Werner and Matte (nee McKnap [?]), born ----; baptized March 24, 1791. Sponsors: father and mother.
Anna Maria of Philip Wagener and Maria, born June 4, 1786; baptized April 15, 1791. Sponsors: parents.
Anna Dorothee of Philip Wagener and Maria, born November 25, 1788; baptized April 15, 1791. Sponsor: Anna Doroth. Rothakern.
son of Philip Wagner and Maria, born November 19, 1789; baptized April 15, 1791. Sponsor: Davis Schmidt.

ST. STEPHEN'S LUTHERAN CHURCH 67

Anna Margr. of the late Mich. Wagner and his widow Maria, born January 2, 1789; baptized April 15, 1791. Sponsor: the mother.
Michel of the late Mich. Wagner and his widow Maria, born May 2, 1790; April 15, 1791. Sponsor: Christoph Rothaker.
Anna Catharina of Philip Bauer and Ann Elisabeth (nee Laoger [?]), born ----; baptized June 7, 1791. Sponsors: Jacob Cass and Anna Catharina.
Anna of Ludolph Peter, Sr., and Catharina, born October 6, 1790; baptized June 19, 1791. Sponsors: Elisabeth Kun. Kels and the father.
Maria Catharina of Nic. Kreel and Catharina (nee Hansecker), born ----; baptized June 20, 1791. Sponsors: Cathr. Lis Foltz, the mother.
Johann Georg of Georg Bauer and Anna Maria, born ----; baptized October 8, 1791. Sponsors: Hinr. Walte and wife and the parents.
Anna Maria of Hinr. Walte and Catharina, born ----; baptized October 8, 1791. Sponsors: Philip Schneider and wife and the parents.
David of Philip Wagener and Elisabeth, born ----; baptized October 8, 1791. Sponsors: David Schmidt and wife.
Marg. of Georg Cruse and Else., born ----; baptized October 8, 1791. Sponsors: Joh. Reineck [?] and the father.
Johann of Nic. Gottshall residing on that side of Philadelphia in Bucks County, born January 19, 1791 [?]; baptized September 26, 1791. Sponsors: John Reineck, Isaac Anglew and wife.
Marg. of Eisett Agnew and Barbara, born ----; baptized October 26, 1791. Sponsors: Elisabeth Kunethet [?] and Christoph Wittmaier.
William of Jean Rabens and Elisabeth, born ----; baptized January 21, 1792. Sponsors: father and mother.
Elisabeth of Nicolaus Popp and Catharina, born ----; baptized February 11, 1792. Sponsors: father and mother.
Johann Adam of Peter Steinberger and Margreth (nee Mies), born October 18, 1791; baptized December 26, 1791. Sponsors: Adam Langstaff and wife and the father.
Elisabeth of Andreas Popp and Susanna (nee Schäfern), born January 10, 1792; baptized February 4, 1792. Sponsors: Adam Langstaff and wife and the mother.
Nicolaus of William Bohr and Mar. Lisab., born ----; baptized February 27, 1792. Sponsors: Nic. Bohr and the father's mother.
Anna Maria of Adam Langstaff and Elisabeth, born ----; baptized March 4, 1792. Sponsors: Adam Schalle and Anne Mar. Depot.
Elisabeth of Jacob Lehmer and Catharina, born May 19, 1792; baptized June 9, 1792 in the church. Sponsor: Elisabeth Kunckeln.
Cathrina of Johannes Schäfer and Hanna, born April 14, 1792; baptized August 5, 1792. Sponsors: Cathrina Schäfern and parents.
Elisabeth of Jo. Spies and Eva, born ----; baptized September 2, 1792. Sponsor: Elisabeth Beckern.
Johann Jacob of Hinr. Keller, born October 18, 1791; baptized June 10, 1792. Sponsors: parents.

Georg of Jo. Georg Klenck and Anna, born May 25, 1792; baptized
September 16, 1792 in the church. Sponsors: Jacob Cast and
Cathrina.
Alexander of Alexander Moore and Mary, born August 1792; baptized
September 30, 1792 in Carlisle in Mr. Joh. Reinecks house.
Michael of Marthin Langsdorf and wife Margretha, born November 6,
1793; baptized November 25, 1793.
Catharina of Darf Hachmeister and Elisabet, born August 17, 1793;
baptized September 22, 1793. Sponsors: Stophel Witmeier and
Catharina.
Johannes of Stophel Witmaier and Catharina, born November 16,
1793; baptized November 25, 1793. Sponsors: Samuel Shäfer and
Elisabeth.
Anna Margaretha of Heinrich Schmidt and Dorothea, born November
13, 1793; baptized November 25, 1793. Sponsor: Anna
Langdorffin.
Elisabeth of Adam Longsdorff and Elisabeth, born December 24,
1793; baptized ----.
Daniel of Samuel Schaefer and Elisabeth, born March 11, 1794;
baptized May 4, 1794. Sponsors: Ludwig Carl Hachmeister and
Elis.
Susana of Joseph Ares and Catarina, born June 2, 1794; baptized
November 30, 1794.
Martin of Christian Herman and Elisabeth, born December 3, 1794;
baptized March 22, 1795. Sponsors: Martin Bauer and Elisabeth.
Johan Georg of Stophel Witmaier and Catarina, born March 19,
1795; baptized April 18, 1795. Sponsors: Georg Bauer and Anna
Maria.
Annamaria of Philip Schneider and Barbara, born September 29,
1795; baptized October 25, 1795. Sponsors: Martin Langsdorf
and Anna Margred.
Martin of Adam Kiefer and Elisabeth, born December 22, 1795
[sic]; baptized February 10, 1795. Sponsor: Martin Stücke.
Johan Adam of Martin Langsdorf and Margreda, born February 10,
1795; baptized April 10, 1795. Sponsors: parents.
Johannes of Samuel Schäffer and Elisabeth, born March 23, 1796;
baptized ----. Sponsors: Christopel Wittmaÿr and Catarina.
Johannes of Christian Herman and Elisabeth, born May 19, 1796;
baptized June 10, 1796. Sponsors: Jacob Kast and Anna
Catarina.
Elisabeth of Christofel Albert and Barbara, born January 22,
1796; baptized ----. Sponsors: Georg Bauer and Anna Maria.
James Geils of Isaac Augney and Barbara, nee Reineckin, born June
4, 1796; baptized June 22, 1796. Sponsor: Johannes Reineck,
grandfather.
Elisabeth of Stophel Witmeÿer and Catharina, born December 3,
1796; baptized March 19, 1797. Sponsors: Saml. Schäfer and
Elisabeth.
Johannes of Philip Schneider and Barbara, born February 22, 1797;
baptized May 7, 1797. Sponsors: Joh. Seiler and A. Maria.
Anna Marg. of Benjamin Clark and Elisabeth, born August 1, 1797;
baptized November --, 1797. Sponsor: A. Marg. Philips.
Willhelm of J. Henr. Keller and A. Christina, born October 12,
1797; baptized November 27, 1797. Sponsors: parents.

ST. STEPHEN'S LUTHERAN CHURCH   69

Joh. of John Evert and Cath., born December 10, 1797; baptized December 31, 1797. Sponsor: Joh. Pope.
Nancy of James McCassal and Elisabeth, born December 4, 1797; baptized December 31, 1797. Sponsors: Richard Coons and Agnis.
Salome of Adam Kiefer and Elisabeth, born February 12, 1797; baptized April 8 [?], 1798. Sponsors: parents.
Joh. Michael of Joseph Ares and Catharina, born February 22, 1797; baptized May 7, 1797. Sponsors: Michl. Haag and Magdalena Philippin.
Margaretha of Christopher Albert and Barbara, born December 30, 1797; baptized May 28, 1798. Sponsors: Andreas Schweitzer and Catharina.
Salome of Martin Hermann and Catharina, born April 25, 1798; baptized July 8 [?], 1798. Sponsors: Adam Kiefer and Elisabeth.
Joh. Wilhelm of Peter Schmidt and Marg., born March 17, 1798; baptized Tuesday after Pentecost, 1798. Sponsors: parents.
Elisabeth Hermann, wife of Christian Hermann, nee Bauerin, of Joh. Bauer and Elisabeth, born April 1, 1774; baptized August 19, 1798. Sponsors: Martin Hermann and wife Dorothea and Joh. Hermann.
Jacob of Christian Hermann and Elisabeth, born June 3, 1798; baptized August 19, 1798. Sponsors: Martin Hermann and wife Dorothea and Joh. Hermann.
Joh. Georg of Henrich Wald and Catharina, born April 6, 1798; baptized August 19, 1798. Sponsors: parents.
Michael of Willhelm Boor and Maria Elisabeth, born May 3, 1798; baptized August 29, 1798. Sponsor: Michael Boor.
Joh. Peter of Georg Ares and Anna Maria, born June 25, 1798; baptized September 2, 1798. Sponsor: Anna Maria Philippin.
Anna Maria of Heinrich Keller and Anna Christina, born December 20, 1798; baptized December 23, 1798. Sponsors: parents.
Maria of Andreas Schweitzer and Elisabeth, born February 15, 1799; baptized April 24, 1799. Sponsor: Elisabeth Kitzmüller.
Jacob of Rudolph Schäfer and Elisabeth, born February 9, 1799; baptized April 28, 1799. Sponsors: Joh. Adam Weiss and Eva.
Anna Maria of Joh. Jac. Kast and Anna Catharina, born July 27, 1799; baptized August 4, 1799. Sponsors: Michael Haag and Apollonia.
Johannes of Adam Kiefer and Elisabeth, born June 24, 1799; baptized August 4, 1799. Sponsors: parents.
Robert of Richard Kerns and Nancy, born February 17, 1799; baptized August 4, 1799. Sponsors: parents.
Elisabeth of James McCarslin and Elisabeth, born August 21, 1799; baptized September 15, 1799. Sponsors: parents.
Elisabeth of Philip Schneider and Barbara, born October 26, 1799; baptized December 15, 1799. Sponsors: Georg Bauer and A. Maria.
Anna Maria of Christian Hermann and Elisabeth, born November 11, 1799; baptized January 12, 1800. Sponsors: parents.
Georg of Martin Langsdorf and Margaretha, born March 5, 1800; baptized March 30, 1800. Sponsors: parents.
Andreas of Joh. Knochen and Margaretha, born September 9, 1799; baptized April 27, 1800. Sponsors: Geo. Forne and A. Maria.

Jacob of Joh. Best and Barbara, born November 8, 1799; baptized
May 25, 1800. Sponsors: Bej. Clark and Elisabeth.
Sarah of Nicolaus Schwardt and Sarah, born March 20, 1800;
baptized June 29, 1800. Sponsors: parents.
Elisabeth of Georg Forney and Margaretha, born May 13, 1800;
baptized May 25, 1800. Sponsor: Elisabeth Langsdorff.
Georg of Joh. Everts and Catharina, born September 16, 1800;
baptized November 16, 1800. Sponsor: Geo. Pope.
Margaretha of Henrich Meyer and Catharina, born September 28,
1800; baptized November 16, 1800. Sponsor: mother.
Anna of Thomas Nicolson and Maria, born November 3, 1800;
baptized April 5, 1801. Sponsor: mother.
David of Henrich Wald and Cath., born December 15, 1800; baptized
April 5, 1801. Sponsors: parents.
Philip Evens of John Kery and Maria, born December 5, 1800;
baptized June 7, 1801. Sponsor: mother.
Martin of Martin Hermann and Catharina, born December 28, 1800;
baptized June 7, 1801. Sponsors: the parents.
Jacob Eversol of Jacob Eversol and Maria, baptized April 17,
1802, aged about 25 years. Sponsors: part of the congregation.

Deaths, 1792

Mr. Philip Bauer in Langstaff, aged 25 years, 10 months.
Mr. Henr. Langstaff in Langstaff, aged 77 years.
Mr. Adam Kiefer's little daughter from across the creek, aged 3
years.

Baptisms
Elisabetha of Michael Schiele and Magdalena, born August 17,
1789; baptized September 6 thereafter. Sponsors: the parents.
Johann David (twin) of Andreas Emminger and Elisabetha, born
November[?] 18, 1789; baptized ----. Sponsor: Martin Kitzsch.
Johann Jacob (twin) of Andreas Emminger and Elisabetha, born
November[?] 18, 1789; baptized ----. Sponsor: Jacob Fahrnÿ.
Elisabeth of Christian Hillman and wife, born November 19, 1781;
baptized July 31, 1805.
Salome of Christian Hillman and wife, born July 17, 1788;
baptized July 31, 1805.

PASTORAL RECORD OF THE REV. JOHN CONRAD BUCHER
1763 - 1769

Baptisms and marriages performed in Cumberland County along with Dauphin and other counties.

Baptisms at Carlisle.
Ludwig David of Jacob Goodling and Anna Margaretha, bapt. Apr 17, 1763. Wit: Ludwig David Ripple, Sybilla Maria.
John Jacob of John Jacob Carl and Christina, b. Apr 23, 1763; bapt. May 19. Wit: Parents and Philip Noller and Maria.
Ludwig David of Ludwig David Ripple and Syblilla Maria, bapt. May 19. Wit: Ludwig Senzer.
Nancy of John McIntosh and Margreth, b. Jan 13, 1763, bapt. --- 4. Wit: John Nicklas Albert and Cathrina Seyler.
Johann Jacob of Conrad Bucher and Maria Magdalena, b. Jan 1, 1764, bapt. Jan 8, 1764. Wit: James Verdier and Sybilla Maria Ripple.
Maria Margareth of Mathias Seyler and Maria Margareth, b. Jan 4, 1764, bapt. Jan 12, 1764, d. Jan 15, 1764. Wit: John Leopold and Anna Maria Herbich.
Johan Philip Ludwig of John Henry Keyl and Anna Elisabeth, b. Feb 17, 1764, bapt. Feb 26. Wit: Philip Noller, Maria his wife and Ludwig David Ripple.
Johannes of Jacob Philip and Anna Maria, b. Mar 24, 1764, bapt. Apr 1, 1764. Wit: Johannes Kraus and Margaretha his wife.
Edward of Samuel Saunders and Christina, b. Mar 1, 1764, bapt. Mar 16. Wit: John Sayler and Elizabeth Smith.
Johannes of Johannes Hamuth and Anna Margaretha bapt. ---. Wit: John Leopold and Eva Kehr Ehring.
Jaques of James Verdier and Susannah b. Jan 17 (1764). Wit: Parents.
Johann Philip of Geo. Fred. Wurzbacher and Margaretha, b. Nov 16, 1764, bapt. Nov 23. Wit: Philip Noller and Margaretha his wife.
Ludwig of Johannes Stark and Dorothea, b. Dec 25, 1764, bapt. Dec 30. Wit: Ludwig Senzer and Margaretha.
Anna Margaretha of Johan Nicklas Albert and Anna Maria, b. Nov 22, 1764. Wit: Philip Noller and Anna Margaretha.
Mathias of John La Forge and Mary, b. Nov 20, 1764, bapt. Dec 25. Wit: Mathias Seyler.
John of Neal McDonald and Jannet, b. Nov 16, 1764, bapt. Apr 2, 1765. Wit: John McDonald, Jannet Mater pueri.
John of Peter Deytes and Mary, b. June 10, (1764), bapt. Apr 7, 1765. Wit: nemor, sed hic ipse.
Theodora Anna Isabel of John Deytes and Elisabeth b. June 15, 1764, bapt. Apr 7, 1765. Wit: John Statskoch, Theo. A. Isabel and his wife.
Johannes of Michael Kunckle and Anna Maria, b. Apr 22, 1765, bapt. July 25, 1765. Wit: Michael Hergesheimer and mater pueri.
Daniel of Jacob Carl and Christina, b. Sep 8, 1765, bapt. Sep 11, 1765, d. Dec 18. Wit: Parents.

Maria Appollonia of Leonard Huber and Christina, b. Jan 5, 1765, bapt. Sep 13, 1765. Wit: S. I. Houseman and Maria Appollonia his wife.
John Ludwig of Mathias Legner and Maria Eva, b. Nov 3, 1765, bapt. Dec 8, 1765. Wit: Ludwig Senzer and Margareth.
Cathrina Friderica of Valentine Dikes and Christina, b. Dec 1, 1765, bapt. Dec 8, 1765. Wit: Fredrick Christly and Ann Cathrina Christly.
John Philip of Georg Kast and Anna Margareth, b. Dec 1, 1765, bapt. Dec 25, 1765. Wit: Philip Noller and Margaretha his wife.
Cathrina of Mathias Seyler and Maria Margreth, b. Feb 16, 1765, bapt. Feb 24, 1766, d. Sep 20, 1768. Wit: Parents.
Susannah of Michael Dill and Maria Elisabetha, b. Jan 5, 1766, bapt. Jan 26, 1766. Wit: Mary Elisab. Schneyder.
Johanes of Johannes Hamuth and Margaretha, b. Feb 1, 1766, bapt. Feb 2, 1766. Wit: John Leopold and Eva Eliz. Kehring.
Cathrina of Jacob Philip and Anna Maria, b. Feb 8, 1766, bapt. Feb 20, 1766. Wit: John Nicklas Albert and Anna Maria, wife.
George Paulus of Fridrich Brose and Eva Maria, b. Mar 21, 1766, bapt. Apr 27, 1766. Wit: Georg Paulus Gresham and Magdalena, wife.
Johan Martin of Joseph Lochbaum and Hannah, b. Apr 13, 1766, bapt. May 8, 1766, d. June 28, 1766. Wit: Martin Huber and Anna Elizabeth, wife.
Cathrina Elisabeth of Michael Mack and Susanna Charlotta, b. Mar 25, 1766, bapt. May 8, 1766. Wit: Martin Huber and A. Elizabeth, wife.
John Michael of Jacob Goodling and Anna Margaretha, bapt. May 25, 1766. Wit: Michael Birckel and Barbara, wife.
Johan Heinrich of John Georg Kistner and Anna Maria, b. July 25, 1766, bapt. Aug 31, 1766. Wit: Joh. Heinrich Lansdorf and Elizabeth, wife.
Elizabeth of J. Christian Sensenbach and Mary Margreth, b. Aug 22, 1766, bapt. Aug 31, 1766. Wit: Michael Dill and Maria Elizabeth, wife.
Barbara of Georg Jacob Houseman and Maria Apollonia, b. Aug 15, 1766, bapt. (Sep) 17, 1766, d. Nov 25 1766. Wit: Conrad Bucher and Mary Magd., wife.
Cathrina of Jacob Carl and Christina, b. Sep 8, 1766, d. July 26, 1768. Wit: Mathias Seyler and Mar. Margr., wife.
Johan Georg of Conrad Bucher and Maria Magdalena, b. Oct 4, 1766, bapt. Oct 12, 1766. Wit: Mathias Seyler and Christina Carl.
Anna Apollonia of Ludwig Senzer and Margaretha, b. Nov 1, 1766, bapt. Nov 9, 1766. Wit: C. J. Houseman and Maria Apollonia.
John of John Leopold and Jenny Coroders, bapt. Oct 1, 1766, bapt. Nov 12, 1766. Wit: Parents.
Mary of Philip Ebers and Elizabeth, b. Nov 14, 1766, bapt. Nov 24, 1766. Wit: Philip Ebers, Peter and Mary Rheyneck.
John Michael of Michael Hagg and Apollonia, b. Dec 25, 1766, bapt. Feb 3, 1767. Wit: John Christ. Albert and Anna, his wife.

PASTORAL RECORD OF REV. JOHN CONRAD BUCHER 73

Johan Heinrich of Christoph Muhleysen and Maria Sarah, b. Dec 14, 1766, bapt. Mar 1, 1767. Wit: Heinrich Freser and Dorothea Stark.
George Jacob of Heinrich Koch and Rebecca, b. Mar 7, 1767, bapt. Mar 15, 1767. Wit: George Jacob Houseman and Maria Apollonia.
Maria Magdalena of J. Nicklas Albert and Anna Maria, b. Mar 27, 1767, bapt. Apr 12, 1767. Wit: Conrad Bucher and Maria Magd., wife.
Johan Georg of Joh. Georg Ziegler and Anna Maria, b. Apr 17, 1767, bapt. Apr 22, 1767. Wit: Joh. Georg Habacher and Anna Margreth, wife.
Joh. Heinrich of Hollman Carlo and Maria Elizabeth, b. Mar 9, 1767, bapt. May 10, 1767. Wit: Joh. Heinrich Moll and mater pueri.
Johan Michael of Michael Dill and Maria Elizabetha, b. Jan 29, 1767, bapt. May 24, 1767. Wit: Jacob Carl and Christina.
Anna Maria of Joseph Lochbaum and Hannah, b. May 8, 1767, bapt. May 28, 1767. Wit: John Adam Stein and Anna Maria, wife.
Jane of William Little and Grisel, b. Apr 1, 1766, bapt. June 15, 1767. Wit: Mater Puella.
Barbara of John Reinbeck and Maria, b. June 17, 1767, bapt. June 24, 1767. Wit: Parents.
Anna Maria of Adam Hoffman and Anna Maria, b. Apr 1, 1767, bapt. July 5, 1767. Wit: Jacob Syler and Ferena, wife.
John Conrad of Martin Huber and Anna Elizabeth, b. July 15, 1767, bapt. July 22, 1767, d. July 26, 1767. Wit: Conrad Bucher and Maria Magd., wife.
Johan Christoph of Michael Kunckel and (Anna Maria), b. July 30, 1767, bapt. July 30, 1767, d. same day. Wit: His parents.
Maria Dorothea of Valentine Digges and Christina, b. July 9, 1767, bapt. Aug 2, 1767. Wit: Johannes Stark and Maria Dorothea, his wife.
Anna Margareth of Heinrich Shado and Maria Cathrina, b. Aug 24, 1767, bapt. Sep 10, 1767. Wit: Johannes Hamuth and Anna Margretha, his wife.
Johannes of Johannes Stark and Maria Dorothea, b. Sep 30, 1767, bapt. Oct 2, 1767. Wit: Peter Schuck and Maria Margretha, his wife.
John of John Buchannon and Mary, b. Sep 11, 1767, bapt. Oct 18, 1767. Wit: his parents.
Johannes of Thomas Heyser and Anna Barbara, b. Oct 10, 1767, bapt. Oct 25. Wit: his parents.
Ann Elizabeth of William Thompson and Sally, b. Dec 25, 1767, bapt. Oct 25, 1767. Wit: Jacob Aller and Ann Elizabeth.
Anna Margretha of Conrad Böhmer and Julianna, b. Dec 9, 1767, bapt. Dec 19, 1767. Wit: his parents.
Johan Adam of J. Mathys Lachner and Maria Eva, b. Dec 28, 1767, bapt. Mar 13, 1768. Wit: Ludwig Senzer and Margreth, wife.
Johannes of Geo. Fred. Wurzbacher and Anna Margreth, b. Jan 12, 1768, bapt. Mar 13, 1768. Wit: Johannes Stark and A. Dorothea, wife.
John Michael of Jacob Philip and Anna Maria, bapt. Apr 10, 1768. Wit: Michael Kunckel and Anna Maria, his wife.

Frederick of John Ulrich Seyler and Elizabeth, b. June 6, 1768, bapt. June 12, 1768. Wit: Jacob Seyler and Ferena, wife.
William of Daniel Lawrence and Mary, b. Apr 12, 1767, bapt. June 24, 1768. Wit: Parents.
Margreth of Jacob Seyler and Ferena, b. July 28, 1768, bapt. July 28, 1768, d. Dec 20, 1768. Wit: J. Ulrich Seyler and Elizabeth, wife.
Johan Georg of Jacob Carl and Christina, b. Dec 128, 1768, bapt. Dec 21. Wit: Parents.
John of Philip Ebers and Elizabeth, b. Nov 25, 1768, bapt. Dec 25, 1768. Wit: John Reineck and Mary, wife.
Anna Maria of Peter Kusser and Anna, b. Nov 14, 1768, bapt. Jan 8, 1769. Wit: Michael Kunckel and Anna Maria, wife.
Johan Georg of Conrad Bohmer and Julianna, b. Dec 25, 1768, bapt. Jan 29, 1769. Wit: J. George Huber and Anna Maria, wife.
Carl of Johannes Stark and Dorothea, b. Mar 23, 1769, bapt. Apr 23, 1769. Wit: Mathys Seyler and Mary Margreth, wife.

Baptisms in Middletown [Dauphin Co.]
Johannes of Johannes Backenstoss and Magdalena, b. Jan 31, 1765, bapt. Mar 10, 1765. Wit: his parents.
Johan Wilhelm of Wilhelm Mass and Margaretha, b. Feb 23, 1758, bapt. Mar 10, 1765. Wit: Christian Roth and Ursula, wife.
Cathrina of Wilhelm Mass and Margaretha, b. Dec 4, 1761, bapt. Mar 10, 1765. Wit: Wilhelm Mass.
Johan Peter of Wilhelm Mass and Margaretha, b. May 16, 1763, bapt. Mar 10, 1765. Wit: Peter Woulds and Lucia Erliss.
Carolus of John de France and Elizabeth, b. Mar 10, 1765, bapt. Mar 10, 1765. Wit: Peter Woulds and Elizabeth.
Deborah of Abraham Bonn and Rebecca, b. Feb 25, 1765, bapt. Feb 25, 1765. Wit: Peter Woulds and Elizabeth.
John of John Dunkan and Eleonora, b. Feb 25, 1765, bapt. Feb 25, 1765. Wit: his parents.
Abraham of Jacob Walter and Juliana, b. May 26, 1765, bapt. June 16, 1765. Wit: his parents.
Johannes of Balthasar Lauber and Elizabeth, b. Sep 1, 1762, bapt. Aug 25, 1765. Wit: Adam Wagoner and Rosina Wagoner.
Johan Adam of Balthasar Lauber and Elizabeth, b. Sep 1, 1764, bapt. July 14, 1765. Wit: Adam Wagoner and Rosina, wife.
Ludwig of Conrad Wolffly and Cathrina, b. Mar 2, 1766, bapt. Mar 19, 1766. Wit: Philip Barthomer and Eva, his wife.
Johan Godfried of Jacob Rudiseller and Barbara, b. Dec 21, 1765, bapt. Mar 30, 1766. Wit: J. Godfried Kretschman and Sophia, his wife.
Catharina of Johannes Bossart and Catharina, b. Oct 28, 1765, bapt. Mar 30, 1766. Wit: George Frey and Cathrina, his wife.
Johan Philip of Wilhelm Mass and Margreth, b. June 3, 1766, bapt. Oct 17, 1766. Wit: Joh; Phil. Bodamer and Anna Eva, wife.
Rebecca of John de France and Elizabeth, b. Nov 3, 1766, bapt. Dec 14, 1766. Wit: Peter Wulds and Elizabeth, wife.
Friedrich of John Backenstoss and Magdalena, b. Jan 2, 1766, bapt. Jan 11, 1767. Wit: Parents.
Johan Jacob of Philip Bodamer and Anna Eva, b. Dec 21, 1766, bapt. Jan 11, 1767. Wit: Conrad Wolffly and Cathrina, wife.

Margreth of John Dunckan and Eleanora, b. Nov 2, 1766, bapt. Feb 8, 1767. Wit: Parents.
William of John Wall and Mary, b. Apr 18, 1767, bapt. July 13, 1767. Wit: Peter Wultz, Jun. and Nanct Wultz and Sorer Petri.
Joh. Philip of Philip Krafft and Anna Maria, b. Nov 23, 1767, bapt. Dec 14, 1767. Wit: Antoni Keller and Barbara, his wife.
Maria Dorothea of Jacob Graff and Eva, b. Nov 6, 1767, bapt. Dec 15, 1767. Wit: Jacob Jistler and Christina, wife.
Cathrina of Christian Spath and Christina, b. Feb 7, 1768, bapt. Mar 6, 1768. Wit: Georg Frey and Cathrina, wife.
Margretha of Johannes Bossart and Cathrina, b. Dec 21, 1767, bapt. Mar 6, 1768. Wit: Heinrich Schaffer and Anna Ferena, wife.
Anna Maria of Conrad Wolffly and Cathrina, b. Apr 17, (176-). Wit: Georg Philip Jaquin and Cathrina, wife.
Anna Maria of Joh. Jacob Burkhard and Anna, b. June 1763, bapt. May 31, 1768. Wit: Jacob Kistler and Christina, wife.
John Jacob of Joh. Jacob Burkhard and Anna, b. Sep 14, 1765, bapt. May 31, 1768. Wit: Jacob Kistler and Christina, wife.
Margreth of Joh. Jacob Burkhard and Anna, b. Feb 15, 1768, bapt. May 31, 1768. Wit: Barbara LaRue.
Eva of Melchior Stahelin and Cathrina, b. Apr 11, 1768, bapt. May 31, 1768. Wit: Jacob Groff and Eva, his wife.
Jane of Edward Betz and Sarah, b. Jan 14, 1768, bapt. May 31, 1768. Wit: Melchior Stahelin and Cathrina, wife.
Mary Dorothea of Jacob Lochman and Barbara, b. July 7, 1768, bapt. July 25, 1768. Wit: Parents.
John Christian of Leon Eshenauer and Margreth, bapt. July 25, 1768. Wit: Christian Alleman.
Elizabeth of Willm. Wall and Elizabeth, b. July 13, 1768, bapt. July 25, 1768. Wit: James Catch and Susanna, wife.
Maria Elisabetha of Adam Meyer and Anna Maria, b. July 22, 1768, bapt. Aug 20, 1768. Wit: Henry Schaffer and Anna Ferena, wife.
Dina of Thomas Brown and Mary, b. June 6, 1768, bapt. Aug 21, 1768. Wit: James Ketch and Susanna, wife.
Mary Elizabeth of Johan Bodamer and Cathrina, b. Sep 13, 1768, bapt. Oct 16, 1768. Wit: Christoph Shap and Margreth, wife.
Anna Maria of John Metzgar and Anna Maria, b. Sep 12, 1768, bapt. Oct 16, 1768. Wit: Barbara LaRue.
Johannes of Jacob Kistler and Christina, b. Aug 23, 1768, bapt. oct 19, 1768. Wit: Jacob Graff and Eva, wife.
Anna Maria of Saml. Ziriacy and Elisabeth, b. Oct 25, 1768, bapt. Jan 16, 1769. Wit: Philip Krafft and Anna Maria, wife.
Cathrina of Michael Fischer and Anna Maria, b. Oct 21, 1768, bapt. Jan 16, 1769. Wit: Georg Gross and Cathrina, wife.

Baptisms in Fredericktown alias Hummelstown [Dauphin Co.]
Melchior of Melchior Ram and Rebecca, b. Feb 15, 1762, bapt. Apr 14, 1765. Wit: his parents.
Eva Christina of Christoph Reichwein and Dorothea, b. Aug 25, 1765, bapt. Sep 25, 1765. Wit: Anna Eva Brouch.
Fredrick of Nb. John Folk and Elizabeth Wolff, b. July 8, 1765, bapt. Oct 20, 1765. Wit: Peter Wolff and Hannah, wife.

Anna Barbara of Martin Stahelin and Mary Margreth, b. Aug 27, 1765, bapt. Dec 15, 1765. Wit: Godfried Campher and Mary Magd. Lambert.
Johannes of Melchior Ram and Rebecca, b. Sep 22, 1765, bapt. Dec 15, 1765. Wit: John Brundle and Cathrina.
Johan Melchior of John Brundle and Cathrina, b. Feb 16, 1766, bapt. Feb 17, 1767. Wit: Melchior Ram and Rebecca, wife.
John Frederick of Balthasar Lauber and Elizabeth, b. Feb 17, 1766, bapt. Mar 9, 1766. Wit: Friedrich Brandstetter and Anna Barbara, wife.
Rebecca of Michael Hook and Margreth, b. Feb 17, 1766, bapt. Mar 31, 1766. Wit: Melchior Ram and Rebecca, wife.
Susannah of Charles Wetherhold and Susannah, b. Sep 7, 1766, bapt. Oct 19, 1766. Wit: Susannah, her mother.
Jonas of Peter Schweyger and Anna Christina, b. Feb 25, 1767, bapt. Mar 10, 1767. Wit: Jonas Voght and Eva, wife.
Joh. Jacob of Andrew Killinger and Anna, b. Feb 20, 1767, bapt. Mar 10, 1767. Wit: Peter Wolff and Hannah, wife.
Susan. Margretha of Christoph Reichwein and Dorothea, b. Dec 5, 1766, bapt. Mar 10, 1767. Wit: Felton Brouch and Susannah Marg., his wife.
Johannes of Lorenz Brundle and Ferena, b. Mar 27, 1767, bapt. Apr 5, 1767. Wit: John Brundle and Cathrina.
Elisabeth of Jacob Burman and Anna Maria, b. Feb 27, 1767, bapt. Apr 5, 1767. Wit: Daniel Burman and Elizabeth Werner.
Susannah of Anthony Eller and Anna Cathrina, b. Feb 5, 1767, bapt. May 4, 1767. Wit: Philip Armbruster and Christina, wife.
Joh. Georg of Georg Held and Magdalena, b. June 1, 1767, bapt. June 29, 1767. Wit: Lorenz Striker and Barbara, wife.
John of Thomas McMahon and Mary, b. Jan 23, 1767, bapt. July 26, 1767. Wit: Philip Armbruster and Christina, wife.
Magdalena of Georg Obermeyer and Barbara, b. Aug 2, 1767, bapt. Aug 24, 1767. Wit: Heinrich Miller and Magdalena, wife.
Cathrina of Lorenz Stricker and Barbara, b. Sep 5, 1767, bapt. Sep 20, 1767. Wit: Jacob Stricker and Magdalena Held.
Antony of Andreas Herauff and Maria Elisabeth, b. Feb 2, 1768, bapt. Apr 4, 1768. Wit: Joh. Antony Emrick and Margaretha, wife.
Johann Heinrich of Balthazar Lauber and Elizabeth, b. Feb 16, 1768, bapt. Mar 6, 1768. Wit: Jacob Krieger and Elizabeth, wife.
Johannes of Patrick Moor and Margretha, b. Feb 22, 1768, bapt. Mar 6, 1768. Wit: Georg Obermeyer and Barbara, wife.
George Michael of Michael Schaffer and Christina Barbara, b. Apr 7, 1768, bapt. May 1, 1768. Wit: Friedrich Forster and Gretha Barbara, wife.
Rosina Cathrina of Peter Pfanenkuchen and Cathrina, b. Apr 1, 1768, bapt. May 1, 1768. Wit: Friedrich Humel and Rosina, wife.
John Jacob of Jacob Burman and Maria, b. Apr 10, 1768, bapt. May 1, 1768. Wit: Jacob Werner and Barbara, wife.
Cathrina of Michael Hook and Margreth, bapt. May 1, 1768. Wit: Adam Greiner and Cathrina, wife.

PASTORAL RECORD OF REV. JOHN CONRAD BUCHER 77

Cathr. Elizabeth of Philip Fisher and Cathrina Margretha, b. May 31, 1768, bapt. July 25, 1768. Wit: John Wunderlich and Elizabeth, wife.
Cathrina of Melchior Ram and Rebecca, b. July 20, 1768, bapt. Aug 21, 1768. Wit: John Brundle and Cathrina, wife.
Cathrina of John Brundle and Cathrina, b. Aug 4, 1768, bapt. Aug 21, 1768. Wit: Melchior Ram and Rebecca, wife.
Cathr. Elisabeth of Georg Ezweiler and Maria, b. Feb 15, 1768, bapt. Aug 21, 1768. Wit: Jacob Albrecht and mater infantis.
Jacob of Abraham Stahelin and Barbara, b. Aug 17, 1768, bapt. Aug 21, 1768. Wit: Jacob Kettering and Rebecca Gunther.

Baptisms at Falling Spring, near Conogethique.
Nicklaus of Antony Schneyer and Anna Maria, b. Jan 3, 2765, bapt. June 2, 1765. Wit: Nicklaus Schneyder.
Anna Maria of Georg Adam Koch and Anna Maria, b. Sep 19, 1764, bapt. June 2, 1765. Wit: Daniel Beinbrecht and Anna Maria, wife.
Christina of John Herman and Christina, b. Feb 10, 1763, bapt. June 2, 1765. Wit: his parents.
Johannes of John Herman and Christina, b. Nov 26, 1764, bapt. June 2, 1765. Wit: his parents.
Johann Adam of Daniel Beinbrecht and Anna Maria, b. Mar 7, 1765, bapt. June 2, 1765. Wit: Georg Adam Koch and Anna Maria, wife.
Johannes of Peter Schneyder and Elizabeth, b. Oct 31, 1764, bapt. June 2, 1765. Wit: Nicklaus Schneyder and Cathrina Stenz.
Mary Margreth of Peter Schuck and Mary Margareth, b. June 8, 1765, bapt. June 30, 1765. Wit: Peter Schneyder and Cathrina Elizabeth.
Johan Adam of Adam Yerg and Mary Sophia, b. Jan 23, 1765, bapt. July 28, 1765. Wit: Adam Stum and Elizabeth Stum.
Cathrina of Charles McCormick and Mary, b. May 31, 1765, bapt. July 29, 1765. Wit: his parents.
Joseph of Joseph Gallidee and Sybilla, b. Jan 8, 1730, bapt. Sep 9, 1765.
Susanna of Joseph Gallidee and Elizabeth, b. Sep 21, 1760, bapt, Sep 9, 1765. Wit: Parents.
Elizabeth of Joseph Gallidee and Elizabeth, b. Aug 3, 1762, bapt. Sep 9, 1765. Wit: Parents.
Johannes of Joseph Gallidee and Elizabeth, b. Nov 25, 1764, bapt. Sep 9, 1765. Wit: Parents.
Johannes of Ludwig David Ripple and Maria Sybilla, b. Aug 26, 1765, bapt. Sep 9, 1765. Wit: Johannes New and Anna Dorothea, his wife.
Susanna of Adam Stump and Elizabeth, b. Oct 7, 1765, bapt. dec 22, 1765. Wit: George Smith and Susanna, wife.
Susanna of Peter Schuess and Elizabeth, b. 1765, bapt. Dec 22, 1765. Wit: Peter Schuess and Peter Beinbrech and Anna Mary, wife.
Anna Barbara of Peter Schneider and Elizabeth, b. Jan 19, 1766, bapt. Apr 20, 1766. Wit: Joh. Georg Koch and Anna Barbara Snyder.
Mar. Elizabeth of Leonhard Stenz and Anna Cathrina, b. Feb 19, 1766. Wit: Peter Schneyder and Elizabeth, wife.

Fanny of Denis Balf and Britchet Brady, b. May 19, 1766, bapt. July 14, 1766. Wit: Parents.
Mary Elizabeth of John Herman and Christina, b. Nov 6, 1766, bapt. Nov 30, 1766. Wit: Parents.
Christian of Geo. Adam Koch and Anna Maria, b. Mar 3, 1767, bapt. Apr 19, 1767. Wit: Georg Hellman and Christina, wife.
Johannes of Philip Hager and Cathrina, b. Mar 21, 1767, bapt. Apr 19, 1767. Wit: Peter Schneider and Elizabeth, wife.
Johannes of Georg Miller and Anna Maria, b. Feb 20, 1767, bapt. Apr 19, 1767. Wit: Johannes Schuez and Elizabeth, wife.
Anna Elizabeth of Georg Herzog and Judith, b. May 14, 1767, bapt. June 14, 1767. Wit: Nicklas Schneyder and Cathrina, wife.
Joh. Jacob of James Smith and Eva, b. Apr 24, 1767, bapt. June 14, 1767. Wit: Jacob Koch and Elizabeth Essig.
Magdalena of Adam Georg and Sophia, b. May 10, 1767, bapt. July 19, 1767. Wit: Matheus Georg, Cathrina, wife.
Magdalena of Joseph Gallidee and Elizabeth, b. May 1, 1767, bapt. July 19, 1767. Wit: Peter Frey and Magdalena, wife.
John Georg of Heinrich Keyl and Elizabeth, b. July 5, 1767, bapt. July 19, 1767. Wit: Georg Smith and Susanna, wife.
Johannes of Peter Schuk and Mary Margreth, b. Feb 27, 1767, bapt. Aug 8, 1767. Wit: Johannes Immel and Mary Gertrud Wernan.
Johan Adam of Philip Stump and Maria Margretha, b. July 23, 1767, bapt. Aug 9, 1767. Wit: Joh. Adam Stump and Elizabeth, wife.
Johann Jacob of Nicklas Schneider and Cathrina, b. Aug 27, 1767, bapt. Oct 4, 1767. Wit: Peter Schneider and Elizabeth, wife.
Maria Magdalena of Joh. Adam Stump and Elizabeth, b. Aug 26, 1767, bapt. Oct 4, 1767. Wit: Philip Stump and Maria Margretha.
Johan Jacob of Jacob Lauzenheiser and Elizabeth, b. Nov 15, 1767, bapt. Dec 27, 1767. Wit: Peter Lauzenheiser and Elizabeth Keller.
Maria Elisabetha of Peter Schneider and Elizabeth, b. Nov 11, 1767, bapt. Dec 27, 1767. Wit: Leonhard Stenz and Maria Cathrina, wife.
Rosina of Andrew Trees and Elizabeth, b. Jan 24, 1768, bapt. Feb 21, 1768. Wit: Adam Stump and Elizabeth, wife.
Sarah of Georg Smith and Susanna, b. Dec 30, 1767, bapt. Feb 21, 1768. Wit: Parents.
Margretha of Conrad Vihman and Margretha, b. Nov 9, 1767, bapt. Apr 17, 1768. Wit: Fred. Krafft and Elizabeth Keller.
Daniel of Conrad Miller and Anna, b. Apr 1741, bapt. May 12, 1768.
Cathrina of John Herman and Christina, b. Apr 15, 1768, bapt. May 13, 1768. Wit: Parents.
Conrad of Daniel Beinbrecht and Anna Maria, b. Feb 24, 1768, bapt. May 15, 1768. Wit: Conrad Bucher and Cathrina Cook.
Franz of Frantz Ury and wife, b. Dec 1, 1767, bapt. May 15, 1768. Wit: Daniel Beinbrecht and Anna Maria, wife.
John Heinrich of Leonhard Stenz and Cathrina, busannah of. Apr 1, 1768, bapt. May 15, 1768. Wit: Peter Schneider and Elizabeth, wife.
John Adam of J. Georg Lang and Cathrina, b. Jan 26, 1768, bapt. May 15, 1768. Wit: John Adam Small and Elizabeth Land.

PASTORAL RECORD OF REV. JOHN CONRAD BUCHER

Elizabeth of Lorenz Stambach and wife, b. Feb 15, 1768, bapt. May 15, 1768. Wit: John Immmel and his wife.
Jacob of James Murray and Anna Maria, b. Mar 1768, bapt. May 15, 1768. Wit: Parents.
Anna Maria of George Spillman and Anna Maria, bp. Mar 26, 1768, bapt. Oct 12, 1768. Wit: Georg Wearah and Anna, his wife.
Elizabeth of Michael Quickle and Ferena (Verena), b. May 28, 1768, bapt. 1769. Wit: J. Philip Beyer and Elizabeth Beyer, soror.

Baptized at different places.
Bedford
Cathrina of Charles Richard and Cathrina, b. Apr 14, 1764, bapt. 1764. Wit: Jacob Kern and Barbara Zoller.
Magdalena of George Sell and Dorothea, b. Dec 14, 1763, bapt. 1764. Wit: his parents.

Fort Pitt
Mary of Maurice Smith and Elizabeth, b. Oct 1, 1764, bapt. Nov 29, 1764. Wit: Samuel Young.
John Heinrich of Christian Miller and Eleonora, b. Feb 25, 1759, bapt. Nov 29, 1764. Wit: Peter Rolleter.
Barb. Dorothea of Christoph Lems and Elizabeth, b. Oct 3, 1764, bapt. Dec 8, 1764. Wit: Philip Baltimore and his wife.

Bedford
Elizabeth of Christian Lang and Elizabeth, b. Nov 15, 1764, bapt. Dec 8, 1764. Wit: Christoph Lems and Elizabeth, wife.
John of Hugh Frazer and Elizabeth, b. Nov 8, 1764, bapt. Dec 9, 1764. Wit: Alexander Cameron and Isabel Dougherty.

Shippenstown
Benjamin of John Schulteys and Cathrina, b. Mar 12, 1765, bapt. July 26, 1765. Wit: his parents.
Ann of Stephen Rhigton and Sophia, b. Mar 17, 1765, bapt. July 26, 1765. Wit: his parents.

On Susquehannah
Johan Peter of Joh. Adam Wirth and Eva Elizabeth, b. Mar 22, 1766, bapt. June 4, 1766. Wit: Jacob Grojean and Mary Magdalene, wife.
Sarah of Thos. Camleton and Mary, b. Jan 2, 1765, bapt. June 28, 1766. Wit: Parents.
Robert of Thos. Camleton and Mary, b. June 6, 1766, bapt. June 28, 1766.
Andreas of Christoph Manz and Margreth, b. July 7, 1766, bapt. Aug 22, 1766. Wit: Andrew Ultch and Ann, wife.
Polly of Josua Rhoddow and Magd. Kistler, bapt. Oct 15, 1766. Wit: Parents.
Sayusannah of Jacob Grojean and Mary Magdalena, b. Aug 24, 1766, bapt. Oct 15, 1766. Wit: Parents.

80 CUMBERLAND COUNTY CHURCH RECORDS OF THE 18TH CENTURY

Sharpsborough
Paul of James Verdier and Susannah, bp. Apr 28, 1766, bapt. May 21, 1766. Wit: Parents.

Shippensborough
William of John Overn and Mary, b. Dec 12, 1766, bapt. May 18, 1767. Wit: Parents.
Johannes of John Engel and Eleonora, b. Feb 16, 1767, bapt. May 18, 1767. Wit: Parents.
David of John Schulteys and Cathrina, b. Mar 13, 1767, bapt. May 18, 1767. Wit: Parents.

On Susquehannah
Johannes of John Goldenberger and Cathrina, b. Dec 3, 1752, bapt. July 1, 1767. Wit: John Goldenberger, pater, and Dorothea, uxor ejus.
Samuel of John Goldenberger and Anna, b. July 25, 1761, bapt. July 1, 1767. Wit: Same witnesses [as above].
Jacob of Fred. Weiss and Cathrina, b. Apr 20, 1767, bapt. July 1, 1767. Wit: Abraham Shorah and Cathrina, wife.
Johannes of James McCoy and Margreth, b. July 31, 1767, bapt. Aug 20, 1767. Wit: Georg Ezweyler and Cathrina, wife.
Salomon of Abraham de Dieu and Anna, b. Mar 16, 1767, bapt. Aug 20, 1767. Wit: Albrecht Deubler and Cathrina, wife.

Coxtown, alias Hestertown.
John of John Wayer and Mary, b. May 16, 1765, bapt. Sep 1, 1767. Wit: John Collighon and Cathrina Deyeo.

Maytown
Jacob of John Creek and Rebecca, b. Oct 12, 1767, bapt. Dec 13, 1767. Wit: Jacob Ohlweyler and Anna, wife.
Mary Elizabeth of Henry Bruhl and Anna Maria, b. Jan 23, 1768, bapt. Mar 8, 1768. Wit: Joh. Nicklas Haapeger & Cathrina.

Manheim
Elizabeth of Lorenz Brundle and Ferena, b. Apr 2, 1768, bapt. Apr 26, 1768. Wit: Matheys Eip and Anna Maria, wife.

Sharpsbourg
Susanna of James Verdier of Susanna, b. June 24, 1768, bapt. Oct 8, 1768. Wit: Parents.

Bick Crossing of Jaghegeny
Jacob of Peter Risner and Maria, b. Aug 13, 1768, bapt. Nov 10, 1768. Wit: Paulus Frohman and Mater pueri.
Cathrina of Nicholaus Christ and Sarah, b. Sep 24, 1768, bapt. Nov 10, 1768. Wit: Paulus Frohman and her mother.

Redstone
Johan Christian of Peter Young and Eva, b. Mar 10, 1767, bapt. Nov 13, 1768. Wit: Parents.
Andreas of Andreas Godshal and Anna Barbara, b. Sep 23, 1767, bapt. Nov 13, 1768. Wit: Johannes Wirbel and Elizabeth, wife.

William of Indian Peters and Mary, b. May 31, 1762, bapt. Nov 17,
1768. Wit: Pater infantum.
Joseph of Indian Peters and Mary, b. Feb 3, 1765, bapt. Nov 17,
1768. Wit: Mater infantum.
Peter of Indian Peters and Mary, b. Aug 8, 1767, bapt. Nov 17,
1768. Wit: Mater infantum.
Robert of John Peters and Mary, b. Mar 26, 1761, bapt. Nov 17,
1768. Wit: Parents.
Mary of James Kelly, N. B. and Mary Hargus, b. May 20, 1766,
bapt. Nov 17, 1768. Wit: John Peters and Mary, wife.
Sarah of Jacob Schnebly and Christy Hargus, b. Sep 27, 1765,
bapt. Nov 17, 1768. Wit: John Peters and Mary, wife.
William of Matthew Williams and Eva, b. Dec 12, 1754, bapt. Nov
20, 1768. Wit: Johanes Weisman and Eva, his wife, quae est
mater pueri.
Elizabeth of John Weisman and Eva, b. June 1, 1765, bapt. Nov 20,
1768. Wit: Parents.
Molly of John Weisman and Eva, b. Nov 9, 1768, bapt. Nov 20,
1768. Wit: Parents.
Jesse of Jesse Martin and Elizabeth, b. Apr 7, 1766, bapt. Nov
21, 1768. Wit: Parents.
Ann of Jesse Martin and Elizabeth, b. Jan 7, 1768, bapt. Nov 21,
1768. Wit: Parents.

Near Fort Cumberland
Joseph of John Tomlinson and Mary, b. Sep 3, 1767, bapt. Nov 24,
1768. Wit: Henry Leane and Rebecca Tomlinson.

Marriage Records of the Rev. John Conrad Bucher, 1763-1769.
Contributed by Luther R. Kelker, in the Pennsylvania Magazine,
Vol. XXVI, 1902. pp. 375-381.

1763
Mar 2   James Findley and Jane McQuisten
May 23   John Mold and Nancy Dougherty
Oct 21   Lawrence Crawford and Jane Bethy
Nov 1   Andrew Gillbreath and Cathrina Smith alias Robinson
Nov 22   Samuel Brady and Jane Simson
Nov 23   John Pirckins and Nancy Dougherty
Nov 28   James Anderson and Elizabeth Poeples
Nov 30   James Hamilton and Margreth Cisney, alias Gallacher
Dec 6   Peter Pearis and Rebecca Ramage
         John Dougherty and Ellse McDonald
         Samuel Leach and Mary Fleming

1764
Jan 3   Jacob Boursman and Eliz. Streith
Jan 17   William Beard and Mary Lucas
Jan 19   Johanes Hamuth and Anna Margretha Herzeller
Jan 23   William Willson and Jane McFall
Feb 3   William Sanderson and Jane Ervine
Feb 20   Johannes Fuhr and Nancy Murphy
Feb 21   Charles Bonner and Ann Gillpatrick
Feb 27   Andrew Schneider and Isabel Grayton

Mar 15   John Davis and Jane Kofine
         William Walker and Mary Herring
Mar 19   William Robinson and Bethy Eager
Mar 27   Thomas Taylor and Ester Harley
Apr 2   William Kellsay and Agnes Goudy
Apr 16   Samuel McCrue and Martha McKnight
Apr 19   Samuel McClure and Elizabeth English
Apr 23   Isaak Botterum and Margreth Gallacher
May 7   Samuel Glen and Elizabeth Morrow
May 17   Abraham Adams and Elizabeth McCormick
May 18   James Kirkpatrick and --- McKellhenny
May 28   John Maghan and Mary Morrow
May 30   Jacob Grojean and Mary Magdalena Kistler
June 12 Thomas Askey and Elizabeth Baker.
June 25 Willm. Gallaghly and Hannah Gardner
July 18 Stephen Delph and Prudence McAlwain.
     25 Joseph Sample and Hannah Wallace
     26 Willm. McCalethon and Jenny Watson
July 31 John Wright and Susannah Armstrong
Aug 4   John Rose and Hannah French
Sep 27   Charles McKennis and Martha Buttler
Nov 30   Peter Rolleter and Judith Hickins
Dec 4   Benjamin Scitmore and Elizabeth Harribel
         James Forster Carson and Sarah Reyanth
      1 James Royl and Mary Willson
         John Hutlass and Elizabeth Frex
     21 John York and Amy Beyers

1765
Jan 5   John Philip Ebers and Elizabeth Taylor
     21 Robert Gelilan and Jane Galliforth
Feb 19   Grafener Mash and Jane Boyd
     25 James Duff and Ester McGill
Mar 5   David Dumbar and Frances Steel
         John Dumbar and Fanny Dumbar
Mar 14   David McBride and Margreth McFarlin
     18 Samuel Simpson and Eliz. Smith
     29 Willm. Collins and Margreth Poeples
Apr 1   Andrew Forster and Elizabeth Guthrie
      4 Willm. Grahams and Mary Ann Brandon
May 2   James Snotgrass and Jane Brown
May 15   Abraham Jones and Mary Beard
May 17   James Collhoon and Mary Willson
June 4   John Coblin and Pheby Ong
     20 Willm. Little and Grezil Means
same day Christoph Quigley and Mary Crawford
same day Francis Ellis and Mary Findley
     27 Patrick Jack and Martha Findley
July 4   Joseph McKenny and Rebecca Latimore
     24 Even Davis and Martha Martin
Aug 8   John Davison and Agnes Grahams
     20 Andrew Wait and Mary James
     27 Samuel Beyers and Agnes Beyers
     28 James Brakon and Mary Dill

PASTORAL RECORD OF REV. JOHN CONRAD BUCHER 83

same day		Georg Smith and Eleonora Grahams
Sep	9	Cookson Long and Rebecca McNight
Sep	13	Robert Dickey and Agnes Dickey
Oct	14	James Clendenen and Isabel Huston
	20	Philip Krafft and Anna Maria Keller
	24	Johannes Goldenberger and Dorothea Lang, nee Grempelman
	28	John Rennels and Sarah Carnoughan
	31	James Maxsell and Mary Leighlin
Nov	4	Thomas Donn and Jane McEntekerd
	14	Moses Kerk and Mary Forster
	12	Nicklas Schneyder and Cathrina Fischer
Nov	22	Samuel Chambers and Jane Crean
	24	Thomas Simpson and Mary Rose
	27	Thomas Hunter and Elizabeth Beard
Dec	9	Richard Long and Margreth Cample
	24	Marcus Hulin and Mercer (Mercy) Dougherty
	27	Thomas Gerdy and Ann Dotton
	28	Jeared Pollock and Jennet Galliford
Dec	30	Henry Dougherty and Sarah Baskin

1766
Jan	30	John Reed and --- Brotherintown
Feb	7	John McDonald and Margreth Mitchell
	13	James McCowan and Eliz. Leard
	18	Edward McDuel and Margret Lormar
	24	Francis Cample and Mary Rees
	26	John McElhathon and Mary Little
Mar	18	Dennis Balf and Britchet Brady
	20	William Patrick and Margreth Dorough
Apr	1	Henry Schatto and Mary Cath. Stahl
	30	Thomas Adams and Jane Shaw
	22	James Thompson and Ann hamilton
May	1	Richard Morrow and Elizabeth Willcock
June	6	John Beadle and Mary Dutton
same day		Georg Roller and A.M.C. Busholtz
	24	John Williams and Eleanor Leard
same day		Peter Dickey and Mary Barckley
July	1	Christoph Laubengeyer and Elizabeth Miller
	6	Andrew Mehlhorn and Mar. Eliz. Breittingross
	29	Willm. Wright and Mary Smith
	30	Hugh Sherang and Elizabeth Armstrong
Aug	9	Fergus Moorhead and Jane White
Aug	11	Jacob Schatz and Prudence Williamson
	12	Georg Habacker and Margreth Fresinger
	21	Stephen Davis and Eleanor Morrison
same day		Willm. Morrison and Mary Carver
	26	James Saye and Mary Reed
	28	John Kistler and An. Marg. Stricker
Sep	1	Jacob Weiser and Jane Michelltree
	18	John Ulrich Seyler and Elizabeth Wolf
	30	Michael Laplin and Ann Dorothea Ramberger

["Illa Mortua est, Mar 16, 1767"]
Oct	5	Samuel Thompson and Mary Nugent
	7	Saln. White and Cathr. Mitchell

```
         15  Josua Rhoddo and Magdalena Kistler
         25  William Martin and Isabel English
Nov  25  William Willson and Margreth Scot
Dec   1  John Brownfield and Elizabeth Clark
      2  William Campbell and Hannah Young
     15  John Fiscus and Cathrina Fans
     23  John McWever and Margret Collins
     27  John Burns and Elizabeth McGill
     29  Samuel Jack and Martha Heran
     31  Johanes Lanweyl and Maria Kistner

1767
Jan   2  Absolom Meret and Mary Cathrina Bubach
     13  John Johnston and Eva Betsy
Feb   3  John Wyle and Eliz. McCibbens
     10  John Philip Lauer and Mary Cathrina Goldstett
     23  John Davis and Isabell Hill
Mar  16  William Gobbins and Esther Rheins
     21  Willm. McMeen and Elizabeth Sherang
     24  James Rotch and Sarah Forster
     25  Georg Thoughly and Susannah Spray
same day James Mappin and Sarah Welsh
     28  David Harkness and Ann Armstrong
Apr   8  Lawrenz Kelleyah and Martha Smith
     20  Philip Wegelin and Feronica Krafft
May   6  John Rothrock and Dorothea Gump
      8  John Hunter and Jane Cuningham
same day Robert Donwan and Martha Turner
     12  Andrew McMaghan and Eleonora Ray
     25  Robert Chester and Eliz. Patterson
June  4  James Turner and Elizabeth Morgan
      9  Samuel Adams and Margreth Fleming
     23  John Arbuckle and Rebecca Ross
July  1  George Ezweyler and Mary Shorah
      2  William Samuels and Sarah Brown
      3  Jacob Seyler and Ferena Sherp
      6  Georg Welsh and Agnes Bethy
      8  James Morrison and Sarah Hodge
     14  David Lewis and Eliz. McGaffy
same day Isaak Worral and Hannah Calvert
same day John Moor and Eliz. More
same day Antony Herbich and Nancy Daviss
     28  Heinrich Hein and Cathrina Kinzler
Aug   3  Samuel Gorman and Nancy Kennedy
      6  Ennis Willson and Isabel Roads
same day Alexander Brown and Deborah Clark
     11  James Ross and Jean Steel
     25  John Kearns and Sarah Galliforth
Sep   9  Clemence McGeary and Rachel Smiley
     11  James Stevenson and Elizabeth Thompson
     22  Sebastian Grewass and Charlotta Pfannekuch
     23  Stephen Hildebrand and Hannah Beals
     30  Francis Worley and Ruth Collins
Oct   6  John Marshall and Agnes Clockstone
```

```
     26   William Herron and Agnes Brown
Nov  5   Alexander McNett and Jenny Piper
     18   William Hunter and Mary Donnely
     24   John Beard and Mary Erwin
Dec  7   Christian Shally and Elizabeth Wattman
      8   Johanes Meyer and Anna Cathrina Shaffer
     17   Archibold Hanah and Margreth Brady
     21   William Forster and Cathrina Lefever
     28   Johan Georg Koch and Maria Elisabetha Schüz
     29   Jacob Frosch and Cathrina Koch

1768
Jan 13   John English and Jane Chambers
     26   Thomas Douglass and Elizabeth Woods
Feb 12   John Cochran and Jane Fisher
     15   Charles McCardy and Mary Skipton
Mar 22   Hugh Hollan and Susannah Reed
same day John McCall and Jane Robinson
Apr  6   William Dorward and Mary Burns
      7   James Newlon and Cathrina Bennett
     16   Jacob Jordy and Ann Kingrich
May 17   Thomas Pumery and Mary Grahams
     24   Jacob Bender and Magd. Stauffer
same day Joh. Nicklas Meas and Susannah Laubsher
     26   Franz Geib and Eliz. Schneider
     27   Adam Keener and Christina Hoch
     31   Abraham Albrecht de Rocke and Elizabeth Graff
June 1   Alexander Setting and Mary Forster
     13   Paul Cohan and Ann Gardner
     20   Durst Thomah and Regina Spicker
     21   Philip Graber and Ann Cathr. Ebrecht
same day John Hemmig and Elis. Thomah
     22   Nichlas Liverich and Cathr. Meyer
     28   Jacob Stricker and Dorothea Saur
same day Franz Elias Daniel Ehinguer and Mary Magd. Cossey
     29   Nichlas Cassel and Rosina Rambach
same day John Morrison and Mary Devire
July 15  William McGee and Sarah Logan
     25   John Albrecht and Marg. Barbara Stoffelman
     26   Robert Armstrong and Isabel Forster
same day Charles Stuarth and Eliz. Hunter
same day Samuel Meek and Cathr. Parkison
Aug  6   Balthazar Fuchs and Dorothea Miller
      8   John Benrad and Sally Davidson
     11   Hugh McCardle and Elizabeth Murray
     18   William McConnal and Rose Kennedy
     30   Peter Blaser and Cathrina Newer
Sep 13   Robert Pickin and Alice Gordon
same day John McAdams and Mary Ann Fisher
     15   Elijah Newland and Ann McGrew
     26   George Lauman and Ester Künig
same day Edward Lee and Elizabeth Money
     28   John McCord and Nancy Sillick
Oct  3   Andrew Fleming and Ann Britewell
```

```
        13   James McCean and Sarah Pierson
        13   Hugh Colhoon and Ann Proctor
        18   Fridrich Kauffman and Barbara Geitlinger
        19   Alexander McGrue and Mary Blackburne
        21   James Curry and Else Abbet
        25   Georg Schank and Susannah Meister
        29   James Driskel and Jane Pierson
        31   Joseph Reed and Mary Holl
Nov     19   John Woodfine and Christy Hargus
        25   John McKinley and Sarah Robertson
Dec     16   Thomas Dillon and Margreth McCrackon
same day     Jacob Sweizer and Rahel Schadow
        20   William Boggs and Eliz. Quirey
        29   George Sweizer and Eleonora Ward
        31   William Poeples and Elizabeth Finley
same day     William Brownfields and Margreth Breyens

1769
Jan 2        Andrew Walker and Mary Grahams
same day     James Thompson and Elizabeth Beyers
same day     Nicklas Obreyan and Susannah McCutcheon
same day     Hugh Logg and Nancy McCully
        9    Charles Mair and Polly Hillman
same day     Nathaniel Miller and Margreth Cuningham
Feb 7        Philip Eckle and Cathr. Becker
        22   Johannes Lauman and Magdalena Zindmeyer
        28   James McEllway and Nancy Lean
Mar 5        Jacob Trewer and Susannah Shnebel
same day     Christoph Bauman and Ann Cathrina Bauman
        8    Martin Billmeyer and Cathrina Thomas
Mar 9        John McClellan and Margery Rippy
same day     Alexander Mitchell and Jenny Moorhead
        20   John Jacob Zufall, V.D.M. and Ferronika Brunner
        22   Abraham Korey and Jane Nees
        27   Philip Schock and Eliz. Sanger
Apr 2        Heinrich Kuntz and Dorothea Pragunier
same day     Jacob Cook and Eliz. Small
        3    Christian Nesler and Sybilla Lincking
        4    Peter Schlosser and Susannah Regnas
        5    Adam Umberger and Mary Gertraut Wernan
        6    Peter Schuck and Maria Margreth Ruth
same day     Georg Danzer and Cathrina Simon
same day     James Crutchlow and Jane Andrew
        14   Wm. Miller and Charity Calvert
        18   Martin Böhler and Ann Eliz. Diffenderfer
same day     Melchior Fortune and Margreth Meyer
        25   Charles Finley and Hester Hodge
```

EXTRACTS FROM SESSION BOOK OF MIDDLE SPRING PRESBYTERIAN CHURCH

Abstracts of personal items from "A session book for the use of the session of the congregation of Middle Spring," 1742-1748.

March 21, 1743. Letter sent by Robt. Henry desiring to be restored.

Apr 1, 1743. Robt. Henry appeared and after conversing with him we find him obstinate and unwilling to submit to the censure of the Presbytery.

May 2, 1743. Hugh Brady appeared and acknowledged his sin in being out of order with liquor and resolves through grace to watch against it.
Charles Cummins informed the session that Willm. McCall, junr., was the worse for liquor at Saml. Culbertson's wedding and was unable to govern himself ... sitting on a bench at the end of the house he fell back over. David Herron was appointed to cite Willm. McCall to appear at John Finley's Friday come week, also to cit Thomas McComb for evidence.

Aug 18, 1743. Andrew Culbertson informed Mr. Blair that Saml. Leard was disordered with liquor coming from James Boyd's wedding. Nathaniel Willson being at John Ervin's house, saw Samuel Leard coming from James Boyd's and noticed that he Saml. Leard did not speak solidly. John Cummings said that Saml. Leard appeared sick. [Evidence judged to be insufficient.]

Sep 5, 1743. Margaret Ervine says thought that Saml. Leard was disordered with liquor. Agnas Boyd says he spilled his drink, riding horseback between John Ervine's and her father's; staggered to dinner at her father's.
Agnas Pattan entered a complaint against Daniel Smith for hurting her character by reporting she had a handkerchief of his which he had lost at Middle Spring Meeting House. Daniel Smith denies saying this. Witnesses: George Hamilton, David Kidd, Martha Hamilton, Mary Simpson, Agnas Hutton.
John Nisbet acknowledged his sin in assenting[?] to more than was just to Robt. Henry in an affair relating to John Killough.

Oct 17, 1743. Willm. Jake acknowledged he was guilty of intemperance in drink at Robt. Wiley's funeral.

Jan 30, 1743/4. James Tate, John Greer, Thomas Greer and John McCall were cited on account of a quarrel they were engaged in at William Dunbar's. Witness: George Finley.

-------------two pages missing--------------
[date unknown] Daniel Smith, John and Elizabeth Henry were cited. Witnesses: James Montgomery, Mary Layson, Mary Stuart.

June 25, 1744. Andrew Murphy objected against Robert McComb's being ordained an elder. Robert McComb denied using abusive language to either Andrew Murphy or his wife. Andrew Neil objected against Robert McComb being ordained an elder. He said that Robert McComb had said he would not forgive Andrew Murphy for setting[?] John Qua.

The affair concerning James Montgomery and Mary Layson resumed. John Henry said he received information form his son William that John Breaddy had intimated that Mary Layson was with child. Elizabeth Henry said while at Hugh Breaddy's one day last winter she enquired at Hannah Breaddy how Mary Layson was and particularly spoke of the trouble she was under. Hannah Breaddy knew not of any signs that Mary Layson was with child. Nathaniel Peebles knew that Mary Layson was living up with James Montgomery at the time of the fright about the Indians and that said Montgomery had offered something indecent to Hannah Layson alias Woods. Other witnesses: Isabell McKee, John Layson regarding his mother Mary Layson; said she talked about making a coffin for her. James Montgomery complained that Daniel Smith had used his character ill in some expressions at Saml' Montgomery's house.

Jan 16, 1744/5. [The following concerns a riotous quarrel involving members of Middle Spring and Big Springs congregations.] Robert Finley complained that George M'Elwain had assaulted him and tore his handkerchief. William Carnachan complained that William McCall assaulted him first. Other persons involved: Joseph Carnachan, James Laughlane, Junr., James Jake, Saml. Smith, John Jake, John Smith, Alexander Fairbairn, Francis McCall, John McCall. Witnesses: Gustavus Henderson, John Curry re a squabble at John Lackey's wedding when some came to see if the bride and groom were in bed; mentions Wm. McCall, Senr. and his son Wm. McCall, John Wiley, Saml. Culbertson. William and John McCall state that someone had mixed stilled liquor in their beer.

Apr 19, 1745. John McNaught was cited for intemperance. Elizabeth Neil professed a desire to give satisfaction for her offense of fornication. James Finley confessed he was guilty of fornication with Elizabeth Neil who has had his child.

June 7. Catherine Petite does not appear to have sense of "the evil she practices."
George Hamilton, Martha Hamilton, Robert Simson and Mary Gay, junr., having sometime ago separated from the congregation and joined Mr. Craighead's party, have since returned.

July 22. Sarah Cotter admits the sin of staying away.
John McCall admits being overtaken in liquor at the Fair.
Witnesses: Willm. McConnel, Charles Cummings, Archibald Machan.

Aug 7. It was reported that Thomas Finley had been intoxicated.
Witnesses: James Montgomery, Robt. Montgomery.

Sep 2. John Henry accuses John Atchison of drunkenness after the session of Big Spring had acquitted him.

March 3, 1745/6. Isaac Miller was cited for being drunk at Robt. Chambers.

July 18, 1746. Willm. Jake, having been cited, appeared and acknowledged that Adam Hoop and he having wrestled sometime before the vandue at Shippensburgh on 16 June last, they had some debated about it on said day of the vandue. James Wallace had tried to reconcile them but Hoop struck him and he had returned the blow.
Neil McClean was cited for strokes given to John Rippy on the day of the vandue. Witness: Saml. Reynolds.
Saml. Laird was cited for intemperance on the day of vandue. Witnesses: Thomas Neil, Adam Turner, Jane Culbertson.
James Doag was cited for taking venison from an Indian and giving him meal and butter for it on a Sabbath day; mentions Willm. Keith.
Regarding Saml. Laird case: James Ward said he observed Saml. Laird staggering and spoke to David Herron to persuade him to go home or go down to widow Piper's and take a bed. Witnesses: Robert Kerr mentions John Reynolds, Saml. Rippy, James McBride.

Dec 4. To enquire into the conduct of David Herron and Mose Moore who went into William Dunlaps to see William Rankin and his company when said Rankin was bringing home his wife.
Wm. Reynolds complained that Thomas Edmiston had called him a rogue; that he kept whores and rogues in his house.

Jan 23, 1746/7. Witnesses in the case of Thomas Edmiston: Deborah Dunlap, Willm. McCall mentioned Wm. Thomson.

Jan 1, 1747/8. Robert Symenton and Hugh Breaddy were cited for being overtaken in drink lately at a funeral.
Thomas Edmiston applied to session re a squabble with William Jack. Witness George Cummins mentioned John Caldwell.

Jan 22, 1747/8. The case re the quarrel between Joseph Bogs and John Lucky. Witnesses: William Cox said Joseph Bogs and George Finley were drunk. Charles Morrow mentioned James and John Montgomery. John Montgomery mentioned Andrew Lucky.

June 17, 1748. Jane McKewn admits the sin of fornication. John McCall is accused of being guilty with her of said sin.

July 29, 1748. Saml. Smith and wife profess their sins of fornication.

Aug 15. Robert Henry, after separation from the congregation, requested to be restored to communion with the congregation. Elenor Cunningham admitted of her sinfulness in her former separation from the congregation.

Sep 22. Robt. McConnel complained that Thomas Finley was drunk at David Scot's vandue.

CUMBERLAND COUNTY CHURCH RECORDS OF THE 18TH CENTURY

Nov 21, 1748. Margrate Peebles complained that Allxdr. McNut prevented her of church privileges.
Witnesses in the case of Thomas Finley [above]: Wm. Barr, George Finley.

Feb 8, 1748/9
Re conduct of Hannah Wallace. Witnesses: James Paxton was at Shippensburgh, frequently in committee with Hannah Wallace - he came upon her sleeping on a log and Charles Morrow on another. It was reported that John Carnachan had seen them in an unseemly posture together but when asked he said he saw no such thing. Mary Paxton said that she and Hannah moved once or twice across the floor to a fiddle - that Hannah appeared to be sick on the day in question from some punch she had drunk.

MARRIAGES AND BAPTISMS PERFORMED BY REV. CUTHBERTSON

Excerpts from Register of Marriages and Baptisms performed by Rev. John Cuthbertson, 1751-1791.

Cumberland County
Big Spring (Near Newville)
1751 Nov 10   Baptized Robert son to Horace Bratton presented by the Mother.
1752 Oct 24   Baptized James son to Allan Scroggs.
1753 Apr. 15 Baptized Esther daugh. to Jo. McClung ... (at Andrew Ralston's, Big Spring)
1753 Sept. 18 Baptized Mary daughter to Horace Bratton.
1754 Apr. 14 Baptized Agnes, daughter to Joseph Junken, and Sam, son to John Glendining.
1754 Aug. 6   Baptized Eleanor daughter to him [Alan Scrogs].
1756 Aug. 9   Baptized Jean daughter to Alan Scrogs.
1758 Nov. 5   Baptized Mathew, son to John McClung.
1758 Nov. 8   Baptized Allan, son to Al. Scrogs; and Margaret daughter to Alex. [Last name?]
1761 May 14   Baptized James son to James Brown.
1762 Aug. 24 Baptized Charles son to John McClung - married John Giffan and Eleanor Heron.
1762 Oct. 12 Baptized Jesse son to Charles Kilgore and Agnes daughter to Wm. Calbreath.
1764 Feb. 9   Baptized Mary, daughter to him [Math. Brown].
1764 Feb. 12 Baptized Alexander, son to James Brown and Esther daughter to James Thorn.
1765 Nov. 16,17 Baptized James son to James Thorn. Robert, son to John Dunbar. Mary daughter to James Dunbar. John, son to John Anderson.
1768 Apr. 12 Married Robert Hamilton and Eleanor Giffe(n).
1768 Apr. 13 Baptized Sara, daughter to Matthew Brown.
1768 Apr. 17 Baptized son to John Taylor and James, son to Wm. Paterson.
1769 Apr. 2   Baptized Agnes daughter to John Giffen.
1770 Mar 8   Baptized Elizabeth to him [???]
1770 June 1   Baptized Jean daughter to Matthew Brown g.a.
1773 Feb. 15 Married William Walker and Margaret Reid.
1775 Aug. 6   Baptized Matthew son to Brother Lind.

Canandugqinet Creek (See also Junkin Tent)
1751 Aug. 21 Baptized Jo., son to Jo. Glendining. John, son to Jo. McClellan and Jean, daughter to Henry Swansie.
1752 Mar. 15 Baptized Jas. son to Walter Buchanan. Jas. son to Jo. Gardner, Isaac son to Alex Laverty and Jean daughter to Adam Colqhoun.
1752 Mar 16   Married Isaac Dowglas and Mary Sloan.
1765 Apr. 3   Rode 8 miles to Walter Buchanan's. ... Baptized Agnes.
1766 Feb. 12 Baptized Sarah to Sam Leipers.
1770 Apr. 17 Married Alexander McCulloch and Hannah Dixon.
1770 Apr. 18 Baptized James, son to Peter Wilson.
1775 Dec 20   Baptized William son to James Glen and baptized Rebecca (his daughter).
1777 Feb. 26 Married Jas. Ramsay and Margaret Stuart.

CUMBERLAND COUNTY CHURCH RECORDS OF THE 18TH CENTURY

1783 Mar. 26 Baptized Jean to James Glen and Mary to Gilbert Buchanan.

Carlisle
1752 Oct. 17 Married Jo. McCormick and Mary Strehon...
1753 July 15 Baptized Daniel son to John McClellan and Wm. son to And. Giffen.
1753 Sept. 23 Baptized James son to Sam Colghoun.
1755 Aug. 3 Baptized Mary and Mary daughters to John McClellan and John Mitchel.
1755 Sept. 22 Married Reid and Margaret Hamilton.
1759 May 20 Baptized Arch, Thomas, William and Mary, to John Smielie and Margaret daughter to Walter Buchanan.
1760 Mar. 30 Baptized William, son to Robert Bonar.
1764 Oct. 28 Baptized John son to John Garner.
1765 May 12 Baptized John Laferty, adult at Wm. Parkieson's.
1765 May 19 Baptized Agnes, daughter to Agnes McConel.
1767 May 18,19 Married John Navin and Martha Swansie.
1769 Apr. 17 Married W. Thomson, Jean Duncan.
1771 Aug. 6 Baptized Walter son to James Braeden and Margaret to Matthew Richie.

Junken Tent. near Kingston and about ten miles from Harrisburg, on the farm of Joseph Junken.
1752 June 23 Baptized Rachel daughter to Wm. Rose and Groyn, daughter to Wm. Walkter.
1752 Dec. 12 Married Jas. Loughhead and Eleanor M.
1753 Aug. 5 Baptized Wm. son to Alex. Lockey.
1753 Oct. 22 Married Ben. Brown and Mary Mitch.
1754 Mar. 19 After riding 5 miles to Jo. Sloans, marrying Hew Coulter and Mary Sloan.
1754 Apr. 4 Rode 3 miles to Joseph Junkens ... married Walter Buchanan and Mary Coulter.
1754 Apr. 7 Baptized Ann, daughter to Sam Gay; John, son to William Walker and Ruth, daughter to William Rose, presented by the mother, father gone to ---.
1755 July 31 Baptized Samuel to Sam Cal.
1756 Apr. 27 Baptized John son to Joseph Junken and John son to Robert Bonar. ... Rode 7 miles to W. Walkers ... baptized David son to W.W.
1756 Aug. 8 Baptized Agnes daughter to Wm. Rose - and Elizabeth daughter to Jo. Garner.
1757 Jan. 30 Baptized Mary daughter to Benjamin Brown. - At David Mitchel's, whose wife died the 19th.
1757 Feb. 17 Rode 1 mile to Joseph Junkens ... baptized John son to Walter Buchanan.
1758 Mar. 21 Baptized Katharine daughter to John Glendining. Rode 4 miles to William Parkieson's ... baptized David, his son.
1759 May 23 Baptized Mary, daughter to W. Wal.
1761 May 17 Baptized Benjamin son to Joseph Junken.
1761 May 18,19 Baptized James to Walter Buchanan. Wm. son to Robert Brison. Daniel son to Hugh Hail and Martha daughter to Wm. Spoedy.

1762 Feb. 4 Baptized David son to Sam Calhoun.
1762 Oct. 17 Baptized Robert son to John Leiper.
1763 Apr. 26 Baptized Robert son to Sam Calhoun and Eliz. to Joseph Junkens.
1764 Feb. 5 Baptized Henry son A. Brown. Jonathan, son W. Walker. Jean daughter to Robert Brison.
1764 Apr. 15 Baptized David, son to Barth. Hains.
1764 May 22 Married Alexander Robieson and Martha McCormick.
1765 Nov. 25,26 Married James Grahams and Ruth Little.
1766 Apr. 3 Baptized James, son to David Mitchel.
1766 Aug. 7 Baptized Rebecca daughter to James Howston.
1766 Aug. 18 Baptized Sam son to Robert Brison.
1766 Sept. 21 Baptized Sarah, daughter to Sam Calhoun.
1767 Mar. 29 Baptized James son to Katharine McClellan.
1767 June 8 Rode 10 miles; fasted after marrying Robert and Marjory Stewart at Sam Bell's.
1767 Oct 29 Baptized Agnes daughter to James Howston.
1768 May 29 Baptized Mary, daughter to Sam Calqhoun and Margaret to James Thorn.
1769 Mar. 24 Married Aud Reid and Esther McBryar.
1769 June 25 Baptized Agnes daughter to James McKt.
1769 Aug. 3 Baptized Ann to S. Colqhoun.
1769 Aug. 6 Baptized Wm. son to Katharine Meek or Parkieson.
1771 Feb 25 Baptized Sarah to Y. Mil. and married Thomas Kennedy and Mary McCalllin.
1771 June 16 Baptized James son to Thomas Finey and Jean daughter to John Hilton.
1771 June 18 Married John Brown and Mary Guililand, James Robertson and Margaret Young.
1772 Apr. 26 Baptized Johns sons to James Leiper and John Neil.
1772 Sept. 27 Baptized Thomas son to William Paterson.
1772 Nov. 9 Baptized Samuel son to Elijah Stewart. Elijah to John Graham. George to John Taylor. David to James McKt. and Martha daughter to James Taylor.
1773 Aug. 11 rode 18 miles to D. Mit. and to Widow Morison's - Janet married ...
1775 Dec. 19 Married Wm. Clark and Mary Rowan.
1781 Feb 21 Baptized Isaac son to Gilbert Buchanan.
1782 Feb. 20, 21 Baptized Joseph to James Walker, Mary to John Brigs, Hannah to John Walker Jun. and Eliza to John Padon.
1783 Dec 4 Baptized Sarah.
1784 Nov. 2 Baptized Barbara to Sam Taylor born Nov. 23, 1783 and Mary to John McCallen born Sept. 1st, '82 and Thomas and Robert sons to Wm. Whigham born March 24th 1779 and March 4th 1783.

Leteart Spring
1753 Apr. 22 Baptized John son to Wm. Paterson and Thos. son to Robert Bonar.
1754 Aug. 10 Baptized Benjamin son to William Parkieson and Margaret, daughter to Robert Gibson.
1758 Mar. 23 Baptized Rob. son to William Pattison. Esther, daughter to Charles Kilgour and Agnes, daughter to Alexander Young.

1764 May 17 Baptized Margaret, daughter to Sam Hodge.

Pennsborough Meeting-house
1751 Nov. 11 Baptized Jo. son to Sam. Colquhoun, And. son to And. Giffan and Ann daughter to Robert Gibson.

Sherman Valley
1762 Baptized Margaret daughter to John Gardner.

Shippensburg
1765 Nov. 13, 14, 15 Baptized Daniel son to J.C.

Susquehanna River
1751 Sept. 3 Married Robert Love and Rachel Sloan at the River.

MARRIAGE LICENSES ISSUED BY JOHN AGNEW, ESQ.

Clerk of the court of Quarter Sessions of Cumberland County, PA, at Carlisle.

Date of Issue
1771
Aug 24 George Gibson to Susanah Wright
Sep 17 John Pollock to Grace Lucas

1772
Mar 4   David Herron to Elizabeth Magee
Mar 21 William Logan to Elizabeth Baxter
May 26 James Young with Margt. Meekey
June 30 Lodwick Long with Christian Vernon
Aug 27 John Hamilton with Marg't. Alexander
Nov 28 John Love with Jane Lockhart
Dec 7   William Straine with Jane Erwin

1773
Jan 23 John Campbell with Marg't. McKinney
Aug 12 Moses Baskens with Unis Richardson
Aug 24 Jas. Alexander with Marg't. Tate
Sep 4   Dug'l. Campble with Marg't. Johnston
Sep 27 John Walker with Mary Gaskins
Oct 12 Jas. Crawford with Isabella McConnell
Nov 10 William Maulsby with Ann Smith
Dec 15 William Stewart with Mary Orr

1774
Jan 12 John Wilson with Isabella McGrew
May 24 John Snider with Elizabeth Spangler
June 10 Marriage license per Mr. Long, Rev. James of Connecheage
June 22 Abm. Lukins with Christian Lewis
June 25 Marriage license per Mr. Long, Rev. James of Connechegue
Aug 12 Thomas Smith with Jane Robinson
Sep 27 Dan'l. Clymer with Sabina Kuhn
Oct 3   James Bennett with Jane Dalton
Dec 3   Sam'l. Mccoskry with Susaana Slegell

1775
Mar 9   Robt. Dunlop with Cath. Dodds
Apr 13 Jos. Williams with Mary Dill
June 5 George Scwert with Mary Lees
June 10 Wm. Crop with Sarah Reezen
Nov 27 Stephen Folk with Cath. Thornburgh
Dec 30 John Haterington with Ruth Smith

1776
Feb 8   --- Dunbarr with --- Wier
Mar 12 --- Laird with --- McNickle

Licenses issued between 13th of March 1779 to Oct 79.
William Camlin with Mary Clark

John Magafoge with Easther Laughlin
Archd. Magwire with Jane McCormick
Barnd. Burst. with Mary Eminger
John Maxwell with Isabella Dodds
John Cochran with Jane Hood (or Wood)
Robt. Barclay with Isabella McWhinie
Samuel Neely with Jane Dodds
John Cohil with Sarah Speers
John Gilmore with Dorothy Helwick
Thomas Boyd with Marg't. Shannon
James Baskins with Elizabeth Martin
David Campble with Mary Berns
Thos. Fullerton with Hannah Kennedy
John Armitage with Ann Glenn
William Hurlbutt with Louisa Reed
William Little with Martha Reely (Riely)
John Semple with Jane Brown

1780
June 19 William Gillespie with Mary McSwean
Oct 14 John Wimp with Mary Fickle
Nov 7 Thos. Campble with Mary McDowell
Nov 7 Lemuel Gustin with Rebeccah Parker
Nov 21 Jas. Gregory with Marg't. Shannon
Dec 29 Robt. McKean with Sarah Martin

1781
Mar 3 Walter Beatty with Nancy Smith
may 4 Samuel McPherran with Marg't. McMullan
May 31 Michl. Huffnagle with Catherine Archer
Aug 29 Joseph McKenney with Mary Warden
Nov 15 John Dickey with Eliz. McCaul

1782
June 1 Col. James Culbertson with Marg't Smith
Aug 21 John Johnston with Ann McDowell
Aug 21 Josiah Smith with Esther Clark

1783
Mar 27 Thomas Kyle with Elizabeth Chambers
June 6 Benjamin Chambers with Sarah Brown
July 31 John Kirpatrick with Catherin McMullan
Sep 5 John Mitchel with Eliz. McCallister
Sep 30 George McCully with Ann Irish
Dec 24 Doctr. John Wilkins with Catherin Stevenson

1784
Apr 12 Danial Fisher with Susannah Heak
Apr 22 John Duncan with Sarah Postlethwaite
Sep 17 William McClure with Ann McKean
Oct 30 Hugh McClelland with Marg't. McFarlane
Nov 13 Daniel Cowhick with Mary Kennedy
Nov 16 Robert Thompson with Eliz. Andrew
Nov 18 Matthew Allison with Marg't. Lamb

MARRIAGE LICENSES ISSUED BY JOHN AGNEW

1785
Jan 22 Alexr. McDowell with Isabella McKinney
Jan 31 Moses Thompson with Elizabeth Fulton
Mar 1 William Work with Polly Eakin
Apr 27 Thos. Duncan, Esqr. with Miss Martha Callendar
May 11 Henry Miller with Margt. Aspell
Aug 30 James Straine with Elizabeth Montgomery
Nov 2 George Smith with Isabella Stevens

1786
Jan 6 Jacob Stuart with Elizabeth Laudermilk
Jan 14 Doctr. Wm. MaGaw with Susannah Boldwin
May 20 John Keen with Polly Whitehill
Nov 3 James Parker with Elizabeth McCallister
Nov 26 Robert Fowler with Elizabeth Reagh

1787
Apr 23 George Swingler with Magdalina Dierick

1788
June 26 Joseph Hays with Ann Gordon

1789
Apr 25 John Moore with Elizabeth Park

MEETING-HOUSE SPRINGS

Condensed from Egle's *Notes and Queries*, Third Series, vol. II, pp 478-479.

"In North Middleton township, Cumberland county, on the Conedoquinet creek, two and a half miles from Carlisle, is the grave-yard of Meeting-House Springs. A correspondent sends us the following record, which for the present we give space to, intending before the cold season prevents to visit that memorable spot and gather up all the records which time and the elements have not defaced."

[Abstracted here. Ed.]

Janet Thompson, wife of Rev. Samuel Thompson, d. Sep 29, 1744, aged 33 years.
Alexander McCullough, d. Jan 15, 1746, aged 50 years.
James Young, seiner, d. Feb 22, 1747, aged 79 years.
Mary Donnel (Meyr donnel) d. Oct 15, 1747, aged 64 years.
Thomas Witherspoon, d. Mar 22, 1759, aged 57.
John and Alexander McKehan (no date).
Major Alexander Parker and his two children, Margaret and John (no date).
Ronald Chambers, d. Dec 24, 1746, aged 60.
William Graham, d. Apr 24, 1761, aged 67.
John Flemming, d. Apr 22, 1761, aged 39.
James McFarlan, b. Dec 24, 1685, d. Oct 31, 1770.
John Kinkead, d. Aug 4, 1772, aged 51.
Mary Kinkead (daughter), d. Aug 1758, aged 17.
James Weakley, d. June 6, 1772, aged 68.
Jane Weakley (wife), d. Nov 30, 1768, aged 53.
James Weakley (infant son of Samuel and Hetty), d. Sep 4, 1777.
Samuel Laird, Esq., d. Sep 1806, in his 74th year.
 [Inscription indicates he was an elder, magistrate and judge.]

MARRIAGES BY REV. ROBERT COOPER, 1786-1794
Middle Spring Presbyterian Church

Nov 13 1786. Samuel Wilson preacher and Jane Mahon.
Nov 21 1786. Robt. Brotherton and Martha Culbertson.
Ditto. Nathaniel Miheson(?) and Mary Referberry(?) of Big Spring.
Dec 21 1786. Moses H--- and Margt. Conningham.
Dec 28 1786. Jas. Robison(?) and Elizabeth Nesbet.
Jan 25 1787. John McCa--- and Bathsheba Herrat.
Mar 1 1787. John Laughlin and Margt. Broaster(?) of Big Spring.
Mar 27 1787. Willm. Nisbet and Ester(?) Robinson(?).
April 5 1787. Jno.(?) Caff---(?) and Mary -aper.
April 26 1787. Joseph McKean and --- --- ine(?)
June
---3 1787. Robt. McKerr(?) and Margt. Greer.
May 15 1787. Thos. Shannon and Margt. Hanna.
June 12 1787. Jas. Brady and Rachel Speer.
Dec(?) 18 1787. Joseph Baldridge and Jane Gibb.
Dec 25 1787. Jas. Johnson and Margaret McMahan.
Jan 8 1788. David Kennedy of Juniata and Isabella Scott of this Congr.
Jan 14 1788. Ben. Blyth, Junr., and Eleanor Beattie.
Feb 26 1788. Saml. Duncan and Sarah Mahon.
Mar 25 1788. James Daugherty of Rocky Spring and Mary Moor of this Congr.

Aug 12(19?) 1788. Kennedy Brown and Martha Beattie, both of this Congr.
Sep 16 1788. Joseph Campble and Jane Hill.
Ditto Sep 16. Benjamin Hutcheson and Mary Vance.
Octob. 28 1788. John McCarroll and Polly McKnight.
Nov 18, 1788. Joseph Duncan and Hannah Brady.
Dec 6 1788. Jas. Allwerth and Margt. Strahn.
Ditto. Edward Strattle(?) and Margaret McMullen.
Jan 6 --- Isaac Stark and widow ---.
Jan 8 1789. John McKee and Anne Hier.

Jan 25 1789. Captn. Robt. Peepbles and Sarah ...
Jan 27 1789. Edward McDonald and Elizabeth Henderson.
Feb 26 1789. Jas. Jack(?) and Nancy McKinney.
Mar. 10 1789. John McCann of Big Spring and Sarah Adamson of this congr.
Mar. 23(?) 1789. John Richie of Chesnut Level and Mary McCune.
April 9 1789. Thos. Wilson and Eleanor McCune, wid.
May 12 1789. Thos. Glenn and Jane Bromfield.
June 18 1789. Paul Martin and Jane Brady.
June 23 1789. Saml. Walker and --- Barr.
July 14 1789. --- and Frances Donavan.
Aug. 18 1789. John --- and Jane Dunlap.
Dec 1 1789. John McDaniel of Big Spring and Mary Sharp of Rocky Spring.
Dec 10 1789. John Murran of Big Spring and Jane McClean of this Congr.

100 CUMBERLAND COUNTY CHURCH RECORDS OF THE 18TH CENTURY

Dec 23 1789. Willm. McClayland(?) and Margt. Culbertson of Rocky Spring.
June 22 1790. John McKibbern and Hannah Beard. Ditto Hugh McKibbern and Agnes Beard.
June 24 1790. John Elder of Path Valley and Sarah Barr of this Congr.
Oct. 10 1790. Benjamin Futhy and Elizabeth Cambridge.
Oct. 24 1790. Willm. Fairman and Prudence Kennedy, both of Path Valley
--- 1790. Willm. Robt. Oram(?) of Path Valley and Margt. ---on of Rocky Spring.
Dec 30 1790. Richard Witherow and Sarah McCormick.
Jan 13 1791. Joseph Davis and Hannah McKibben.
Jan 27 1791. Willm. McConnell and Mary McMullen.
Mar. 22 1791. David Sterret and Elizabeth Hanna.
April 5 1791. Saml. Kirkpatrick and Ruth Weir(?).
Dec 13 1791. John Coffee and Ruth ---.
--- 19 17--. William R--- and ---.

Feb 16 1792. --- Gilmore and Agnes Johnson.
Aug 16 1792. Jesse Kilgore and Jane Clark.
Dec 25 1792. John Sterrat and Mary Patterson.
Ditto Isaac Cook and Margt. Scott.
Dec 27 1792. John Reid of ---town and Elizabeth Hanes(?).
Jan 14 1793. Willm. Leper and Hanah Reynolds.
Feb 12 1793. Thomas Moor and Widow Porter.
Feb 21 1793. John Brittain and Elisa. Reid.
Mar 14 1793. Robt. Patterson and Peggy Lindsay - Andrew Love and Hannah Cambridge(?) - George Sloan and Mary Story.
April 4 1793. Henry --- and Margaret Wyley.

June 6 1793. Isaac(?) Grier and Elizabeth Cooper (Casper?)
Aug 19 1793. Married in Path Valley - --- Witherow and --- Killgore.
Sep 17 1793. Moses Kirkpatrick and Elizabeth McKee
Oct. 29 1793. Doctor Saml. Davis and Mary Neil.
Mar. 11 1794. George Kelly and --- McMullen.
May 6 1794. George Cooper and Margt. Henderson.
June 3 1794. Jas.(?) Ri--- and Margt. Simmeral(?).
June 17(?) 1794. Saml. Ray and Martha ---.
July(?) --- --- and Mary ---.
---one entry entirely obliterated ---

MARRIAGE BONDS

From the J. Zeamer Collection, State Library

"The following Marriage Bonds are filed away among other very old papers in the Court House at Carlisle, Pennsylvania":

Jan 1, 1762. John McCrory to Mary Ross. Bondsmen: John Morrison, James Hutcheson. Wit: Wm. McClay, Ephraim Allen.
July 10, 1761. Samuel McKun to Jean McClean. Bondsmen: John McKun, John McClean. Wit: John W. Cather, Jun., William Maclay.
Dec 8, 1761. Andrew Eaken to Lettie Mahan. Bondsmen: James Eaken, James Pollock. Wit: Robert Callender, William Maclay.
Dec 8, 1762. Thomas Blair to Susanna McClellan. Bondsmen: William Allison. Wit: Hermanus Alricks, Samuel Holmes.
Oct 20, 1763. Lawrence Craford to Jane Bethy. Bondsmen: Lawrence Crafford, James Dean. Wit: Conrad Bucher, Thomas Jeffries.
Oct 11, 17863, William Marsh to Elizabeth Thorps. Bondsmen: William Marsh, Robert Hamersly. Wit: Hermanus Alricks, Samuel Holmes.
Jan 5, 1762. Samuel Johnson to Mary Rayl. Bondsmen: William McCoskey, James Barclay. Wit: Hermanus Alricks, Francis Adams.
March 27, 1762. Robert Galbreath to Mary Hendricks. Bondsmen: Wm. Davenport, Robert Callendar. Wit: William Maclay.
Jan 4, 1762. John Williams to Margaret Steuart. Bondsmen: Robard McWhinny, Clement Harrell. Wit: Harms Alricks, Wm. Maclay.
Nov 14, 1761. William Hendricks to Mary Rheynolds. Bondsmen: Richard Long, Robert Gibson. Wit: Harms Alricks.
Oct 4, 1762. John Sadler to Jane Sadler. Bondsmen: Richard Sadler, Robert Hamersly. Wit: Harms Alricks, Samuel Holmes.
Aug 14, 1761. John McCoy to Margaret McKinley. Bondsmen: Joseph Galbraith, Thomas Park. Wit: John Nicklson, Harms Aldricks.
July 27, 1761. Joseph Sharp to Susannah Dunning, both of Carlisle. Bondsmen: Joseph Smith, William Waddel. Wit: Robert Baird, Harms Alricks.
July 18, 1761. William Buchanan to --- (name omitted). Bondsmen: William Buchanan, Thomas Holt. Wit: Andrew Calhoun, Harms Alricks.
July 2, 1761. William Waddel To Elizabeth Shaw. Bondsmen: William Waddel, Willson Thompson. Wit: William Maclay, John Bird.
Dec 28, 1761. John Chaplin to Elizabeth Christy. Bondsmen: John Chaplin, William Christy. Wit: Harms Alricks.
Jan 31, 1785. Moses Thompson to Elizabeth Fulton. Bondsmen: Moses Thompson, John Pollock, both of the Borough of Carlisle.
Jan 6, 1786. Jacob Stuart to Elizabeth Loudermilk. Bondsmen: Jacob Staurt, Christ. Smith. Wit: David Rowan, John Agnew.
Oct 29, 1761. William Little to Mary Steel. Bondsmen: William Little, James Saron. Wit: John Little, Robert Huston.
Oct 30, 1761. James Templeton to Sarah Ardly. Bondsmen: James Templeton, William Russell. Wit: Robert Cummins, Harms Alricks.

Oct 30, 1761. James Templeton to Sarah Ardly. Bondsmen: James Templeton, William Russell. Wit: Robert Cummins, Harms Alricks.
Sep 17, 1784. William McClure to Ann McKean. Bondsmen: william McClure, Wm. Wallace. Wit: Henry Long, John Agnew.
Oct 30, 1784. Hugh McClelland to Margaret McFarland. Bondsman: Hugh McClelland. Wit: Wm. Montgomery, John Agnew.
Dec 20, 1762. Robert Hamersly to Mary Rankin. Bondsmen: Robert Hamersly, Stephen Foulk. Wit: Jos. Neilson, Samuel Holmes.
Jan 2, 1762. James McConnel and Margaret Huston. Bondsmen: James McConnel, Robert Semple, Abraham Holmes. Wit: Harms Alricks, Wm. Maclay.

Marriages and Deaths from the
Carlisle Gazette, And The Western Repository Of Knowledge.

The following are marriages and deaths of persons who were or may have resided in Cumberland County at some time. Marriages and deaths reported in the Gazette pertaining to persons outside the county have been omitted.

The Gazette was founded August 10, 1785 by George Kline and George Reynolds. It was published on Wednesdays. A complete coverage of genealogical gleanings of Newspapers for York and Cumberland counties was published in the series, *Abstracts of South Central Pennsylvania Newspapers* by Family Line Publications for the period, 1785 -1800, in three volumes.

Feb 15, 1786: James Oliver, teacher of mathematics, died on Feb 11th, from slight jag of a nail; buried at Silver Spring.

May 10, 1786: Married Wednesday evening last in this town, Doctor Thomas Parker, to Miss Lydia M'Dowell.

June 28, 1786: John O'Neal states his wife, Mary, has left him and taken up with Jeremiah Miller of Carlisle.

July 26, 1786: Married Thursday evening last, at Middlesex, by Rev. Nisbet, George Thompson, Esq., to Miss Maria Callender.

Nov 1, 1786: Married Monday evening last at the seat of the late General Thompson, George Read, esq. of Delaware, to Miss Maria Thompson.

Nov 22, 1786: Died Nov 1st, after a short illness, Miss Jane Holmes, daughter of John Holmes, senr., of this place.

Dec 6, 1786: Died Wednesday 29 November last, Mrs. Jane Glen, in her 89th year.

Jan 3, 1787: Married Dec 21st at Bohemia [Cecil County, Md.], Joshua George, Esq., to Miss Betsy Thompson, 4th daughter of the late Rev. Thompson.

Jan 17, 1787: Died Jan 9, 1787, in her 67th year, Mrs. Elizabeth Young, relict of James Young, long a resident of the vicinity of this borough; buried at Presbyterian Church of Carlisle.

March 14, 1787: Died Friday last, after a lingering illness, Captain William M'Murray.

May 23, 1787: Carlisle - Died on Monday the 14th, John Caldwell, late merchant of Shippensburgh, during a long indisposition.

May 23, 1787: Died on April 29th, Rev. Samuel Thompson, in his 96th year, for many years pastor of the First Presbyterian Congregation of this place, later at Conewago, York Co.; buried in Sharpsburgh, Virginia where he resided.

Aug 1, 1787: Married at York-town, 5th ult., James Hall, Esq., M.D., of Philadelphia, to Miss Eleanor Hartley, daughter of Colonel Thomas Hartley.

Sep 5, 1787: Married Thursday last by Rev. Dr. Charles Nesbit, Dr. George Stevenson, to Miss Molly Holmes.

Feb 20, 1788: On Wednesday, 13th instant, died John Byers, Esq., in his 73rd year. Remains will be interred in the old burying ground, belonging to the Presbyterian Church of Carlisle, of which church he had long been a member.

March 19, 1788: Died Monday morning last at his seat near Carlisle, in his 36th year, after a short illness, Major James Armstrong Wilson, leaving wife and children.

April 16, 1788: Died on the morning of the last Sabbath, after a tedious and lingering disorder, Mrs. Rosanna Ross, consort to James Ross, professor of languages in Dickinson College.

July 2, 1788: Married Thursday last at the seat of James Irwin, Joseph M'Clellan, to Miss Polly Irwin.

Oct 1, 1788: Died Thursday, 25 September, in her 49th year, after a few days affliction, Mrs. Mary Pollock, wife of James Pollock, at his dwelling house, 10 miles from this place; and on Saturday her remains were interred in the burying place adjacent to the town.

Jan 28, 1789: Married Thursday the 15th instant, at the seat of James Dill, Fermanagh Township, James Rogers to Miss Margaret Dill.

March 11, 1789: Died Wednesday night, 18th ult., after a short illness, Colonel Robert M'Pherson, at his house in Marsh Creek settlement, York County. Died suddenly on Thursday night, John Hofack, of the same place.

June 10, 1789: Married at Marietta (Muskingum) by Arthur St. Clair, Esq., Capt. David Zeagler, to Miss Sheffield, from Rhode Island.

Nov 18, 1789: Died on Wednesday last after a short illness, at his farm near this town, Matthew Gregg. Died Thursday, Colonel Cooke, of Dauphin Co., member of the convention for said county. Died on Monday after a few days illness, James Stuart of this town.

Feb 3, 1790: Died at Middlesex, near Carlisle, on 25th of January last, in his 39th year, after a painful illness, James R. Ried, Esq., late a major in the armies of the United States. Having his education at Princeton College and received the degree of

B.A. at an early period of his life, and in the first stage of the war, entered the service of his country as a lieutenant. He was appointed as delegate to the late Congress twice.

Feb 17, 1790: Robert Dickie, taylor, in Middletown Township, died from a house fire.

April 14, 1790: Died on the 8th instant, John Agnew, Esq., in his 60th year. He long exercised the office of Magistrate.

June 1, 1790: Died after a short illness, on Monday, 24th ult., in the city of Philadelphia, John Miller, merchant and son of Robert Miller, Esq., both of this town. He had arrived but a few days in the city before he took sick. He left a wife and 3 small children.

June 16, 1790: Died after an illness of about 48 years, early on Sunday morning last, Mrs. Elizabeth Smith, wife of Robert Smith, innkeeper of this town; remains interred in the burying ground adjacent to this borough.

Sep 22, 1790: Married on the evening of 7th instant, by Rev. Morrison, Rev. John Bryson, of Cumberland Co., to Miss Jenny Montgomery, of Northumberland.

Oct 6, 1790: Died Tuesday, 28th ult., Lieutenant Joseph Collier of the late Pennsylvania Line.

Nov 17, 1790: Died in the town of Carlisle, in his 26th year, on 9th of present month, Lieutenant Nathaniel Smith. He entered the army about the 16th year of his age. His last illness was long and trying. Died at his farm in Newton Township, Cumberland Co., 2nd instant, David Sterrett, after a tedious illness; interred at the Big Spring burying ground.

Feb 2, 1791: Died in East Pennsborough on Thursday night, 27th of January, Isabel Hoge, wife of Jonathan Hoge, Esq., in her 64th year. On the Saturday following her remains were attended by a large and respectable train and interred in the burial ground at Silver-Spring. Her husband was absent, attending his duty in the Legislature of the state. Her health had been for a long time declining.

April 20, 1791: Died at Middle Octorara, of a lingering illness, in his 73rd year, on 10 March 1791, Rev. John Cuthbertson.

Sep 21, 1791: Died 14th instant, at his own house, after a few weeks painful illness, James Smith; remains interred at burying ground at Carlisle.

Aug 24, 1791: Died Thursday, 11th instant, aged 39 years, after a long and lingering illness, Mrs. Mary Peebles, wife of Col. Robert Peebles, at his seat near Shippensburgh. died suddenly on Monday morning last, Mrs. Brown, wife of John Brown of Carlisle.

She was hearty and well on the Saturday evening preceding; interred in burying ground adjoining this borough.

Oct 12, 1791: Died 1st instant after a few days illness, Robert Davidson Cooper, son of Charles Cooper of Carlisle, age about 4 years. The parents lost a child of the same name with this a few years ago, and another, a few weeks since, named Samuel M'Coskry Cooper, both very young.

Oct 19, 1791: Married Thursday last, William Turnbull of Pittsburgh, to Miss Maria Nisbet, daughter of Rev. Dr. Charles Nisbet, Principal of Dickinson College, Carlisle. Died on Friday night last, Mrs. Herr, wife of David Herr, of this borough. Died on the 15th instant, Mrs. Mary Stevenson, in her 65th year.

Oct 26, 1791: Died Tuesday, 18th instant, at his farm, about 4 miles form Carlisle, Andrew Macbeth, in an apoplectic fit.

Nov 2, 1791: Died Wednesday last after a short illness, Joseph Given, merchant of this town.

Nov 16, 1791: Married on the 8th instant, Jacob Walters of Chambersburgh, merchant, formerly of this town, to Miss Patty Stuart, of this town. Married on the 9th, William Wallace of this town, to Miss Jean Gray. Died Thursday last, after a tedious and painful sickness, Mrs. Margaret Steel, aged 24 years, wife of Joseph Steel, clock maker, of this town.

Dec 7, 1791: Married at the seat of David Hoge, Esq., James Blaine to Miss Jean Hoge, daughter of David Hoge.

Dec 14, 1791: Married at Shippensburgh on Friday last, Joseph Duncan to Miss Ruth Rippey, daughter of Capt. Wm. Rippey.

March 21, 1792: Married at Carlisle on the 20th instant, by Rev. Meyer, Samuel Shaver to Miss Elizabeth Ritchwine.

Feb 8, 1792: Married Tuesday, 24th of January last, at Trindle's Spring, William Gilson of East Pennsborough Township, to Mrs. Sarah Trindle, widow of Capt. Alexander Trindle. Married Tuesday, 31st, at Carlisle, William Trindle to Miss Betsy Gilson, son and daughter of the above.

March 28, 1792: Died Wednesday, 21st instant, after 3 days illness, William Blair, Junr., of Carlise, in his 32nd year, leaving wife and 4 small children. Died Saturday, 24th instant, in a sudden manner, John Rodgers, in his 50th year.

April 11, 1792: Married on Tuesday, 3rd of April, Richard Sheldon of Cumberland Co., Iron Master, to Miss Susannah Foulk, daughter of Stephen Foulk, Senr., at his seat near Carlisle.

May 30, 1792: Married Thursday last, Rev. Nathaniel Snowden of Philadelphia to Miss Sally Gustain, daughter of Dr. Gustain of

Carlisle.

June 6, 1792: Married Thursday, 31st ult., by Rev. Dr. Davidson, Rev. Samuel Mahon to Miss Nancy Duncan, daughter of Stephen Duncan, Esq. (Carlisle).

July 4, 1792: Married Thursday last by Rev. Dr. Davidson, at the seat of Ralph Sterrett, Adam Logue of Carlisle to Miss Nancy Sterrett.

Sep 19, 1792: Died on 8th instant, after a short illness, John Irwin, at his house near Shippensburgh in Franklin Co.; remains interred in the burying ground at Middle Spring Meeting House.

Oct 17, 1792: Died last Saturday morning, after an illness of considerable duration and severity, Miss Susanna Thompson, daughter of late Parson Thompson, in her 19th year; interred at the Episcopal church in this town.

Oct 31, 1792: Died at Shippensburgh on Sunday morning last, after a severe illness, Robert Colwell, merchant of that town, in his 28th year.

Nov 7, 1792: Died last Monday morning, aged 36 years, after a very long and painful illness, Mrs. Ann Holmes, consort of John Holmes of Baltimore, merchant; interred in the Presbyterian burying ground.

Nov 14, 1792: Died last Saturday morning, David Allen of Carlisle, in his 58th year. Married Thursday last by Rev. Dr. R. Davidson, William Kelso to Miss Betsy Chambers, daughter of Col. William Chambers, near Carlisle. Died Monday on the 12th instant, Mrs. Susan M'Coskry of Carlisle, consort of Dr. Samuel A. M'Coskry.

Dec 5, 1792: Married Tuesday, 20th ult., at the farm of Robert Sanderson, by Rev. Dr. Davidson, Dr. James M'Clean of Leesburg to Miss Patty Sanderson, daughter of Robert.

Feb 6, 1793: Died Friday 1st instant, after a tedious illness, Mrs. Amelia M'Clure, wife of Charles M'Clure, leaving a husband and 4 small children.

Feb 13, 1793: Married Thursday last by Rev. Dr. Davidson, at the farm of John Dunbar, Thomas Urie to Miss Margaret Dunbar, daughter of John Dunbar.

March 20, 1793: Died Saturday morning last, Mrs. Mary Kleinhoof, about her 80th year, after nearly 3 months illness.

April 3, 1793: Died at Ligonier on the evening of the 24th March, John Buchanan, formerly a citizen of Carlisle.

April 17, 1793: Married Thursday last by Rev. Dr. Davidson, Samuel Simison to Miss Peggy Denny, both of this town. Died in Carlisle, Monday morning, in her 24th year, after a short illness, Mrs. Jane Blaine, wife of James Blaine.

April 24, 1793: Died Monday 22nd instant, in his 42nd year, after a short illness, Hugh Patten, for some years an inhabitant of this borough. Died Saturday in the morning of the 20th instant, at York Town, Mrs. Martha Gibson, in her 81st year; remains taken to Lancaster and interred in family burying ground.

May 15, 1793: Married Tuesday the 14th instant, by Rev. Dr. Davidson, James Fleming to Miss Fanny Randolph. Married at this borough on Wednesday last, George Hamilton, aged 86 years, to Catharine Bow, aged 73; each had been married twice before.

July 31, 1793: Married on Thursday last by Rev. Dr. Davidson, Rev. David Denny to Miss Peggy Lyon, daughter of William Lyon, Esq. of this borough.

Aug 7, 1793: Married June 25th, 1793, at the farm of John Williams, by Rev. Samuel Waugh, Andrew Parker of Cumberland Co., to Miss Margaret Williams, daughter of John Williams.

June 26, 1793: Killed in a duel last Saturday morning, John Duncan, leaving a wife and 5 children; he was shot and killed by James Lamberton. The duel was fought near Carlisle.

July 10, 1793: Married at Pittsburgh on Monday the first instant, Ebenezer Denny, merchant, to Miss Nancy Wilkins, daughter of John Wilkins, Esq.

Aug 21, 1793: Married Thursday, 8th instant, at Shippensburgh, by Rev. Long, Joseph Kerr, merchant of Strasburgh, to Miss Isabella Rippey, daughter of Capt. William Rippey of Shippensburgh.

Nov 9, 1793: Married at Shippensburgh, Tuesday, 29th ult., by Rev. Cooper, Dr. Samuel Davis, of Shippensburgh, to Miss Mary Neil, daughter of William Neil, late of Baltimore. Died at Pittsburgh Thursday last, Samuel Alexander, merchant, lately an inhabitant of this town.

Feb 12, 1794: Died Friday last at his farm in East-Pennsborough Township, in his 80th year, James Parker; his remains interred in the old burying ground on Conodoguinet, about one mile from this borough.

March 5, 1794: Died on Friday last, after a short illness, in her 56th year, Mrs. Sarah Allen, relict of David Allen.

March 19, 1794: Died in her 44th year, in a very sudden manner, Monday morning last, Mrs. Mary Cooper, wife of Charles Cooper of this borough, leaving husband and 4 children.

April 16, 1794: On Monday last, Lieut. Richard Hazlewood was thrown from his horse and killed, on the mountain near Strasburgh; interred in the burying ground adjoining this borough. Married on the 15th instant, by Rev. Dr. Davidson, John Miller of Mount Rock, to Miss Jean Semple, daughter of Robert Semple.

May 14, 1794: Married Thursday last by Rev. Dr. Davidson, Major Samuel Jackson of Mifflin Town to Miss Peggy Ramsay, daughter of James Ramsay of this town. Married the same evening, John Woodart to Miss Jane Clendinan, both of East Pennsborough Township. Died Thursday last, Andrew Colhoon, carpenter of this town.

June 18, 1794: Died Thursday last, after a lingering illness, Mrs. Alexander, wife of Thomas Alexander, of this town.

June 25, 1794: Married last week, Dr. John Geddes of Newville to Miss Elizabeth Peebles.

Aug 13, 1794: Died Monday, 11th instant, after a few weeks indisposition and in her 20th year, Miss Betsey Neil, daughter of the late William Neill, merchant of Baltimore.

Jan 28, 1795: Married Thursday 15th instant, by Rev. Dr. Davidson, James Blaine, merchant of Carlisle, to Miss Peggy Lyon, daughter of Samuel Lyon.

Feb 11, 1795: Died Thursday, 5th instant, after a long and continued scene of affliction, Mrs. Rebecca Blaine, consort of Col. Ephraim Blaine.

Feb 18, 1795: Died Friday last, in his 71st year, Alexander Gordon, of this town; remains interred in burying ground adjoining this town.

March 4, 1795: Married Tuesday, 24th ult., at the farm of William Flemming by Rev. Dr. Davidson, Charles Gregg to Miss Nancy Flemming, daughter of William Flemming.

March 11, 1795: Died Monday last in this borough, in his 78th year, General John Armstrong.

April 15, 1795: Died on the 9th instant, after a very short illness, in her 45th year, Mrs. Eleanor Lyon, wife of Samuel Lyon, living in the vicinity of Carlisle, from a stroke.

April 29, 1795: Died Sunday last, Mrs. Elizabeth Pattison, after a lingering illness, in her 55th year; remains interred in the burying ground adjoining this town.

May 6, 1795: Died Saturday after a long illness, in her 54th year, Mrs. Margaret Chambers, consort of Robert Chambers, living near this town; remains buried in the burying ground adjoining this borough.

May 13, 1795: Died Thursday last, after a short illness, in the prime of life, Christly Fisher, innkeeper of this borough. Died Monday morning, a son of Oliver Pollock, Esq., Silver Spring, by the fall off a horse the day before.

June 3, 1795: Died Tuesday morning, Thomas Stevens, fuller.

June 24, 1795: Married Thursday evening last by Rev. Dr. Davidson, at the farm of Col. Chambers, Mordecai M'Kinney, merchant of Middletown, to Miss Polly Chambers, daughter of Col. William Chambers.

Aug 5, 1795: Married Thursday evening last by Rev. Dubendorf, Wendel Michael, merchant of this town, to Miss Margaret Clouser of this county.

Aug 26, 1795: Died Friday morning last, at the age of 93 years, Mrs. Agness Moore. Died on Sunday after a very short sickness, Mrs. Catharine Weise, wife of George Weise, saddler.

Sep 9, 1795: Died Saturday, John Webber, merchant of this town, after a short illness. Died Monday, Mrs. Egolf, wife of Michael Egolf.

Oct 14, 1795: Died Saturday morning, 10th instant, at his farm near Shippensburgh, after a short illness, Capt. David Somerville.

Oct 31, 1795: Died Wednesday last, Mrs. Sarah M'Donald of this borough; on Thursday Mrs. Jean Craine; on Sunday, William Simmonds - in the vicinity of this borough, all in advanced age.

Nov 4, 1795: Married 24th of October by Dr. Robert Davidson, James Smith to Miss Betsy Dunlap, both of this county.

Nov 11, 1795: Died Tuesday the 10th instant, in his 72nd year, Robert Miller, senior.

Nov 18, 1795: Married Thursday last by Rev. Dr. Davidson, Hance Morrison of Pittsburgh to Miss Margaret Pollock, daughter of John Pollock of this town. Died 6 May 1795, Charles Quin of Westpennsborough Township, in his 37th year, he having a number of books lent to different persons; his sister Margaret Quin, now living in Newville at Capt. Archison(?) Laughlin's in said town, desires that they be conveyed to her.

Jan 13, 1796: Died on the evening of 31st ult., in her 60th year, after a lingering illness, Mrs. Mary Gordon, relict of Alexander Gordon, inhabitants of this borough.

Feb 27, 1796: Died after a long and tedious sickness, at an advanced age, Ralph Sterrett, citizen of this county; remains

MARRIAGES AND DEATHS FROM THE GAZETTE

interred in burying ground adjoining this town.

April 27, 1796: Married Tuesday, 12th instant, by Rev. Dr. Nesbit, William Noland of Virginia, to Miss Catharine Callender of this town. Married Thursday, 14th instant, by Rev. Dr. Davidson, William Dunbar, to Miss Betsey Forbes, both of this county.

May 18, 1796: Married Thursday last at the farm of John Dunbar, by Rev. Dr. Davidson, Dr. John Creigh, of Lewistown, Mifflin County, to Miss Nelly Dunbar, daughter of John Dunbar. Died Saturday, 14th instant, at Shippensburgh, Mrs. Margaret Heap, wife of John Heap, Esq., of that place, during a lingering illness.

June 8, 1796: Married 31st of May by Rev. Dr. Davidson, John Officer of this town, to Mrs. Officer of this county. Married 31st of May by Rev. Dr. Davidson, Nathan Woods, to Miss Jean Weakley, daughter of James Weakley, both of this county.

July 6, 1796: Died Saturday 25th ult., in an advanced age, the celebrated philosopher, David Rittenhouse, Esq.

July 27, 1796: Died 5th instant, after a long and lingering illness, Ezekiel Dunning, Esq., one of the first settlers in this county.

Aug 3, 1796: York: Died at 2 o'clock on the morning of Sabbath last, at the age of 27 years, Miss Anna Kennedy, daughter of Robert Kennedy; funeral to held at Presbyterian church.

Sep 14, 1796: Married last week, Joseph Steel, clock maker, to Miss Johnston.

Sep 21, 1796: Married at York Town on Wednesday last by Rev. Cambell, David Watts. Esq., of this town, to Miss Juliana Miller, daughter of General Henry Miller of York Town.

Oct 26, 1796: Married Tuesday, 18th instant, by Rev. Dr. Davidson, Robert Evans, Esq., of Maryland, to Mrs. Isabella Alexander of this town.

Nov 2, 1796: Died last week, Charles Gregg.

Nov 9, 1796: Daughter of Mr. Briggs, about 10 years old, died from burns suffered Thursday night last, when the Silver Spring Tavern burned. Mr. Briggs was the tavern keeper.

Nov 16, 1796: Died in this town, Thursday evening, Miss Jean Thompson, daughter of the late Rev. Thompson; remains were interred in the vault in the church.

Nov 23, 1796: Married last week by Dr. Robert Davidson, Robert Kenny to Miss Polly Davis - and Thomas Craighead to Miss Rebecca

Weakley - and Archibald Loudon to Mrs. Hannah Holcham.

Nov 30, 1796: Married by Dr. Robert Davidson, Thursday, 24th instant, Paul Randolph to Miss Susanna Fleming, both of this county.

Dec 14, 1796: Died 29th November, Mrs. Tobitha M'Bride, consort of Alexander M'Bride, Jun., of Dickinson Township.

Dec 28, 1796: Married Tuesday, 20th instant, Thomas Jones to Miss Margery O'Donnell, daughter of Edward O'Donnell, all of Juniata Township, Cumberland County.

Jan 4, 1797: Married Tuesday, 20th of December last, by Rev. Linn, Joseph Eaton, fuller, to Miss Jane Maxwell, daughter of James Maxwell, all of Toboyne Township.

Jan 18, 1797: Married Thursday evening in this town by Rev. Dr. Davidson, William Brown, of Baltimore, to Miss Nancy Loughridge, daughter of Abraham Loughridge.

Feb 1, 1797: Died Wednesday last in Mifflintown, Mifflin County, in his 60th year, James Ramsey, for a number of years an inhabitant of this borough. Died on 22 January last, aged 68 years, Mrs. Jean Dill, wife of Col. Matthew Dill.

Feb 8, 1797: Married Thursday last by Rev. Herbst, Henry Ream of Baltimore, to Miss Polly Crever, daughter of John Crever of this borough. Married Sunday night last, by Rev. Dr. Adams, Thomas Armor, to Miss Serah Hogue, both of this place.

Feb 22, 1797: Died in this town on Thursday last, William Haslet, age 100 years and 9 months.

March 8, 1797: Married in this town, Thursday evening last, George Wise, saddler, to Mrs. Fisher.

March 15, 1797: Died Thursday, 9th instant, in her 41st year, Mrs. Mary Holmes, after a long and continued illness. Married on the 9th instant, by Dr. Robert Davidson, Charles M'Clure to Mrs. Rebecca Parker, daughter of William Blair. "(This correspondent notes that this is the third marriage by this gentleman and each time the family name of each of his wives was Blair.)"

April 12, 1797: Married on Thursday last by Rev. Dr. Davidson, John Logan, to Miss Peggy Chambers, daughter of Robert Chambers, all of this county.

June 21, 1797: Died Wednesday evening last, after a few days illness, Mrs. Elizabeth Peterson, widow of the late Doctor Henry Peterson, of the state of Delaware. This lady who was in the prime of life, resided since the death of her husband with her mother, Mrs. Susannah Thompson of this borough; in four years since Mrs. Thompson settled here, she has attended the funeral of

MARRIAGES AND DEATHS FROM THE GAZETTE   113

three of her daughters. Died Monday, 12th instant, Mrs.
Buchanan, wife of General Thomas Buchanan. Died Saturday last,
Mrs. M'Farlane, wife of Major William M'Farlane; remains interred
in the old Presbyterian burying ground near this borough.

Aug 30, 1797: On Saturday evening a Mr. Leonard who lived about 3
miles from this town, in attempting to cross the Conodoguinet
Creek on horseback, was drowned.

Sep 6, 1797: Married Tuesday last by Rev. Waugh, in the Lower
Settlement, Samuel Criswell, of this town, to Miss Margaret
Morrison. Married Thursday last in this town by Rev. Dubendorff,
David Alter of Westpennsborough to Miss Betsey Mell.

Sep 20, 1797: Married Thursday, 17th Aug, in Juniata Township,
Shearmans Valley, by Rev John Linn, Rev. John Hogg, aged 82, to
Miss Rossana M'Ewen, aged 38, of the same place.

Sep 27, 1797: Married Thursday evening last by Rev. Robert
Davidson, Col. Ephraim Blaine, to Mrs. Sarah Duncan of this
borough.

Oct 11, 1797: Married on the 26th September in Harrisburgh, by
Rev. Nathaniel Snowden, John Robertson, teacher of youth, to Miss
Jane M'Cracken, daughter of William M'Cracken, weaver, both of
East Pennsborough Township, Cumberland Co.

Nov 8, 1797: Married 31st ult. in Lisburn by Rev. Samuel Waugh,
James Ligget, of Newbury Township, York Co., to Miss Isabella
Hannah, of Lisburn, Allen Township. Married at Pittsburgh, Jacob
Keller, saddler, to Mrs. M'Coumb.

Nov 15, 1797: Died on 12th instant, in her 75th year, Jannet
M'Keehan, wife of Alexander M'Keehan, of this borough, after a
painful and lingering illness; remains interred at the old
burying ground.

Nov 22, 1797: Died on 16th instant, in her 78th year, Mrs.
Rebecca Armstrong, relict of the late General John Armstrong, of
this borough, having received several paralytic shocks by which
her faculty of speech and powers of mind were much affected.
Died on 15th instant in her 36th year, Mrs. Eleanor M'Curdy, wife
of John M'Curdy of this borough, labouring for 3 years under a
lingering disease and for 3 weeks previous to her death, her
sufferings were great. Died 15th instant, Philip Pendergrass, in
his 72nd year, of this borough.

Jan 24, 1798: Died 5th of January in her 25th year, Miss Jane
Chambers, daughter of Robert Chambers; interred in the burying
ground at Carlisle.

Feb 14, 1798: Died Sunday, 4th instant, in his 62(?)nd year,
William Denny, of this borough, after a few weeks of extreme
illness which had been preceded by a great infirmity of many

years.

March 7, 1798: Died Monday morning, 26th February, in his 59th year, on his plantation in Eastpennsbro' Township, John Carothers, Esq., one of the justices of the peace of this county; remains interred in the burying place at Silver Spring Meeting house.

March 14, 1798: Died Friday last in this town, John Wallace; remains interred in the burying ground adjoining this town.

April 11, 1798: Died Sunday last, George Morrow, student in the Dickinson College, from North Carolina; about two weeks ago he was seized with the small pox which proved his death. Married Tuesday, 3rd instant, by Dr. Davidson, James Neely of York Co., to Miss Peggy M'Beth of Cumberland Co.

April 25, 1798: Died Sunday last after a short illness, Philip Baker of Middleton Township; his remains were interred in the German burying ground in this town.

May 2, 1798: Died Sunday evening last, Robert Gibson, old inhabitant of this county.

May 23, 1798: Died at his seat in Shippensburgh, Sunday last, about half after ten in the morning, Capt. Mathew Scott, parent and husband, long a resident of this little town; served in the revolutionary War; taken prisoner in the battle of Long Island; remains interred in the public burying ground.

June 6, 1798: Died Saturday, 2nd instant, Mrs. Flemming, wife of James Flemming, in the vicinity of this borough. Died last Sunday evening in her 58th year, after an illness of some months, Mrs. Mary Carothers, widow of John Carothers, Esq., late of Eastpennsborough Township; her remains interred in the Silver Spring burying ground.

June 13, 1798: Committed to the jail of this county on Monday last, Sarah Clark, on suspicion of being the person who has poisoned the family of John Carothers, Esq. in the lower settlement of which Mr. Carothers and his wife have died and several of the family are now very ill.

Aug 8, 1798: Died Saturday last, Mrs. Riddle, consort of John Riddle, Esq., of Chambersburgh.

Aug 15, 1798: Died Friday night last, Samuel Gray, merchant of this town; remains were interred in the burying ground adjoining this town.

Aug 22, 1798: Died 18th instant, in his 72nd year, William Flemming. Chambersburg - died Friday evening last, after a long and severe indisposition, Mrs. Elizabeth Riddle, consort of Hon. James Riddle, Esq.

Oct 24, 1798: Married 18th instant, by Rev. Dr. Davidson, Rev. Thomas Hoge, of Northumberland, to Miss Betsey Holmes, of this town.

Nov 14, 1798: Married Tuesday last (13th instant), by Rev. Dr. Davidson, David Harris, merchant of the town of York, to Miss Sally Montgomery, daughter of John Montgomery, Esq., of this borough.

Nov 21, 1798: Married on 20th instant by Dr. R. Davidson, Robert Wright of this borough, to Miss Nancy Holmes, daughter of Thomas Holmes of York County.

Dec 5, 1798: Married Thursday last by Rev. Waugh in East Pennsbro., Jonathan Hoge, jun., to Miss Eleanor Briggs, both of East Pennsborough.

Dec 19, 1798: Married 13th instant by Dr. R. Davidson, Robert Elliot, to Miss Rebecca Fleming. Also John Lytle to Miss Barbara Lefevre.

Jan 23, 1799: Died 17th instant, in his 76th year, William Woods, after a tedious affliction. Died on 13th instant, James Anderson, proprietor of the ferry on the Susquehanna, of that name, after a short illness, in his 59th year. Died on the 10th instant, Mrs. Margaret Pollock, of distinguished birth and family, wife of Oliver Pollock, Esq., aged 52 years; her remains were deposited near the present residence of the family, at Silver's Springs; she left a husband and 7 children; she was born in Ireland and descended from the O'Briens of the house of Clare and Kennedy of Ormand.

March 13, 1799: Died last week at Newville, Rev. Wilson.

March 27, 1799: Died Sunday, 24th instant, after a short illness, Mrs. Mary Blaine, wife of Alexander Blaine.

April 3, 1799: Married on the 25th ult., in the city of Philadelphia, by Rev. Dr. Rogers, Robert Hamilton, of that city, to Miss Jesse M'Naughton, daughter of Patrick M'Naughton, Esq., of this county.

April 17, 1799: Married in this borough on Thursday last, by Rev. Dr. Davidson, Dr. James Postlethwait, to Miss Betsy Smith, daughter of the late Major James Smith of this county. Married in East Pennsborough, on the same day, David Bell, to Miss Isabella Hoge, daughter of Jonathan Hoge, Esq. Married in this borough, Saturday last, John Hanna, to Miss Hannah Smith, daughter of John Smith, blacksmith of this town.

April 24, 1799: Married last week by Rev. Waugh, in East Pennsborough Township, Matthew Miller, of Middletown Township, to Miss Jane Galbreath, daughter of Andrew Galbreath, Esq., of East Pennsborough.

May 1, 1799: Died in this town last week, Miss Sally Calhoon, daughter of Andrew Calhoon, deceased.

May 15, 1799: Died on Tuesday, 7th instant, in Lewistown, after a very short illness, Jerman Jacobs.

May 29, 1799: Died last week after a long and painful illness, Mrs. Weiss, wife of Jacob Weiss, of Middleton Township.

July 17, 1799: Married 9th instant, by Rev. Snowden, at Silver's Springs, Dr. Samuel Robinson, to Miss Polly Pollock, eldest daughter of Oliver Pollock, Esq.

Aug 7, 1799: Died Monday, 29th July last, Margaret Logan, wife of John Logan, and daughter of Robert Chambers, in her 24th year, of a lingering disorder.

Aug 21, 1799: Died yesterday morning, Adam Logue of this town.

Aug 28, 1799: Died Saturday morning, 24th instant, at half past 7 o'clock, at Shippensburgh, Pa., in her 20th year, after a three weeks painful disease, Miss Elizabeth Shippen, daughter of Joseph Shippen, Esq., of Plumley farm, Chester Co. Died on the 25th instant, Col. William Lusk; his remains were interred at Newville. Married in Philadelphia on Thursday, 15th instant, John Hoff of Lancaster, to Miss Mary Boyer, daughter of Frederick Boyer of this town.

Sep 4, 1799: A child of Mr. Bradley of this town of 2 years was Saturday last near the Square, run over by a wagon.

Sep 18, 1799: Died Thursday, 12th instant, aged about 70 years, Mrs. Elizabeth Miller. Married Thursday last by Rev. Hautz(?), Samuel Krop, to Miss Catharine Spotswood, both of this place. Died at Fort Fayette, on the 1st instant, Lieut. David Thompson, of the 2d U.S. Regiment of Infantry, after a painful and tedious illness.

Oct 30, 1799: Married Thursday last by Rev. Waugh, John Chain to Sidney Moffatt, both of East Pennsborough Township.

Nov 6, 1799: Died Sunday last, after a tedious illness, Miss Margaret Davis, daughter of Col. John Davis, deceased; remains interred in the old Presbyterian burying ground. Sarah Clark was executed Wednesday last on the commons east of this town, convicted of poisoning the family of John Carothers.

Nov 27, 1799: Died at Fort Wayne, on 21st ult., Capt. Daniel Britt of the 1st Regiment of Infantry. Died Saturday night last, Mrs. Rebeckah Parker, relict of James Parker of East Pennsborough; remains were interred in the old Presbyterian burying ground. Married Thursday last, Joseph Latshaw to Miss Polly Riddle, both of this place.

MARRIAGES AND DEATHS FROM THE GAZETTE   117

Dec 11, 1799: Died - John Jordan, Esq., one of the Associate Judges of the Court of Common Pleas in this county; his remains were interred in the burying ground adjoining this town; he had been Whig during his life; served in the militia during the Revolutionary War; elected in 1783 a Justice of the Peace.

Jan 8, 1800: Died Wednesday last in his 75(?)th year, John M'Dannel; remains were interred in the Presbyterian burying ground at Newville. Married Saturday last at York Town, Lieut. Anthony Gale, of the Marine Corps, Philadelphia, to Miss Kitty Swope of this town.

Jan 22, 1800: Died Monday last, Mrs. James Leyburn of this borough, after a short illness.

Jan 29, 1800: Died Monday morning last, after a lingering sickness, Miss Gitty(?) Thompson, daughter of the late Rev. Thompson; her remains were interred in the burying ground of this town.

Feb 12, 1800: Died January 30th 1800, in his 52nd year, John Rippeth of Westpennsborough, leaving 6 children; his remains were interred in the burying ground at the Big Spring.

Feb 19, 1800: Died at Pittsburgh on Wednesday, 5th instant, David Hoge, of that town.

Feb 26, 1800: Married Thursday, 13th instant, by Rev. Dr. Davidson, Jereat Pollock to Miss Polly Briggs, both of this county.

March 12, 1800: Married on the 6th instant, by Rev. Robert Davidson, Samuel Duncan, Esq., Attorney at Law, to Miss Elizabeth Creigh, daughter of John Creigh, Esq. Died at Pittsburgh on Thursday morning last, 6th instant, in her 27th year, of a lingering and painful illness, Mrs. Catharine Semple, consort of Steel Semple, Esq., of that place.

March 26, 1800: Married Wednesday, 12th instant, by Rev. M'Connel, at the farm of Joseph Junkin, in East Pennsborough Township, John Findley of Westmoreland County, to Miss Elizabeth Junkin, daughter of Joseph Junkin of this county.

April 9, 1800: Married Monday evening, 31st March, by Rev. Dr. Davidson, Lieut. Ofley, quarter master of the 10th Regiment, to Miss Polly Greer.

April 23, 1800: Died Saturday, 19th instant, in his 71st year, after an illness of two days, which we are informed was by a stroke of the palsey, Jonathan Hoge, Esq., one of the Associate Judges of this county.

May 7, 1800: Married on Thursday, 24th April, at New Castle, by Rev. Robert Clay, Jh. L. D'Happart, to Miss Elizabeth Thompson, daughter of the late General William Thompson.

May 21, 1800: Died last week, Dr. James Forbes, son of John Forbes of this county.

June 11, 1800: Died Wednesday morning last, in her 30th year, after a long and painful sickness, Mrs. Margaret Weakley, wife of Nat. Weakley; remains were interred in the burying ground adjoining this town. Married last week by Rev. Dr. Nesbit, William Holling, of Virginia, to Miss Jean Sanderson, daughter of Robert Sanderson, of Middleton Township, in this county.

July 2, 1800: Married Thursday last by Rev. Dr. Davidson, Lieut. Potts of the 10th U.S. Regiment, to Miss Betsey Hughes, daughter of John Hughes, Esq. of Carlisle.

July 9, 1800: York - Died on Monday night last at the house of Capt. Gossler, in this borough, Lieut. John Douglas, late of the 10th U.S. Regiment. Died on Monday last, Alexander Blaine; interred in the burying ground adjoining this borough.

Aug 20, 1800: Married Wednesday last, at the farm seat of William Godfrey in York County, by Rev. Campbell, John Oliver, merchant of Carlisle, to Miss Hannah Godfrey, daughter of William Godfrey.

Sep 3, 1800: Died Monday last after a short illness, James Pollock, one of the earliest inhabitants of this county.

Sep 24, 1800: Died at Landisburgh, Shearmans Valley, George Crook, lately from Baltimore; it is believed he died from the Yellow Fever. Died Monday, 15th, at Baltimore, Dr. Charles Stimmeckie, formerly of this town. Died Wednesday last, at the mouth of the Juniata, Daniel Clark, oldest son of the late John Clark, deceased. Married Tuesday, 16th last, by Rev. Waugh, Charles Pattison, of Carlisle, to Miss Polly Mateer, of Allan Township.

Oct 1, 1800: Married in Adams County, on Thursday last, by Rev. Samuel Waugh, James Ramsay, merchant of Carlisle, to Miss Elizabeth Smith, daughter of Capt. John Smith of Adams County. Married on the same evening in Carlisle, by Rev. Dr. Nesbit, Mr. Knix, late a Lieutenant in the 10th Regiment, to Miss Hannah Douglas, daughter of John Douglas, merchant of Carlisle.

Oct 8, 1800: Married Thursday, 25th September last, by Robert Lusk, Esq., Henry Hill, of Hopewell Township, to Miss Grizzy Cupels, of Mifflin Township. John Chain was killed when he attempted to stop his horses from running off as he was run over by the wagon; he left a wife and mother.

Nov 12, 1800: Died Saturday last, after a very painful illness, Mrs. Nancy Craighead, wife of Major Gilson Craighead; remains were interred in the burying ground adjoining this town. Died Saturday, 8th instant, after a lingering and painful disease,

Capt. John Steel, of the U.S. Army. Died Sunday last, Richard Hemming.

Nov 26, 1800: Died Thursday last at his farm adjoining this town, Stephen Foulk, Sen.; his remains were interred at Huntingdon, York County; he was in an advanced stage of life, a long-time sick.

Dec 3, 1800: Married on Tuesday, 25th ult., Rowland Curtain, merchant of Bell Fount, to Miss Margary Gregg, daughter of John Gregg of this county.

Dec 24, 1800: Married Thursday last by Rev. Francis Herron, Abraham Smith of this county, to Miss Jane Linn, daughter of William Linn, of Franklin County. Died Wednesday, 17th instant, Mrs. Margaret Wilson, wife of James Wilson, merchant of Landisburgh, in her 38th year, long time affected with a painful disease; remains interred at the Centre Meeting house; she left a husband and 5 small children.

Dec 31, 1800: Died Sunday morning, 31st instant, Major Gen. Hartley, in hi 52nd year; represented York County in Congress; remains interred at St. John's Church.

BAPTISMS PERFORMED AT CARLISLE AND RECORDED IN THE REGISTER OF
ST. JAMES EPISCOPAL CHURCH, LANCASTER, PENNSYLVANIA.

An Account of Christenings in the Year 1755.

Francis of Francis and Dorothy West, bapt. June 5 in Carlisle.
James of Rich. and Mary Baldrick, bapt. June 15 in Carlisle.
Hannah of Ludwick and Marg. Chanar, bapt. June 15 in Carlisle.
Martha Maria of James and Catherine Bole, bapt. June 15 in Carlisle.
Martha Maria of Rob't and Hannah Kirkpatrick, bapt. June 15 in Carlisle.
Eleanor of Luke and Elizab'th Sexton, bapt. June 15 in Carlisle.
Martha of Wm. and Mary Miller, bapt. June 15 in Carlisle.
John of Timothy and Catherine Donehow, bapt. June 16 in Carlisle.
David of David and Mary Clayton, bapt. July 6 in Carlisle.
John of Andrew and Mary Swilehan, bapt. July 6 in Carlisle.
Henry of Adam and Charity Hays, bapt. July 6 in Carlisle.
John of John and Mary McDowel, bapt. July 6 in Carlisle.
Sarah of Joshua and Ann Drumond, bapt. July 6 in Carlisle.
Philip and Margaret of Sam'l and Cathrine B-aton, bapt. July 23 in Carlisle.
Isaac of Rich'd and Ann Kirkpatrick, bapt. July 28 in Carlisle.
Rebekah of Jam's and Christian Kenedy, bapt. July 28 in Carlisle.
Joseph of John and Margaret Walsh, bapt. August 24 in Carlisle.
Thomas and Sarah of Lawrence and Eliz'th Donohow, bapt. August 24 in Carlisle.
Susanna of John Haggan and Susanna, bapt. August 24 in Carlisle.
William of John and Elinor Halkett, bapt. September 14 in Carlisle.
Elizabeth of Alister and Agnus Ryan, bapt. September 14 in Carlisle.
Stephen of Thomas and Margaret Sisney, bapt. September 15 in Carlisle.

Baptism of Adults:
Sarah, the wife of Roger Walton, July 6, 1755, in Carlisle
Rachel, the wife of Howel Harris, May 30, at Carlisle
Sarah Fluke, May 30, at Carlisle

INDEX

Readers are cautioned that the original records were often difficult to read and contained a wide range of spellings and misspellings. Attempt to be creative in researching family names. You are also reminded that the name may appear more than once on the page; scrutinize the entire page.

-A-
ABBET, Else, 86
ACKMAN, John, 27
  Mary, 27
ADAIR, Rosian, 30
ADAM, Johann, 46
ADAMS, Abraham, 22, 82
  Agnes, 31
  Elizabeth, 22
  Esther, 1
  Francis, 101
  Isaac, 22
  Jenny, 31
  John, 34
  Mary, 22
  Rev. Dr., 112
  Richard, 31
  Samuel, 31, 84
  Thomas, 31, 83
ADAMSON, Sarah, 99
ADIBEN, Cathar., 26
AEI, Chatharina, 52
  Magdalena, 52
  Stephen, 52
AGNEW, Barbara, 67
  Eisett, 67
  John, 101, 105
  Marg., 67
  Nancy, 38
ALBERT, Anna, 72
  Anna Margaretha, 71
  Anna Maria, 71
  Barbar, 65
  Catharine, 19
  Christofel, 68
  Christopher, 69
  Elisabeth, 68
  Henry, 19
  J. Nicklas, 73
  Johan Nicklas, 71
  Johann Christoph, 65
  Johannes, 21
  John Christ., 72
  John Nicklas, 71

  Margaretha, 69
  Maria, 20, 63
  Maria Barbara, 21
  Maria Magdalena, 73
ALBRECHT, Barbara, 52
  Catharina, 46
  Elisabet, 46
  Heinrich, 52
  Jacob, 46, 77
  John, 85
  Maria Catharina, 52
ALCORN, James, 1
ALEXANDER,
  Isabella, 1, 111
  James, 1, 37, 95
  John, 1
  Joseph, 1
  Margaret, 95
  Mrs. 109
  Samuel, 1, 108
  William, 1, 109
ALLEMAN, Christian, 75
ALLEN, Agnes, 1
  Alexander, 35
  Catharine, 1
  David, 35, 107, 108
  Elizabeth, 1, 35
  Ephraim, 101
  Hugh, 35
  Isabella, 35
  Jennet, 35
  Jenny, 1, 35
  John, 35
  Margaret, 1
  Nancy, 29
  Sarah, 108
  William, 1
ALLER, Ann Elizabeth, 73
  Jacob, 73
ALLISON, Mary, 36
  Matthew, 96

  William, 101
ALLSWORTH, Mr., 34
ALLWERTH, James, 99
ALRICKS, Harms, 101, 102
  Hermanus, 101
ALTER, David, 113
ALTICH, Anna, 41
  David, 41
ALTIG, Daniel, 42
  Elisabeth, 42
ANDERSON, Hannah, 30
  James, 1, 37, 81, 115
  John, 1, 91
  Joseph, 1
  Letitia, 1
  Mary, 1, 40
ANDERWOOD, Mary, 60
ANDREW, Elizabeth, 96
  Jane, 86
  Margaret, 1
ANGLEW, Isaac, 67
ANSTADT, Georg, 45
  Magdalena, 45
APPELBY, ---, 39
APPELL, Catharina, 57
  John, 57
APPLEBY, Eliza, 31
  J., 31
  Jane, 31
  John, 31
  Nancy, 31
  William, 31
ARBUCKLE, John, 84
ARCHER, Catherine, 96
ARDILER, Caleb, 35
  Jane, 35
ARDLEY, Sarah, 101
ARES, Anna Maria, 69
  Catarina, 68
  Catharina, 69

Georg, 69
Joh. Michael, 69
Joh. Peter, 69
Joseph, 68
Susana, 68
ARMBRUSTER,
  Christina, 76
  Philip, 76
ARMITAGE, John, 96
ARMOR, Thomas, 112
ARMSTRONG, ---, 39
  Ann, 84
  Elisabeth, 44
  Elizabeth, 83
  James, 1, 37, 44
  John, 109, 113
  Mary, 38
  Rebecca, 29, 38, 113
  Robert, 1, 37, 85
  Sarah, 38
  Susannah, 82
  Thomas, 1
  William, 44
ARNDT, Catharina, 51
  Huyses, 51
  Jacob, 51
ARNOLD, Peter, 1
ARTHURS, John, 1
ASKEY, Thomas, 82
ASPELL, Margaret, 1, 97
ASPEY, Rachel, 37
ATCHISON, Benjamin, 37
  Catherine, 34
  Elizabeth, 37
  Jacob, 37
  James, 37
  John, 88
  Joseph, 37
AUGNEY, Barbara, 68
  Isaac, 68
  James Geils, 68
  Mary, 1
AULD, Christiana, 27
  Martha, 27
  Mary, 27
  Sarah, 39
  William, 27
AULL, Jean, 1
AUNE, Elisabet, 47

Heinrich, 47

-B-
B-ATON,
  Cathrine, 120
  Margaret, 120
  Philip, 120
  Samuel, 120
BAAK, Johann
  Philip, 45
  Johann Wilhelm, 44
  Johannes, 44
  Magdalena, 44
  Margaretha, 44
  Maria Magdalena, 45
  William, 44
BACKENSTOSS,
  Friedrich, 74
  Johannes, 74
  John, 74
  Magdalena, 74
BAHMER, Christina, 47
  Georg, 47
  Julianna, 47
BAIL, Cathrine
  Jenan, 59
BAILEY, Elizabeth, 1
  Jonathan, 57
  Mary, 57
BAINER, Christina, 49
  Friedrich, 49
BAIRD, Robert, 101
BAKER, Elizabeth, 82
  Philip, 114
BALDRICK, James, 120
  Mary, 120
  Richard, 120
BALDRIDGE, Joseph, 99
BALF, Denis, 78
  Dennis, 83
  Fanny, 78
BALMER, Elisabetha, 49
BALTIMORE, Philip, 79
BANKS, Mr., 34

BARCKLEY, Mary, 83
BARCLAY, James, 101
  Robert, 96
BARKER, Martha, 1
BARNES, David, 33
  Grizel, 33
  Margaret, 33
  Robert, 33
  Thomas, 33
BARR, ---, 99
  John, 1, 38
  Robert, 35
  Sarah, 100
  William, 90
BARTHOMER, Eva, 74
  Philip, 74
BASKENS, Moses, 95
BASKIN, Sarah, 83
BASKINS, James, 96
BAUER, A. Maria, 69
  Anna Catharina, 67
  Anna Elisabeth, 67
  Anna Eva, 23, 62
  Anna Maria, 52, 67
  Catha, 52
  Catharina, 23, 55, 62
  Elisabeth, 54, 65, 68
  Georg, 67
  Joh., 69
  Johan, 23, 62
  Johann Georg, 67
  Johannes, 26, 62
  John, 52, 55
  Maria Magdalena, 65
  Martin, 68
  Philip, 67
  Phillip, 65
BAUERIN, Christian, 69
BAUMAN, Ann
  Cathrina, 86
  Christoph, 86
BAXTER, Elizabeth, 95
BAYLE, Martha, 28
  Samuel, 28
BAYLES, Betsey, 1
BEADLE, John, 83

INDEX

BEALS, Hannah, 84
BEARD, Agnes, 100
  Anne, 37
  Elizabeth, 37, 83
  Hannah, 100
  James, 37
  John, 85
  Margaret, 1, 37
  Mary, 82
  Robert, 37
  William, 81
BEATTIE, Eleanor, 99
  Martha, 99
BEATTY, Jean, 60
  Samuel, 1
  Walter, 96
BECK, Catharine, 17
  George, 17
  Henry, 17
BECKER, Cathr., 86
BECKERN, Elisabeth, 67
BECKWITH, Ann, 1
BEECK, Anna
  Margaretha, 53
  Deacon Johannes, 53
  Johannes, 53
  Magdalena, 54
  Maria Madgalena, 53
BEERS, Alexander, 1
BEHL, Johannes, 46
  Magdalena, 46
BEHR, Jac., 26
  Johannes, 43
  M. Magdalena, 43
  Sara, 43
BEIDTENER, Jacob, 50
  Lydia, 50
  Wilhelm, 50
BEINBRECH, Anna
  Mary, 77
  Peter, 77
BEINBRECHT, Anna
  Maria, 77
  Conrad, 78
  Daniel, 77
  Johann, 77
BEISTEL, Marga, 54
BEITEL, Anna Maria, 45

Christoph, 45, 51
Margareth, 51
Maria Elisabeth, 51
Samuel, 45
BEITELMAN, Abr., 50
  Abraham, 51
  Gertraut, 51
BEITELMANN,
  Abraham, 46
  Gertraut, 46
  Johannes, 46
BEITER, Elisabeth, 44
BEITZEL,
  Margaretha, 50
BELL, Agnes, 38
  Agness, 2
  Andrew, 32
  Betsy, 32, 38
  Catharine, 2
  David, 32, 115
  Elizabeth, 29
  George, 30
  James, 2
  Jane, 30
  Jenny, 35
  John, 29, 32
  Joseph, 30, 37
  Katharine, 30
  Margaret, 39
  Martha, 35
  Matty, 32
  Peggy, 32
  Robert, 29, 32, 37
  Sam, 93
  Samuel, 2, 32
  Thomas, 30
  Walter, 32
  William, 30
BENDER, Adam, 43
  Jacob, 85
  Magdalena, 20
  Martin, 19
BENNETSCH,
  Catharina, 63
  Georg, 63
BENNETT, Cathrina, 85
  James, 95
BENNITSCH, Elis., 26
  Johan, 26

BENRAD, John, 85
BERCHTEL, Andres, 52
  Anna Catharina, 52
  Barbara, 52
BERND, Anna Mary, 17
  John, 17
BERNHARD,
  Catharina, 53
BERNHART, Maria
  Sarah, 42
BERNS, Mary, 96
BESAHARD, Catharina
  Elisabeth, 66
  Johann, 66
BEST, Barbara, 70
  Jacob, 70
  Joh., 70
BETHY, Agnes, 84
  Jane, 81, 101
BETSY, Eva, 84
BETZ, Edward, 75
  Jane, 75
  Sarah, 75
BEUTEL, Abr., 48
  Gertrud, 48
  Sara, 48
BEYER, Elizabeth, 79
  J. Philip, 79
BEYERS, Agnes, 82
  Amy, 82
  Elizabeth, 86
  Samuel, 82
BEYMER, Christina, 41
  Friedrich, 41
  Wilhelm, 41
BILLMEYER, Martin, 86
BIRCKEL, Barbara, 72
  Michael, 72
BIRD, John, 101
BLACK, Margaret, 2
BLACKBURNE, Mary, 86
BLAIN, Robert, 37
BLAINE, Alexander, 115, 118
  Ephraim, 109, 113

124   CUMBERLAND COUNTY CHURCH RECORDS OF THE 18TH CENTURY

James, 2, 106, 108, 109
Jane, 108
Jean, 2
Mary, 115
Rebecca, 109
BLAIR, ---, 37
Charity, 37
Daniel, 37
Jenny, 37
John, 2, 37
Mary, 2
Randle, 37
Thomas, 101
William, 106, 112
BLASER, Elizabeth, 19
Henry, 19
Peter, 19, 85
Samuel, 20
BLUM, Adam, 46
Catharina, 46
Margaretha, 46
BLYTH, Ben. Junr., 99
BOB, Andreas, 66
Susana, 66
BOBB, Catharina, 65
Maria, 65
Nicolaus, 65
BOBENMEIER, Maria Charlotta, 20
BOBENMEYER, Gabriel, 19
BOBINMEIER, Catharine, 19
Gabriel, 19
BOBMEIER, Gabriel, 20
BOCKER, Susanna, 53
BODAMER, Anna Eva, 74
Cathrina, 75
Joh. Phil., 74
Johan, 75
Johan Jacob, 74
Mary Elizabeth, 75
BOEMER, Conrad, 47
BOGER, Christian, 59
Magdalena, 59
BOGGS, William, 86
BOGS, Joseph, 89

BOHER, David, 45
Johannes, 45
Magdalena, 45
BOHLER, Martin, 86
BOHMAN, Christina, 51
Friedrich, 51
Magdalena, 51
BOHMER, Anna Margretha, 73
Conrad, 41, 73
Friedrich, 53
Georg, 53
George, 47
Jacob, 41
Johan Georg, 74
Johan Peter, 43
Johannes, 53
Julia, 47
Juliana, 43
Julianna, 41, 73
Maria, 46
Philip, 45
BOHR, Anna Margretha, 65
Mar. Lisab., 67
Maria Elisabeth, 66
Maria Magdalena, 65
Michel, 65
Nic., 67
Nicolaus, 67
Wilhelm, 65
William, 67
BOLDWIN, Susannah, 97
BOLE, Catherine, 120
James, 120
Martha Maria, 120
BOLLINGER, Conrad, 2
BOMER, Conrad, 48
Juliann, 48
BONAR, John, 92
Robert, 92
Thomas, 93
William, 92
BONN, Abraham, 74
Deborah, 74
Rebecca, 74
BONNER, Charles, 81

BOOCHER, Johannes, 54
BOOCKER, Johannes, 55
BOOR, Maria Elisabeth, 69
Michael, 69
Willhelm, 69
BOOS, Catharina, 56
Jacob, 56
Maria Barbara, 56
BOSSART, Catharina, 74
Cathrina, 75
Johannes, 74
Margretha, 75
BOTTERUM, Isaak, 82
BOURSMAN, Jacob, 81
BOVARD, Charles, 2
BOW, Catharine, 2, 108
Nancy, 2
BOWMAN, Eliza, 32
BOYD, Agnes, 87
Deborah, 37
Eleanor, 37
George, 37
James, 37, 87
Jane, 82
John, 2, 37
Joseph, 2
Robert, 28
Thomas, 96
William, 2
BOYER, Frederick, 116
Mary, 116
BRADLE, Georg Christian, 56
Thomas Wilson, 56
BRADLEY, Margery, 2
Mary, 2
Mr., 116
BRADY, Britchet, 78, 83
Hannah, 39, 99
Hugh, 87
Jane, 99
James, 99
Margreth, 85
Samuel, 81
BRAEDEN, James, 92
Walter, 92
BRAKON, James, 82

INDEX

BRANDON, Mary Ann, 82
  Sarah, 2
  Thomas, 38
BRANDSTETTER, Anna
  Barbara, 76
  Friedrich, 76
BRANDT,
  Christopher, 2
BRANDTLEIN,
  Lorentz, 47
BRANNAN, James, 33
  John, 33
  Mary, 33
  Thomas, 33
  William, 33
BRATTON, Adam, 28
  Anne, 28
  Horace, 28, 91
  Martha, 28
  Mary, 91
  Robert, 91
BRAUSS, Anna Mary, 18
  Jacob, 18
BREADDY, Hannah, 88
  Hugh, 88, 89
  John, 88
BREITELMAN,
  Abraham, 49
  Gertrud, 49
BREITTINGROSS, Mar.
  Elizabeth, 83
BREMER, Anna Maria, 49
  Peter, 49
BRENDEL,
  Elisabetha, 42
  Peter, 42
  Samuel, 42
BRENTZ, Catharina, 24
  Georg, 24
BRETS, Freiderich, 59
  Simon, 59
BRETZ, Abraham, 23
  Adam, 26
  Anna Catharina, 23
  Conrad, 25
  Elizabeth, 23
  Freidrich, 23
  Magdalena, 23
BREYENS, Margreth, 86
BRICE, Mary, 2
BRIGGS, Eleanor, 115
  Mary, 2
  Mr., 111
  Polly, 117
BRIGS, John, 93
  Mary, 93
BRINES, Buhard, 35
BRISBY, Betsy, 29
  John, 29
  Nancy, 29
  Sarah, 28
  William, 28
BRISLAND, Sarah, 2
BRISON, Jean, 93
  Robert, 92
  Sam, 93
  William, 92
BRITEWELL, Ann, 85
BRITT, Daniel, 116
BRITTAIN, John, 100
BROADLEY, Daniel, 2
BROASTER, Margt., 99
BROMFIELD, Jane, 99
BROOKS, James, 2
BROSE, Eva Maria, 72
  Fridrich, 72
  George Paulus, 72
BROTHERINTOWN, ---, 83
BROTHERTON, Robert, 99
BROUCH, Anna Eva, 75
  Felton, 76
  Susannah Marg., 76
BROWN, Adam, 34
  Agnes, 28, 85
  Alexander, 2, 38, 84
  Ann, 34
  Ben, 92
  Benjamin, 92
  Betsey, 2
  Dina, 75
  Elizabeth, 34
  Hannah, 34
  Henry, 93
  Isabella, 2
  James, 28, 91
  Jane, 82, 96
  Jean, 91
  John, 2, 28, 34, 93, 105
  Joseph, 2, 34
  Katharine, 29
  Kennedy, 99
  Margaret, 34
  Martha, 28
  Mary, 28, 34, 75, 91
  Math., 91
  Moses, 2
  Mrs. 105
  Polly, 38
  Rebecca, 2
  Robert, 2
  Sara, 91
  Sarah, 84, 96
  Thomas, 75
  William, 2, 28, 38, 112
BROWNFIELD,
  Elizabeth, 39
  John, 84
BROWNFIELDS,
  William, 86
BROWNLEE, Margaret, 2
BROWSTER,
  Alexander, 30
  Ann, 30
  William, 30, 37
BRUCHMAN, Anna
  Elisabeth, 23, 62
  Valentine, 23, 62
BRUCKER, Catharina, 54
  Elisabeth, 53
  Johann, 53
  Peter, 53
BRUCKMANN, Maria
  Catharine, 20
BRUHL, Anna Maria, 80
  Henry, 80
  Mary Elizabeth, 80
BRUMBACH, Anna
  Maria, 41
  Catharina, 41

Elizabeth, 41
Peter, 41
BRUNDLE, Cathrina, 76
Elizabeth, 80
Ferena, 76
Johan Melchior, 76
Johannes, 76
John, 76
Lorenz, 76
BRUNNER, Ferronika, 86
BRUSTMAN,
Elisabeth, 48
Maria, 48
Philip, 48
BRUSTMANN, Jacob, 48
Maria, 48
Philip, 48
BRYAN, Patrick, 2
BRYSON, Hugh, 36
John, 105
Margaret, 36
Rebecca, 36
Samuel, 36
William, 36
BUBACH, Mary
Cathrina, 84
BUCHANAN, Agnes, 29, 91
Gilbert, 92
Isaac, 93
James, 91, 92
John, 92, 107
Margaret, 92
Mary, 92
Mrs., 113
Robert, 2, 29
Sheriff, 59
Thomas, 29, 113
Walter, 91
William, 101
BUCHANNAN, Arthur, 2
Nancy, 2
William, 29
BUCHANNON, John, 73
Mary, 73
BUCHER, Conrad, 71, 101
Johan Georg, 72
Johann Jacob, 71

John Conrad, 71
Maria Magd., 73
Maria Magdalena, 71
Mary Magd., 72
BURKE, Elizabeth, 2
BURKHARD, Anna, 75
Anna Maria, 75
Joh. Jacob, 75
Margreth, 75
BURKHOLDER,
Elizabeth, 2
John, 2
BURMAN, Anna Maria, 76
Daniel, 76
Elisabeth, 76
Jacob, 76
John Jacob, 76
BURNS, John, 84
Mary, 85
BURST., Barnd., 96
BUSCHIN, Anna
Margretta, 56
BUSHOLTZ, A.M.C., 83
BUTTLER, Martha, 82
BYERS, John, 104

-C-

C--, Daniel, 94
J., 94
CAFF---, Jno.(?), 99
CAINER, George, 58
CAL., Sam, 92
CALBREATH, Agnes, 91
William, 91
CALDWELL, Ann, 27
Elizabeth, 27
James, 27
John, 27, 89, 103
Samuel, 2, 27
CALENDAR, Pattey, 2
CALHOON, Andrew, 116
Sally, 116
CALHOUN, Andrew, 101
David, 93
Robert, 93
Sam, 93
Sarah, 93

CALLENDAR, Martha, 97
CALLENDER,
Catharine, 111
Maria, 103
Robert, 101
CALQHOUN, Mary, 93
Sam, 93
CALVERT, Charity, 86
Hannah, 84
John, 31
CAMBELL, Archibald, 2
Rev., 111
William, 2
CAMBLE, Nancy, 2
CAMBRIDGE,
Elizabeth, 100
Hannah, 100
CAMERON, Alexander, 79
CAMLETON, Mary, 79
Robert, 79
Sarah, 79
Thomas, 79
CAMLIN, William, 95
CAMPBELL, Eleanor, 2
John, 2, 95
Rev., 118
William, 84
CAMPBLE, David, 96
Dug'l., 95
Joseph, 99
Thomas, 96
CAMPHER, Godfried, 76
CAMPLE, Francis, 83
Margreth, 83
CANNING, Charles, 3
CARELSON,
Catharine, 55
CARITHERS, James, 36
Mary, 30
CARL, Catharina, 52
Cathrina, 72
Christina, 71, 72, 73, 74
Daniel, 71
Georg, 52
Jacob, 71, 72, 73, 74

Johan George, 74
John Jacob, 71
Sarah, 52
CARLL, Catharina, 54
CARLO, Hollman, 73
Joh. Heinrich, 73
Maria Elizabeth, 73
CARNACHAN, Joseph, 88
William, 88
CARNAHAN, Adam, 36
Agnes, 36
Elizabeth, 36
James, 36, 38
Joseph, 36
Judith, 36
Martha, 36
Nancy, 39
Robert, 36, 38
William, 36
CARNOUGHAN, Sarah, 8
CAROTHERS, James, 3
Jared, 3
John, 3, 114, 116
Mary, 114
Rogers, 3
CARR, Rebecca, 61
CARRICK, Katharine, 39
CARSON, Elisha, 27, 38
Hannah, 27
James, 36
James Forster, 82
Janet, 36
John, 27
Mary, 36
Priscilla, 27
Ruth, 34
CARVER, Mary, 83
CASCADON, William, 3
CASPER, Elizabeth, 100
CASS, Anna Catharina, 67
Jacob, 67
CASSEL, Nichlas, 85
CAST, Cathrina, 68
Jacob, 68
Jo. Mich., 60

CASWELL, Catharine, 3
CASZLER, Catharina, 24
Jacob, 24
Maria, 24
CATCH, James, 75
Susanna, 75
CATHER, John W., Jr., 101
CEFERRY, Christian, 56
Christina, 56
Justina, 56
CHAIN, John, 116, 118
CHAMBERS, Benjamin, 96
Betsey, 3, 107
Elizabeth, 96
Jane, 85, 113
Margaret, 3, 109
Mary, 3
Peggy, 112
Polly, 3, 110
Robert, 89, 109, 112, 113, 116
Ronald, 98
Samuel, 83
William, 107, 110
CHANAR, Hannah, 120
Ludwick, 120
Margaret, 120
CHAPLIN, John, 101
CHAPMAN, James, 3
Mary, 40
Sally, 36
CHESTER, Robert, 84
CHRIST, Adam, 48
Catharina, 49
Cathrina, 80
Christina, 46, 47, 48, 51, 52
Daniel, 46
Elisabet, 48
Jacob, 48
Johannes, 48
Nicholaus, 80
Philip, 46, 47, 48, 51
Philipp, 49, 52
Sara, 51
Sarah, 80
Wilhelm, 47

CHRISTIE, Mary, 3
CHRISTLY, Ann Cathrina, 72
Fredrick, 72
CHRISTY, Elizabeth, 101
William, 101
CISNEY, Margreth, 81
CLADDY, Catharina, 51
Maria Magdalena, 51
Martin, 51
CLARK, Agnes, 29
Alexander, 31
Anna Marg., 68
Benjamin, 68, 70
Daniel, 118
Deborah, 84
Elisabeth, 68, 70
Elizabeth, 84
Esther, 96
Henry, 38
Jane, 100
John, 29, 118
Mary, 95
Sarah, 3, 114, 116
William, 29, 93
CLAWSON, Elsie, 3
CLAY, Robert, 117
CLAYTON, David, 120
John, 3
Mary, 120
CLELLAND, Adam, 31
Jane, 31
CLENDENAN, Isabella, 3
Jean, 3
CLENDENEN, James, 83
CLENDINAN, Jane, 109
CLERK, James, 60
CLINTON, Alexander, 3
CLOCKSTONE, Agnes, 84
CLOTHLAN, Paul M., 51
CLOUSER, Margaret, 110
CLOYD, Jenny, 38

128   CUMBERLAND COUNTY CHURCH RECORDS OF THE 18TH CENTURY

CLYMER, Dan'l., 95
COBLIN, John, 82
COCHRAN, Isabella, 3
  John, 85, 96
COFFEE, John, 100
COHAN, Paul, 85
COHIL, John, 96
COINER, George, 59
COINERN, Rosina, 59
COLGHOUN, James, 92
  Sam, 92
COLHOON, Andrew, 109
  Hugh, 86
COLLHOON, James, 82
COLLIER, Joseph, 105
COLLIGHON, John, 80
COLLINS, Margret, 84
  Ruth, 84
  Willm., 82
COLQHOUN, Adam, 91
  Ann, 93
  Jean, 91
COLQUHOUN, Jo., 94
  Sam., 94
COLWELL, Robert, 107
CONE, Heinrich, 52
  Johann Benjamin, 53
CONELLY, Adam, 29
CONNELLY, Betsy, 39
  Charity, 29, 39
  Elizabeth, 29
  James, 29
  Jane, 3
  William, 29
CONNINGHAM, Margt., 99
COOK, Cathrina, 78
  Isaac, 100
  Jacob, 3, 86
  Ruth, 32
COOKE, Colonel, 104
COONS, Agnis, 69
  Richard, 69
COOPER, Adam, 3
  Charles, 106, 108
  Elizabeth, 100
  George, 100
  Mary, 108

  Rev., 108
  Robert Davidson, 106
  Samuel M'Coskry, 106
COOTS, Margaret, 3
COOVER, Henry, 3
COPELY, Samuel, 3
CORODERS, Jenny, 72
CORRY, Aisett, 58
  Barbara, 58
  Nancy, 58
COSSEY, Mary Magd., 85
COST, Jacob, 66
COTTER, Sarah, 88
COULTER, Henry, 3
  Hew, 92
  Mary, 92
COWDEN, William, 38
COWHER, Agness, 3
COWHICK, Daniel, 96
COWLY, Patty, 27
COX, William, 89
CRABER, ---, 58
  Jacob, 58
  John, 58
CRAFFORD, Lawrence, 101
CRAFORD, Lawrence, 101
CRAFT, Gershom, 3
CRAIG, Mary, 37
  Peggy, 40
CRAIGHEAD, Gilson, 3, 118
  John, 3
  Mr., 88
  Nancy, 118
  Rachel, 3
  Thomas, 3, 111
CRAINE, Jean, 110
CRAIR, Sarah, 39
CRANE, Richard, 3
CRAWFORD, Agnes, 3
  James, 95
  Joseph, 3
  Katharine, 31
  Lawrence, 81
  Mary, 82
  Nancy, 38
CREAN, Jane, 83
CREEK, Jacob, 80
  John, 80

  Rebecca, 80
CREIGH, Betsey, 3
  Elizabeth, 117
  Isabella, 3
  John, 3, 111, 117
CRETZBERGER, Hinr., 23
CREVER, John, 112
  Polly, 112
CRISWELL, Samuel, 113
CROCHET, Elizabeth, 3
CROCKET, Elsie, 3
  James, 3
  Sarah, 3
  Thomas, 3
CRODDERS, Polle
  Pegge, 57
CROMLEY, John, 3
CROOK, George, 118
CROP, William, 95
CROSSON, Mary, 3
CROW, Eleanor, 37
  George, 38
CROWEL, ---, 38
  Samuel, 38
CROWELL, Rachel, 38
CRUSE, Else., 67
  Georg, 67
  Marg., 67
CRUTCHLOW, James, 86
CUHN, Johann
  Benjamin, 41
  Johann Heinrich, 41
  Johann Peter, 41
  Maria Barbara, 41
CULBERTSON, Andrew, 87
  Col. James, 96
  Jane, 89
  Joseph, 3
  Margt., 100
  Martha, 99
  Samuel, 87, 88
CULVER, Levi, 38
CUMMINGS, Charles, 88
  John, 87
CUMMINS, Charles, 87
  Elizabeth, 39

INDEX

George, 89
Robert, 101
CUNINGHAM, Jane, 84
Margreth, 86
CUNNINGHAM, Elenor, 89
Mary, 3
CUPELS, Grissy, 118
CURRY, James, 86
John, 88
CURTAIN, Rowland, 119
CUTHBERTSON, John, 91, 105

-D-

DAELHAUSEN, Anna
Catharine, 18
Daniel, 18
Henry Daniel, 18
DALTON, Jane, 95
DANIEL, Thomas, 3
DANZER, Georg, 86
DAUGHERTY, Eleanor, 3
James, 99
DAVENPORT, William, 101
DAVIDSON, Ann, 3, 37
Dr., 114
Francis, 38
James, 37
John, 3, 37, 38
Leacy, 37
Mary, 4
Matthew, 37
R., 107, 115
Rev. Dr., 107, 108, 109, 110, 112, 115, 117
Sally, 85
Samuel, 4
DAVIS, Charity, 35
Elizabeth, 4
Even, 82
John, 82, 84, 116
Joseph, 100
Margaret, 116
Margery, 4
Polly, 4, 111
Rachel, 4
Samuel, 100, 108
Stephen, 83

DAVISON, John, 82
DAVISS, Nancy, 84
DAY, John, 4
DE DIEU, Abraham, 80
Anna, 80
Salomon, 80
DE FRANCE, Carolus, 74
Elizabeth, 74
John, 74
Rebecca, 74
DE ROCKE, Abraham
Albrecht, 85
DEAN, James, 101
DEARMON, Margaret, 40
DECKER, Heinrich, 41
Mary, 4
DEDERICK, Magdalina, 4
DEEL, Cristina, 43
Elisabetha, 43
Robert, 43
DEISELER, Daniel, 42
Elisabeth, 42
Michael, 42
DELONG, Rebecca, 60
DELPH, Stephen, 82
DEMANN, Christian, 57
DENISON, Sarah, 33
DENNEY, William, 4
DENNY, David, 4, 108
Dennis, 4
Ebenezer, 108
James, 27
Peggy, 4, 108
William, 113
DEPOT, Anne Mar., 67
DER, Margaret, 20
DERRINGER, Barbara, 54
Joh., 54
Johann, 54
DEUBLER, Albrecht, 80
Cathrina, 80
DEVINPORT, William, 28

DEVIRE, Mary, 85
DEWAIN, Friederich, 53
DEWALD, Erf., 26
Jacob, 25
DEWALT, John, 18
Polly, 18
DEWEIN, Freidrich, 54
DEWER, William, 61
DEWIS, Sarah, 57
DEYEO, Cathrina, 80
DEYRMOND,
Elizabeth, 4
DEYTES, Elisabeth, 71
John, 71
Mary, 71
Peter, 71
Theodora Anna
Isabel, 71
D'HAPPART, Jh. L., 117
DICKEY, Agnes, 83
John, 96
Peter, 83
Robert, 83, 105
DICKSON, Andrew, 4
DIELER, Caspar, 66
Christina, 66
Salomon, 66
DIERICK, Magdalina, 97
DIESSLER, Maria, 51
Peter, 51
Susanna, 51
DIETRICH, Anna
Margaretha, 45
Elisabeth, 55
Johann, 54
Johannes, 41, 42, 43, 45, 50
John, 55
Margareth, 53
Margaretha, 41, 42, 43, 53, 54
DIFFENDERFER, Ann
Eliz., 86
DIGGES, Christina, 73
Maria Dorothea, 73
Valentine, 73

DIKES, Cathrina
　Friderica, 72
　Christina, 72
　Valentine, 72
DILL, James, 104
　Jean, 112
　Margaret, 104
　Johan Michael, 73
　Maria Elisabetha,
　　72
　Maria Elizabeth,
　　72
　Maria Elizabetha,
　　73
　Mary, 82, 95
　Matthew, 112
　Michael, 72, 73
　Susannah, 72
DILLER, Casper, 61
　July, 61
　Martin, 60
　Molle, 61
DILLON, Thomas, 86
DIMSEY, Fergus, 4
　Mary, 4
DIPPEL, Ludwig, 54
　Margaretha, 54
DIXON, Hannah, 91
DOAG, James, 89
DODDS, Cath., 95
　Isabella, 96
　Jane, 96
　Thomas, 4
DOET, Bas, 42
　Catharina, 42
　Christina, 42
DOMMA, Marthin, 21
DONALDSON, Jean, 4
　John, 4
DONAVAN, Frances,
　　99
DONEHOW, Catherine,
　　120
　John, 120
　Timothy, 120
DONN, Thomas, 83
DONNEL, Francis, 28
　Mary, 98
DONNELL, Francis, 4
DONNELLY, John, 4
DONNELY, Mary, 85
DONOHOW, Elizabeth,
　　120
　Lawrence, 120

Sarah, 120
Thomas, 120
DONOWAY, Ellenor,
　　36
DONWAN, Robert, 84
DOROUGH, Margreth,
　　83
DORREN, Mar. Magd.,
　　26
DORWARD, William,
　　85
DOTTON, Ann, 83
DOUDS, William, 4
DOUGHERTY, David,
　　33
　Henry, 83
　Isabel, 79
　John, 81
　Mercer, 83
　Nancy, 81
DOUGLAS, Agnes, 30
　Hannah, 118
　John, 30, 38, 118
　Margaret, 30
　Mary, 30
　William, 30
DOUGLASS, Jane, 4
　John, 4
　Margaret, 38
　Thomas, 85
DOUY, Eve, 4
DOWDS, Andrew, 4
DOWGLAS, Isaac, 91
DRAHER, Anna
　　Elisabeth, 56
　Johan Georg, 56
　John Peter, 56
DRECHSLER, Anna
　　Maria, 50
　Conrad, 50
　Elisabeth, 44
　Michael, 44
　Pfronica, 50
DRECKSLER, Alena,
　　52
　Conrad, 52, 54
　Fronica, 52, 54
　Johi, 52
　Schimine, 52
DRECKSTLER,
　Johannes, 41
　Michael, 41
DREICHSLER, Conrad,
　　55

DREISER, Christian,
　　51
　Christina, 51
DRESSLER,
　Elisabeth, 43,
　　44
　Michael, 43, 44
DRIDGE, Mary, 38
DRISKEL, James, 86
DRUGON, Katharine,
　　38
DRUMMOND, Ann, 120
　Joshua, 120
　Sarah, 120
DUBENDORF, Rev.,
　　110
DUBENDORFF, Rev.,
　　113
DUFF, James, 82
DUFFY, Catharine, 4
DUGAN, Agnes, 4
DUI, Adam, 17
　Margaret, 17
DUMBAR, David, 82
　Fanny, 82
　John, 82
DUNBAR, Eleanor, 4
　Elizabeth, 4
　James, 91
　John, 91, 107,
　　111
　Margaret, 4, 107
　Mary, 91
　Nelly, 111
　Robert, 29, 91
　William, 4, 111
DUNBARR, ---, 95
DUNCAN, Anne, 4
　David, 4
　James, 4, 38
　Jean, 92
　John, 96, 108
　Joseph, 99, 106
　Margaret, 35
　Mrs. ---, 4
　Nancy, 107
　Samuel, 4, 99,
　　117
　Sarah, 113
　Stephen, 107
　Thomas, 4, 97
　William, 35, 38
DUNCKAN, Eleanora,
　　75

John, 75
Margreth, 75
DUNKAN, Eleonora, 74
John, 74
DUNLAP, Betsey, 4, 110
Deborah, 89
Jane, 99
DUNLAPS, William, 89
DUNLOP, Robert, 95
DUNNE, Elisabeth, 59
DUNNING, Ezekiel, 111
Susannah, 101
DURBARA, Isaac, 33
Jane, 33
John, 33
Reuben, 33
DURBARROW, ---, 38
DUTTON, Mary, 83

-E-
EAGER, Bethy, 82
Margaret, 37, 38
EAGOLF, Polly, 4
EAKARD, Susanna, 4
EAKEN, Andrew, 101
James, 101
Mary, 4
EAKIN, Polly, 97
EARLS, William, 4
EATON, Joseph, 112
EBBRICH, Adam, 57
Samuel, 57
EBERS, Elizabeth, 72, 74
John, 74
John Philip, 82
Mary, 72
Philip, 72, 74
EBERT, Elisabeth, 55
Elisabetha, 65
Maria, 55
Philip, 65
Sara, 65
EBLE, A. Maria, 24
Anna, 24, 62
Georg, 24, 62
Jacob, 24, 62
Samuel, 24, 62

EBRECHT, Ann Cathr., 85
ECKLE, Philip, 86
ECKLES, Deborah, 4
EDEBACH, Elizabeth, 59
EDELBLAT,
 Elisabeth, 57
 Jacob, 57
EDMISTON, James, 4
 Samuel, 4
 Thomas, 89
EDMONSTON, Agnes, 29
 Joseph, 29
EGOLF, Michael, 110
 Mrs., 110
EGOLFF, Henry, 58
 Maria Magdalena, 58
EHINGUER, Franz
 Elias Daniel, 85
EHRHART, Sophia, 53
EHRING, Eva Kehr, 71
EICHELBERG, Elis., 26
EICHELBERGER,
 Barbara, 25, 64
 Christ., 26
 Christoph, 22, 64
 Jacob, 22, 64
 Joh. Jac., 26
 Johanne, 22
 Margaret, 22
 Maria, 25, 64
EICHENBERGER,
 Barbara, 23, 62
 Christoph, 23, 62
 Christopher, 62
 Sara, 62
 Sarah, 23
EILER, William, 20
EIP, Anna Maria, 80
 Matheys, 80
ELDER, John, 38, 100
ELLER, Anna
 Cathrina, 76
 Anthony, 76
 Susannah, 76
ELLIOT, Martha, 4
 Peggy, 4
 Robert, 5, 115

ELLIOTT, Agnes, 34
 Alexander, 34
 Catharine, 34
 James, 4
 Jannet, 34
 Mary, 34
ELLIS, Francis, 82
EMERICH, Joh., 25
EMINGER, Mary, 96
EMMERICH, Joh., 64
EMMETT, Samuel, 38
EMMINGER, Andreas, 70
 Elisabetha, 70
 Johann David, 70
 Johann Jacob, 70
 Susanna, 65
EMRICHEN, Maria, 62
EMRICK, Joh.
 Antony, 76
 Margaretha, 76
ENDSLEY, John, 5
ENGEL, Eleanora, 41
 Eleonora, 80
 Elisabeth, 53
 Heinrich, 54
 Johannes, 41, 80
 John, 80
ENGELL, Anna
 Elisabeth, 44
 Elisabeth, 53
 Johann Heinrich, 44
ENGENI, Barbaras, 65
 Isaac, 65
 Reinick, 65
ENGLISH, Elizabeth, 82
 Isabel, 84
 John, 85
ERDINGER, Anna
 Maria, 41, 43, 46
 Christian, 41, 43, 45, 46
 Johannes, 41
 Maria Magdalena, 43
ERFURT, Dewald, 23, 62, 64
 Magdalena, 23, 62
ERLANGER, Anna
 Maria, 46

Christian, 46
Philip, 46
ERLINGER, Anna
    Maria, 46
    Christian, 46
ERLISS, Lucia, 74
ERNST, Andrew, 19
    Catharine, 19
    Daniel, 20
    John, 19
ERNSTBERGER, Anna,
    25, 64
    Henrich, 25, 64
ERTINGER, Anna
    Mary, 46
    Christian, 46
ERVIN, John, 87
ERVINE, Jane, 81
    Margaret, 87
ERWIN, Jane, 95
    Mary, 85
ESHENAUER, John
    Christian, 75
    Leon, 75
    Margreth, 75
ESPEY, Ann, 30
    Christian, 38
    Elizabeth, 30
    James, 30
    John, 38
    Margaret, 30
    Peggy, 40
    Rachel, 30
    Robert, 30
    Thomas, 30
    William, 30
ESPY, John, 29
ESSIG, Elizabth, 78
    Simon, 18
EVANS, Robert, 5,
    111
EVERSOL, Jacob, 70
    Maria, 70
EVERT, Anna Maria,
    41
    Cath., 69
    Catharina, 41
    Joh., 69
    John, 69
    Nicolaus, 41
EVERTS, Catharina,
    70
    Georg, 70
    Joh., 70

EWERS, Maria, 66
EWING, Alexander,
    31
    Anna, 31
    David, 28
    Elizabeth, 28, 39
    James, 31
    Jane, 31
    John, 31
    Mariana, 31
    Martha, 27, 31,
       40
    Mary, 31, 38
    Matthew, 31
    Nancy, 31
    Rebecca, 31
    Robert, 31
    Sarah, 31
    Thomas, 31
    William, 31
EWINGS, Jane, 5
EZWEILER, Cathr.
    Elizabeth, 77
    Georg, 77
    Maria, 77
EZWEYLER, Cathrina,
    80
    Georg, 80
    George, 84

-F-

FAHCLERN,
    Elisabeth, 58
FAHRNY, Jacob, 70
FAIRBAIRN,
    Alexander, 88
FAIRMAN, Willm.,
    100
FALKNER, Margaret,
    39
FANS, Cathrina, 84
FARHNER, Prudence,
    27
FASELER, George, 61
    Mistress, 59
FASELERN, Rosina,
    59
FAUST, Cathrina
    Fischbach, 61
    Philip, 50
FECHERT, George, 61
FEE, Patrick, 5
FEGER, Elisabeth,
    24, 63

Jacob, 24, 63
FEHLER, Andrew, 17
    Christian, 18
    Christina, 18
    Elizabeth, 17
    Jacob, 18
    Mary Elizabeth,
       18
    Nicholas, 17
    Susanna, 17
FEILE, Georg, 56
    Johannes, 56
    Sara, 56
FEININGER, Regina,
    58
FELTEN, Catharina,
    22
FENCK, Jacob, 52
    Johannes, 52
    Magdalena, 52
FENTON, Ann, 33
    James, 33
    John, 33
    Mary, 33
    Robert, 33
    Samuel, 33
FERBER, Bernhart,
    51
    Elisabeth, 51
    Maria Elisabeth,
       51
FERGUSON, George, 5
    Margaret, 5
    William, 28
FERTIG, Mary, 38
FESSLER, Catharina,
    63
    Jacob, 63
    Maria, 63
FETTER, Catharina,
    58
    Elisabeth, 58
    Jacob, 58
FICKLE, Mary, 96
FIELDS, Rebecca, 5
FINDLAY, Samuel, 27
FINDLEY, James, 81
    John, 117
    Martha, 82
    Mary, 82
FINEY, James, 93
    Thomas, 93
FINKENBEINER, Anna
    Mary, 18

Elisabeth, 18
John, 18
FINLEY, Charles, 86
  Elizabeth, 86
  George, 87, 89
  James, 88
  John, 07
  Robert, 88
  Samuel, 38
  Thomas, 88
FISCHER, Anna
  Maria, 75
  Cathar., 26
  Catharina, 52
  Cathrina, 75, 83
  Michael, 75
  Philip, 52
FISCUS, John, 84
FISH, Elizabeth, 5
FISHER, Catherine, 17
  Cathr. Elizabeth, 77
  Cathrina
    Margretha, 77
  Christly, 110
  Danial, 96
  Jane, 85
  Mary Ann, 85
  Mrs., 112
  Philip, 17, 77
  Tobias, 5
FLEMING, Andrew, 85
  James, 5, 38, 108
  Margreth, 84
  Mary, 81
  Nancy, 5
  Polley, 5
  Rebecca, 5, 115
  Susanna, 5, 112
FLEMMING, James, 114
  John, 98
  Mrs., 114
  Nancy, 109
  Sally, 5
  William, 109, 114
FLIN, Lillian M., 27
FLUKE, Sarah, 120
FOLK, Fredrick, 75
  Nb. John, 75
  Stephen, 95

FOLTZ, Cathr. Lis, 67
FORBES, Betsey, 5, 111
  James, 117, 118
  John, 118
FOREE, Henry, 22
FORNE, A. Maria, 69
  George, 69
FORNEY, Elisabeth, 70
  Georg, 70
  Margaretha, 70
FORSTER, Andrew, 82
  Friedrich, 76
  Gretha Barbara, 76
  Isabel, 85
  Mary, 83, 85
  Sarah, 84
  William, 85
FORSYTH, Isbel, 5
FORTUNE, Melchior, 86
FOSTER, Elizabeth, 5
  James, 5
FOULK, Stephen, 102, 106, 119
  Susannah, 106
FOULKE, Lewis, 5
FOWLER, Elizabeth, 31
  John, 31, 38
  Robert, 31, 97
FOX, John, 38
FRANK, Daniel, 21
  Dorothea, 21
  Johann Georg, 21
FRANKLIN, Anna
  Maria, 44
  Elisabeth, 44
FRAZER, Elizabeth, 79
  Emelia, 5
  Hugh, 79
  Isabella, 5
  John, 79
  Nancy, 5
FREAK, Jakobus, 48
  Johannes, 48
  Magdalena, 48
FRECK, Johannes, 49
  Magdalena, 49

Samuel, 49
FREISCH, Jakob, 49
  Johan, 49
  Maria, 49
FRENCH, Cathr., 60
  Hannah, 82
  Martha, 5, 33
  William, 5
FRESER, Heinrich, 73
FRESINGER,
  Margreth, 83
FRETZENINGER,
  Jacob, 58
  Magdalena, 58
  Rosina Elisabeth, 58
FREX, Elizabeth, 82
FREY, Abraham, 45
  Adam, 48
  Anna Christina, 45
  Anna Margaret, 50
  Anna Maria, 50
  Catharina, 49
  Cathrina, 74, 75
  Elisabeth, 44
  Elisabetha, 48
  Georg, 45, 75
  George, 48, 50, 74
  Jacob, 46, 48, 49, 50, 55
  Johann, 44
  Johannes, 46
  Magdalena, 78
  Margaretha, 45
  Peter, 48, 78
  Rudolph, 53
  Susanna, 45, 46, 48, 49, 50
FRIED, Jacobus, 47
  Johannes, 47
FRIEDERICH, Anna
  Maria, 46
  Loweina, 46
  Michael, 46
FRITZ, Adam, 46
  Georg, 45
  Louisa, 45
  Lowisa, 46
  Michael, 45, 46
FROHMAN, Paulus, 80
FROSCH, Jacob, 85

134 CUMBERLAND COUNTY CHURCH RECORDS OF THE 18TH CENTURY

FROTHER, Joseph, 38
FUCHS, Balthazar, 85
FUHR, Johannes, 81
FULLERTON, Adam, 40
  Alexander, 40
  Eliza, 5
  Isabel, 27
  James, 40
  Thomas, 96
  Thomas E., 27
  Thomas Elder, 38
FULTON, Elizabeth, 97, 101
  Katharine, 40
FUNK, Samuel, 5
FUTHY, Benjamin, 100

-G-
GABBY, William, 5
GAILLY, Sarah, 38
GALASPE, William, 59
GALBRAITH, Eleo, 31
  Joseph, 101
GALBREATH, Andrew, 115
  Jane, 115
  Rebecca, 5
  Robert, 101
  Sam, 5
GALE, Anthony, 117
GALLACHER,
  Margreth, 81, 82
GALLAGHLY, Willm., 82
GALLESPIE, Ann, 33
  Elizabeth, 33
  Martha, 33
  Mary, 33
  Millie, 33
  Nancy, 33
  Nathaniel, 33
  Nelly, 33
  Robert, 33
  Samuel, 33
  William, 33
GALLIDEE,
  Elizabeth, 77
  Johannes, 77
  Joseph, 77
  Magdalena, 78
  Susanna, 77

Sybilla, 77
GALLIFORD, Jennet, 83
GALLIFORTH, Jane, 82
  Sarah, 84
GAMBLE, Anne, 38
  Elizabeth, 5
GARDNER, Ann, 85
  Hannah, 82
  James, 91
  Jo., 91
  John, 94
  Margaret, 94
GARNER, Elizabeth, 92
  Jo., 92
  John, 92
  Polle, 60
GARROLL, Catharina, 51
  Johann, 51
  Johann Jacob, 51
GASKINS, Mary, 95
GASS, James, 5
GAW, John, 5
GAY, Ann, 92
  Mary, 88
  Sam, 92
GEACH, Ann, 5
GEBFORD, Abraham, 18
  Mary Catharine, 18
GEBSER, Johann, 50
GEDDES, John, 38, 50, 109
  James, 38
GEES, Elizabeth, 40
GEHR, Anna Maria, 60
  Joseph, 60
GEIB, Franz, 85
GEIGESON, Maria Judith, 66
GEIGLE, Anna Judith, 56
  Catharina, 56
  Georg Jacob, 56
  John Jacob, 56
  Sara, 56
GEITLINGER,
  Barbara, 86
GELILAN, Robert, 82

GELTEN, Catharina, 49
  Salome, 49
  Wilhelm, 49
GENSMER, George, 20
  John, 20
GEORG, Adam, 78
  Barbara, 19
  Cathrina, 78
  John Jacob, 19
  Magdalena, 78
  Martinus, 19
  Matheus, 78
  Sophia, 78
GEORGE, Joshua, 103
  Martin, 19
  Nancy, 5
  Thomas, 59
GERDY, Thomas, 83
GERISTEN, Catarina, 58
GEST, Anna, 5
GIBB, Jane, 99
GIBBON, John, 5
GIBSON, Ann, 94
  Elizabeth, 5
  George, 95
  Jane, 5
  Margaret, 93
  Martha, 29, 108
  Patrick, 29
  Robert, 93, 101, 114
GIESE, Johannes, 53
GIESEMAN,
  Catharina, 44
  Georg, 44
  Johannes, 44
GIESENER, Wilhelm, 48
GIESS, Conrad, 18
  Mary Catharine, 18
GIFFAN, And., 94
  John, 91
GIFFE, Eleanor, 91
GIFFEN, Agnes, 91
  And., 92
  Gennet, 5
  James, 5
  John, 91
  William, 92
GIFFIN, Betsy, 28
  Elenor, 28

INDEX

Sally, 28
William, 28
GILLBREATH, Andrew, 81
GILLESPIE, David, 38
 Elleanor, 29
 George, 5, 29
 James, 29
 Jane, 29
 Mat. M., 29
 Nancy, 40
 William, 29, 96
GILLMOR, Margaret, 5
GILLPATRICK, Ann, 81
GILMORE, ---, 100
 John, 28, 96
GILSON, Betsy, 106
 William, 106
GIVEN, James, 5
 Jospeh, 106
GADNEY, William, 5
GLATEISS, Cath., 54
GLEN, Alexander, 30
 David, 37
 Elizabeth, 30
 Gabriel, 28
 James, 91
 Jane, 28, 103
 Jean, 92
 Jenny, 28
 John, 30
 Mary, 37
 Rebecca, 91
 Samuel, 82
 Thomas, 30
 William, 28, 91
GLENDENNING, James, 38
GLENDINING, John, 91
 Katharine, 92
 Sam, 91
GLENN, Alexander, 38
 Ann, 96
 John, 5
 Thomas, 99
GOBBINS, William, 84
GODDRIE, Lisabeth, 59

GODFREY, Hannah, 118
 William, 118
GODSHAL, Andreas, 80
 Anna Barbara, 80
GOLANDER, Anna Maria, 58
 Catharina, 58
 Jo. Christian, 58
GOLD, Joseph, 5
GOLDENBERGER, Anna, 80
 Cathrina, 80
 Johannes, 80, 83
 John, 80
 Samuel, 80
GOLDSTETT, Mary Cathrina, 84
GOODLING, Anna Margaretha, 71, 72
 Jacob, 71, 72
 John Michael, 72
 Ludwig David, 71
 Samuel, 30
GOORLEY, Sarah, 6
GOPOCK, Robert M., 36
GORDON, Alexander, 109, 110
 Alice, 85
 Ann, 6, 97
 Jane, 30
 Jean, 6
 Mary, 110
GORDRICK, Samuel, 45
GORLY, James, 29
GORMAN, Samuel, 84
GORREL, Isabella, 35
 John, 35
GOSSLER, Capt., 118
GOTTHRIE, Jean, 57
 Prudentia Ellis, 57
 Sarah, 57
GOTTSHALL, Johann, 67
 Nic., 67
GOUDY, Agnes, 82
GOURD, Joseph, 31
 Margaret, 31

GOURLEY, Samuel, 6
GRABER, Anna Maria, 48
 Jacob, 48
 Philip, 85
GRAFF, Elizabeth, 85
 Eva, 75
 Jacob, 75
 Maria Dorothea, 75
GRAHAM, Agness, 6
 Arthur, 28, 38
 Elijah, 93
 Francis, 38
 Isaiah, 28, 38
 James, 28
 Jane, 6
 Jared, 28
 Jenny, 28
 John, 93
 Margaret, 6
 Martha, 38
 Susannah, 28
 Thomas, 28
 William, 82, 98
GRAHAMS, Agnes, 82
 Eleonora, 83
 James, 93
 Mary, 85, 86
GRAMLICH,
 Elisabeth, 21
 Eva, 21
 Friedrich, 21
 Magdelena, 21
GRAY, Jean, 106
 Katharine, 30
 Samuel, 6,114
GRAYSON, Jean, 6
 William, 6
GRAYTON, Isabel, 81
GREEN, Adam, 6
 John, 29, 38
 Mary, 6
GREER, John, 87
 Margt., 99
 Patrick, 6
 Polly, 117
 Thomas, 87
 William, 6
GREGG, Agnes, 6
 Charles, 6, 109, 111
 Elizabeth, 6

Jane, 6
John, 119
Margary, 119
Matthew, 104
GREGORY, Elizabeth,
  6
James, 96
GREIN, Catharina,
  44
GREINER, Adam, 76
  Cathrina, 76
GREIST, Catharina,
  50
  David, 50
  Johannes, 50
GREMPELMAN,
  Dorothea, 83
GRESHAM, Georg
  Paulus, 72
  Magdalena, 72
GREWASS, Sebastian,
  84
GRIEL, Christina,
  65
  Johannes, 65
  Maria Elisabetha,
  65
GRIER, Isaac, 100
  Jane, 30
  Jenny, 6
  Polly, 6
  Sally, 36
  Thomas, 30
GRIFFIN, Mary, 6
GROFF, Eva, 75
  Jacob, 75
GROJEAN, Jacob, 79,
  82
  Mary Magdalene,
  79
  Sayusannah, 79
GROSS, Cathrina, 75
  Georg, 75
GRUBER, Peter, 52
  Susanna, 52
GRUENEWALTER,
  Catharina, 22
  Maria, 22
GRUNEWALD,
  Elisabeth, 45
  Eva, 45
  Heinrich, 45
GUERIE, Elisabeth,
  66

Jean, 66
Maria, 66
GUILILAND, Mary, 93
GUMP, Dorothea, 84
GUNCKEL, Elisabeth,
  66
  Johannes, 66
GUNTHER, Rebecca,
  77
GUSTAIN, Dr., 106
  Sally, 106
GUSTIN, Lemuel, 96
  Sally, 6
GUTHRIE, Elizabeth,
  82
  Polley, 6

-H-
H---, Moses, 99
HAAG, Apollonia, 69
  Magdalena
  Philippin, 69
  Michael, 69
HAAPEGER, Cathrina,
  80
  Joh. Nicklas, 80
HAAS, Jacob, 25
HABACHER, Anna
  Margreth, 73
  Joh. Georg, 73
HABACKER, Georg, 83
HABERLANDER,
  Louise, 57
HACHMEISTER, Carl
  Ludwig, 61
  Catharina, 68
  Darf, 68
  Elis., 68
  Elisabet, 68
  Ludwig Carl, 68
HACK, Apelonia, 65
  Apollonia, 65
  Michael, 65
HADDEN, Thomas, 38
HAG, Apelonia, 65
  Michael, 65
HAGER, Cathrina, 78
  Johannes, 78
  Philip, 78
HAGERTY, Nancy, 6
HAGG, John Michael,
  72
  Michael, 72
HAGGAN, John, 120

Susanna, 120
HAGUE, Elizabeth, 6
HAIL, Daniel, 92
  Hugh, 92
HAINS, Aaron, 36
  Barth., 93
  David, 93
HALBERT, Joseph, 30
HALKETT, Elinor,
  120
  John, 120
  William, 120
HALL, Isabella, 6,
  32
  James, 6, 29, 104
HAMAN, Elisabeth,
  49
  Johann Jacob, 49
  Lorentz, 50
  Margaretha, 50
  Martin, 49, 50
HAMERSLY, Robert,
  101
HAMILTON, Ann, 83
  George, 6, 32,
  87, 88, 108
  James, 32, 81
  John, 95
  Margaret, 92
  Martha, 87, 88
  Robert, 91, 115
  Ruth, 32
HAMMON, Jacob, 54
  Johann Jacob, 53
  Martin, 52, 53,
  54
  Phillip, 52, 53,
  54
HAMMSCHIER,
  Johannes, 47
  Leonhart, 47
  Maria Catharina,
  47
HAMSCHER, Ann
  Margaret, 50
  Bernhart, 50
  Catharina, 50
HAMSHIER,
  Catharina, 49
  Leonhardt, 49
  Maria Catharina,
  49
HAMUTH, Anna
  Margaretha, 71

Anna Margretha,
73
Jacob, 58
Johanes, 72, 81
Johannes, 71, 72,
73
Margaretha, 72
Margreth, 50
HANAH, Archibold,
85
HANDELS, Elisabeth,
54
HANES, Elizabeth,
100
HANNA, Elisabeth,
100
James, 38
John, 115
Lydia, 39
Margaret, 99
William, 35, 37
HANNAH, Isabella,
113
HANSECKER,
Catharina, 67
HARBRID, Ebenezer,
60
HARDY, Catharine, 6
William, 6
HARGUS, Christy,
81, 86
Mary, 81
HARKNESS, David, 84
HARLEY, Ester, 82
HARMAN, Anna
Margaretha, 46
Catharina, 65
Johannes, 65
Margaretha, 46
Martin, 46, 65
HARPER, Barbara, 39
Margaret, 31, 37
Nancy, 39
William, 38
HARRELL, Clement,
101
HARRI, Nancy O., 60
HARRIBEL,
Elizabeth, 82
HARRIS, David, 6,
115
Howel, 120
Rachel, 120
J. Adam, 26

HART, John, 59
Matthew, 6
HARTEL, Micha, 52
Susanna, 52
HARTEN, Magdalene,
59
HARTLEY, Eleanor,
104
Major Gen., 119
Thomas, 104
HARWICH, James, 60
HARWICK, Elizabeth,
6
HASLET, William,
112
HASSON, Samuel, 6
HATERINGTON, John,
95
HATTEN, Johannes,
49
Juliann, 49
HAUG, Anna Hag, 42
Anna Margaretha,
42
Johannes, 42
HAUN, Anna, 46
Johannes, 46
HAUPT, Anna Maria,
44
Valentin, 44, 48
HAUSER, Anna
Barbara, 18
Eva, 17
John, 17
Mary, 17
HAUSKNECHT,
Magdalena, 53
HAUTZ, Rev., 116
HAUZER, Anna Maria,
48
Valentin, 48
HAUZZERT, Anna
Maria, 47
Valentin, 47
HAWKES, John, 38
HAWKS, Mary, 40
HAWTHORNE, James,
29
Margaret, 29
Samuel, 29
HAY, Samuel, 6
HAYES, Joseph, 6
Margaret, 6
Mary, 6

HAYS, Adam, 29, 120
Anne, 29
Charity, 120
Henry, 120
Joseph, 29, 97
HAZLEWOOD, Richard,
109
HEAK, Susannah, 96
HEAP, John, 111
Margaret, 111
HECK, Jacob, 62
Johannes, 25, 64
Maria, 62
Maria Barbara, 62
HECKEDORN, David,
47, 48
Elisabet, 48
Elisabeth, 47
HECKMAN, Anna
Maria, 19
John George, 20
John Philip, 19
Maria Magdalena,
19
Philip, 20
HEDSON, Joseph, 60
HEHN, Johannes, 53
Peter, Jr., 53
HEIL, Anna Maria,
51
Johann, 51
HEILMAN, Binna
Maria, 41
George, 41
Johann Georg, 41
HEIN, Heinrich, 84
HEIT, Jacob, 23
Maria, 23
Maria Barbara, 23
HELD, Georg, 76
Joh. Georg, 76
Magdalena, 76
HELL, Barbara, 19
Nicholas, 19
HELLMAN, Christina,
78
Georg, 78
HELM, Christina,
43, 45
Jacob, 43, 45, 49
Rosina, 49
Susanna, 49
HELWICK, Dorothy,
96

HEMKEN, Magdalena, 58
HEMMIG, John, 85
HEMMING, Richard, 119
HEMPHILL, James, 38
HENDERSON,
　Elizabeth, 99
　Gustavus, 88
　Margt., 100
HENDRICKS, Mary, 101
　William, 101
HENRICH, Eva Maria, 17
　John, 17
HENRY, Abraham, 18
　Anna Mary, 17
　Elisabeth, 18, 60
　Elizabeth, 87, 88
　Eva, 17
　Eva Margaret, 18
　John, 17, 87, 88
　Robert, 87, 89
　Susanna, 18
HERAFF, Jacob, 19
HERAN, Martha, 84
HERAUFF, Andreas, 76
　Antony, 76
　Maria Elisabeth, 76
HERAUG, Catharine, 19
　George, 19
　Jacob, 19
HERB, Ana Maria, 50
　Anna, 50
　Johannes, 50
HERBICH, Anna Maria, 71
　Antony, 84
HERBST, John, 17
　Rev., 112
HERGESHEIMER,
　Michael, 71
HERMAN, Cathrina, 78
　Christian, 68
　Christina, 77, 78
　Elisabeth, 68
　Johannes, 68, 77
　John, 77, 78
　Martin, 68

Mary Elizabeth, 78
HERMANN, Anna Maria, 69
　Catharina, 69, 70
　Christian, 69
　Dorothea, 69
　Elisabeth, 69
　Jacob, 69
　Joh., 69
　Martin, 69, 70
　Salome, 69
HERN, Anna Maria, 52
　Jacobus, 52
　John, 52
HERON, Eleanor, 91
HERPOUCH, Anna
　Dorothea, 44
　Johannes, 44
HERR, David, 106
　Mrs., 106
HERRAT, Bathsheba, 99
HERRAUF, Catharina
　Elisabeth, 56
　Catrina, 56
　Jacob, 56
HERREN, Reuben, 6
HERRING, Mary, 82
HERRON, David, 6, 87, 89, 95
　Francis, 119
　Robert, 6
　William, 85
HERSCHMAN,
　Elisabeth, 51
　Elisabetha, 51
　Johannes, 51
HERTINER, Johannes, 42
HERTZ, Adam, 24, 63
　Johannes, 24, 63
　Maria, 24, 63
HERZELLER, Anna
　Margretha, 81
HERZOG, Anna
　Elizabeth, 78
　Georg, 78
　Judith, 78
HEWES, Caleb, 6
HEYSER, Anna
　Barbara, 73
　Johannes, 73

Thomas, 73
HICKERNEL, Phil., 25, 64
HICKINS, Judith, 82
HIER, Anne, 99
HILD, Anna
　Elisabeth, 44
HILDEBRAND,
　Stephen, 84
HILL, Henry, 118
　Isabell, 84
　Jane, 99
HILLMAN, Christian, 70
　Elisabeth, 70
　Polly, 86
　Salome, 70
HILTON, Jean, 93
　John, 93
HIRSCHMAN, Elijah, 47
　Elizabeth, 52
　Johann Georg
　Gell, 47
　Johannes, 47, 52
　Michael, 52
HIRSCHMANN,
　Catharina, 48
　Elisabet, 48
　Johannes, 48
HOB, Cassber, 21
　Johan Cassber, 21
HOBLING, Abraham, 55
HOCH, Christian, 51
　Christina, 85
　Elisabeth, 21
　Johann Adam, 51
　Johannes, 21
　Maria, 51
　Phillip, 21
HOCK, Barbara, 56
　Christian, 56
HODGE, Agnes, 34
　Hester, 86
　John, 34
　Margaret, 94
　Sam, 94
　Sarah, 84
HOEKIN, Mrs. S., 60
HOFACK, John, 104
HOFELMAN, Arnold, 24
　Eva, 24

INDEX

Johan Georg, 24
HOFELMANN, Arnold, 63
  Eva, 63
  Johann Georg, 63
HOFF, John, 116
HOFFER, Isaac, 6
  Melchor, 6
HOFFMAN, Adam, 73
  Anna Maria, 73
HOGE, David, 106, 117
  Isabel, 105
  Isabella, 115
  James Read, 6
  Jean, 106
  Jonathan, 105, 115, 117
  Thomas, 115
  William, 6
HOGG, John, 113
  Martha, 6
  Thomas, 6
HOGUE, Serah, 112
HOHN, Anna, 47
  Johannes, 45, 47, 48
  Juliann, 48
  Susanna, 45
HOLCHAM, Hannah, 6, 112
HOLD, Catharina, 47
  Elisabet, 48
  Elizabeth, 47
  Thomas, 47, 48
HOLL, Anna, 20
  John, 20
  Mary, 86
HOLLAN, Hugh, 85
HOLLING, William, 118
HOLMES, Abraham, 6, 102
  Agness, 6
  Ann, 107
  Betsey, 7, 115
  Daniel, 7
  George, 38
  Isaac, 7
  Jane, 103
  Jenny, 7
  John, 7, 103, 107
  Jonathan, 7
  Mary, 112

Nancy, 7, 115
  Polly, 7
  Samuel, 101, 102
  Thomas, 115
HOLT, Thomas, 101
HOLTZAPFEL, Adam, 58
  Jacob, 58
  Maria, 57
HOLTZINGER,
  Benjamin, 47
  Elisabeth, 47
  Simon, 47
HOLTZOPPEL, Peggy, 7
HOLZAPFEL, Adam, 56
  Johannes, 58
  Lydia, 56
  Margretha, 56
  Mr., 58
HOMES, Nancy, 31
HON, Philip, 20
  Valentine, 20
HOOD, Jane, 96
HOOK, Cathrina, 76
  Margreth, 76
  Michael, 76
  Rebecca, 76
HOOP, Adam, 89
  Maria Magdalena, 58
HOUK, Adam, 7
HOUSEMAN, Barbara, 72
  C.J., 72
  Georg Jacob, 72
  George Jacob, 73
  Maria Apollonia, 72, 73
  Maria Appollonia, 72
  S.I., 72
HOUSTON, Isabel, 37
  James, 30, 37
  Robert, 37
HOUTZ, Anna Catharina, 43
  Anna Catherina, 44
  Johann Wilhelm, 44
  Lorentz, 43, 44
HOWSTON, Agnes, 93
  James, 93

Rebecca, 93
HUBER, Anna Elisabeth, 17
  Anna Elizabeth, 72, 73
  Christina, 72
  Daniel, 17
  Frederick, 17
  John Conrad, 73
  Leonard, 72
  Magdelena, 17
  Maria Appollonia, 72
  Martin, 72, 73
HUBERN, Polle, 59
HUEPHLER, Johannes, 21
HUFFMAN, Christina, 47
  Peter, 47
HUFFNAGLE, Michl., 96
HUGHES, Betsey, 7, 118
  John, 118
HUGHS, Thomas, 38
HUHN, Betty, 17
  Christopher, 17
  Mary, 17
HUMEL, Friedrich, 76
  Rosina, 76
HUMELDORF, Daniel, 25
  Eva, 25
HUNEBERGER,
  Catharina, 45
  Heinrich, 45
HUNT, Letitia, 7
HUNTER, ---, 37
  Agnes, 28
  Eliz., 85
  Elizabeth, 31
  Genny, 7
  James, 28
  Jane, 27
  John, 84
  Lathie, 28
  Mary, 7, 57
  Robert, 7
  Sally, 39
  Sam., 57
  Samuel, 57, 59
  Thomas, 7, 83

William, 7, 27,
  31, 85
HURLBUTT, William,
  96
HUSTON, Andrew, 7,
  30
  Elizabeth, 7
  Isabel, 83
  Jane, 30
  John, 30, 38
  Margaret, 38, 102
  Martha, 29
  Nancy, 29
  Peggy, 29
  Robert, 29, 38,
    101
  Sarah, 30
HUTCHESON,
  Benjamin, 99
  James, 101
HUTCHINSON,
  Francis, 7
HUTCHISON,
  Elizabeth, 7
  Martha, 35
  Mary, 34
  Nancy, 34
  Robert, 34
  Rosannah, 35
HUTLASS, John, 82
HUTTON, Agnas, 87

-I-
IHLE, Andreas, 50,
  51
  Barbara, 46
  Catharina, 51
  Elisabeth, 50, 51
  Georg, 46
  Johannes, 46
  Maria, 50
IHLY, Christina, 44
ILY, Barbara, 25,
  64
  Hanna, 25, 64
IMMEL, Johannes, 78
IMMMEL, John, 79
IRISH, Ann, 96
IRWIN, Agnes, 30
  Catharine, 7
  Eleanor, 35
  Isabel, 35
  James, 35, 104
  John, 35, 107

Mary, 7, 35
Polley (Polly),
  7, 104
ISETT, Henry, 7
ISSET, John, 7

-J-
JACK, Andrew, 36
  Cynthia, 36, 38
  Hannah, 36
  James, 36, 99
  Jane, 36
  Patrick, 82
  Samuel, 84
  William, 89
JACKSON, Samuel, 7,
  109
JACOB, Elenor, 28
  Elizabeth, 28
  Mary, 28, 38
  Thomas, 34
JACOBS, Garman, 35
  Jerman, 116
  Katherine, 35
JACOBY, Elisabeth,
  18
  Peter, 18
  Regina, 18
JAIG, Eva, 24, 63
  Johanes, 24, 63
  Magdalena, 24, 63
JAKE, James, 88
  John, 88
  Willm., 87, 89
JAMES, Mary, 82
JAMESON, Francis, 7
  Hannah, 7
  Rachel, 7
JAQUIN, Cathrina,
  75
  Georg Philip, 75
JEFFRIES, Thomas,
  101
JIST, Christopher,
  60
JISTLER, Christina,
  75
  Jacob, 75
JOAP, Jo., 57
  Johannes, 57
  Magdalena, 57
JOHN, Anna Maria,
  25, 64
  David, 25, 64

Elisabeth, 24, 63
Emrick, 24
Enick, 63
Henrich, 25, 64
Margaretha, 25,
  64
Mary, 24, 63
Willhelm, 25, 64
JOHNSON, ---, 37
  Agnes, 100
  Andrew, 38
  Betsy, 32
  Elizabeth, 38
  Esther, 7
  James, 29, 99
  Jean, 37
  Jenny, 29
  Margaret, 27, 37
  Martha, 29
  Mary, 37
  Peggy, 29
  Robert, 27
  Samuel, 101
  Thomas, 37
JOHNSTON, Adam, 7
  Alexander, 29, 38
  Ann, 31
  Elizabeth, 7
  George, 7
  James, 27
  Jane, 29
  John, 7, 29, 84,
    96
  Margaret, 7, 95
  Mary, 29
  Miss, 111
  Robert, 31
  Salley, 7
  Samuel, 7
JONES, Abraham, 82
  Benjamin, 7
  Hugh, 38
  James, 38
  Thomas, 112
JORDAN, John, 117
JORDY, Jacob, 85
JOTTI, Hinr., 60
  John, 60
JOURDAN, Elizabeth,
  7
JUMANS, John, 17
  Joseph, 17
  Sally, 17
JUMPER, Jean, 7

JUNG, Philip, Jr.,
    45
JUNGEN, Magdalena,
    60
JUNGST, Ana
    Cathar., 24
    Catharina, 24, 63
    Christina, 24, 63
    Henrich, 24, 63
    Peter, 24, 63
JUNKEN, Agnes, 91
    Benjamin, 92
    John, 92
    Joseph, 91, 92
JUNKENS, Eliz., 93
JUNKIN, Elizabeth,
    117
    Joseph, 117

-K-
KAISER, Barbara, 42
    Catharina, 43, 46
    Jacob, 43, 46
    Johannes, 42
    Maria Margaretha,
    53
KAKET, Elisabeth,
    57
KAPP, Catharina, 48
    Conrad, 48
    Elisabet, 48
    Johannes, 48
KAPPENHEIMER,
    Benjamin, 49
    Elisabeth, 49
KARCHER, Anna
    Catharina, 44
    Michael, 44
KARR, Andrew, 60
KAST, Anna
    Catarina, 68
    Anna Cath., 66
    Anna Catharina,
    66, 69
    Anna Margareth,
    72
    Anna Maria, 69
    Georg, 72
    Jacob, 66, 68
    Joh. Jac., 69
    John Philip, 72
KATZ, Elisab., 54
    Margaretha, 46
    Peter, 46

KAUFFMAN, Fridrich,
    86
KAUFMAN, Catharina,
    41
    Elizabetha, 41
    Friedrich, 41
    Henrich, 49
    Isaac, 41
    Jacob, 41
    Johannes, 41
    Magdalena, 41
    Margaretha, 41
    Salomea, 41
KAUP, Anna Maria,
    57
    Maria, 57
    William, 57
KAYSER, Adam, 46
    Catharina, 44, 45
    Jacob, 44, 45, 53
    Johannes, 46
    Sara, 46
KEARNS, John, 84
KEEN, John, 97
KEENER, Adam, 85
KEEPERS, Stephen, 7
KEHRBACH, Anna
    Dorothea, 47
    Johannes, 47
KEILLER, Johannes,
    42
KEITH, Willm., 89
KELKER, Luther R.,
    81
KELLER, A.
    Christina, 68
    Anna Christina,
    69
    Anna Maria, 56,
    69, 83
    Antoni, 75
    Barbara, 75
    Bernhard, 56
    Catharina, 56
    Catherina, 56
    Elizabeth, 78
    Heinrich, 69
    Hinr., 67
    J. Henr., 68
    Jacob, 56, 113
    Johann Jacob, 67
    Leon, 56
    Willhelm, 68

KELLEYAH, Lawrenz,
    84
KELLSAY, William,
    82
KELLY, Ann, 30
    Archibald, 7
    Christian, 30
    Daniel, 30
    Elizabeth, 30
    George, 100
    Grace, 7
    James, 39, 81
    Margaret, 39
    Mary, 81
    Richard, 30
    Samuel, 8
    William, 30
KELS, Elisabeth
    Kun., 67
KELSO, William, 8,
    107
KELSY, Elizabeth,
    29
    George, 29
    Jane, 29
KENEDY, Christian,
    120
    James, 120
    Rebekah, 120
    Thomas Eliot, 8
KENNEDY, Ann, 36
    Anna, 111
    David, 99
    Hannah, 96
    Harris, 8
    Jane, 39
    Jesse, 8
    John, 38
    Juniata, 99
    Mary, 96
    Nancy, 84
    Prudence, 100
    Robert, 111
    Rose, 85
    Thomas, 93
KENNY, Eleanor, 8
    Robert, 8, 111
KER, William, 38
KERBACH, Anna
    Dorothea, 43
    Johann Peter, 43
    Johannes, 43
KERK, Moses, 83
KERLE, Bille, 58

Elisabeth, 58
KERN, Anna Maria, 20
  Elizabeth, 20
  Henry, 20
  Jacob, 79
  Salome, 20
KERNS, Nancy, 69
  Richard, 69
  Robert, 69
KERPACH, Anna
  Dorothea, 53
  Johannes, 52, 53, 54
KERR, Joseph, 108
  Matthew, 39
  Robert, 89
KERREN, Jean, 60
KERY, John, 70
  Maria, 70
  Philip Evans, 70
KETCH, James, 75
  Susanna, 75
KETTERING, Jacob, 77
KEYL, Anna
  Elisabeth, 71
  Elizabeth, 78
  Heinrich, 78
  Johan Philip
  Ludwig, 71
  John Georg, 78
  John Henry, 71
KIDD, ---, 8
  David, 87
KIEBLER, Anna
  Maria, 57
  Georg, 57
KIEFER, Adam, 58, 68, 69, 70
  Anna Maria, 57
  Elisabeth, 58, 68, 69
  Greta, 57
  Johann George, 58
  Johannes, 69
  Magdalena, 50, 51
  Marg., 58
  Margaretha, 61
  Martin, 68
  Peter, 50, 51
  Salome, 69
KIEFFER, Elizabeth
  C., 41

KIEMMEL, Elizabeth, 22
KIESECKER, Cath., 64
KILGORE, Charles, 91
  David, 8
  Elizabeth, 8, 40
  Isabel, 40
  Jesse, 8, 40, 91, 100
  Jonathan, 27
  Robert, 39, 40
  Ruth, 27
  William, 40
KILGOUR, Charles, 93
  Esther, 93
KILLGORE, ---, 100
KILLINGER, Andrew, 76
  Anna, 76
  Anna Margreth, 66
  Joh. Jacob, 76
KILLOUGH, John, 87
KINGRICH, Ann, 85
KINKEAD, John, 8, 98
  Mary, 98
KINTZLE,
  Elisabetha, 43
  Jacob, 43
KINZLER, Cathrina, 84
KIRCHER, Eva, 46
  Johann Peter, 50
  Magdalena, 50
  Michael, 46
  Peter, 50
KIRCHERTNER, Eva, 54
  Michael, 54
KIRK, Mary, 8
KIRKENLUBER,
  George, 8
KIRKPATRICK, Ann, 120
  Elizabeth, 39
  Hannah, 120
  Hugh, 35
  Isaac, 120
  James, 39, 82
  Martha Maria, 120
  Miss, 34

Moses, 100
Richard, 120
Robert, 120
Samuel, 100
KIRPATRICK, John, 96
KISECKER, Anna
  Margaretha, 25
  Elisabeth, 25, 64
  Nicolaus, 25, 64
KISTLER, Christina, 75
  Jacob, 75
  Johannes, 75
  John, 83
  Magd., 79
  Magdalena, 84
  Mary Magdalena, 82
KISTNER, Anna
  Maria, 72
  Johan Heinrich, 72
  John Georg, 72
  Maria, 84
KITZMULLER,
  Elisabeth, 69
KITZSCH, Martin, 70
KLEIN, Catharina, 56
  Conrad, 19
  Georg, 56
KLEINHOOF, Mary, 107
KLENCK, Anna, 68
  Georg, 68
  Jo. Georg, 68
KLEPPINGER, Anna
  Margaretha, 46, 47, 54, 55
  Antonio, 55
  Antony, 54
  Henrich, 54
  Johannes, 46, 47
  John, 52
  Marga., 52
  Margaretha, 47
KLINDENNER,
  William, 60
KLINE, Johanna
  Maria, 8
KLIPPENGER, Anna
  Margaretha, 51
  Anna Maria, 51

INDEX 143

Anton, 51
KNETTLE, Catharine, 17
George, 17
KNITTLE, Henry, 8
KNOCHEN, Andreas, 69
Joh., 69
Margaretha, 69
KNOX, Mr., 118
KNUPPEL, Anna Maria, 58
K'NUSEN, Janne, 60
KOBER, Eva, 25, 64
Georg, 25, 64
Johannes, 25, 64
Sarah, 25, 64
KOCH, Anna Maria, 23, 62, 77, 78
Cathrina, 85
Christian, 78
Elisabeth, 25, 64
Elisabett, 25
George Adam, 77, 78
George Jacob, 73
Heinrich, 73
Jacob, 78
Joh. Georg, 77
Johan Georg, 85
Johannes, 25, 64
Joseph, 23, 62
Philip, 25, 64
Rebecca, 73
Susana, 23, 62
KOENIG, John, 20
Maria Charlotta, 20
Samuel, 20
KOFINE, Jane, 82
KOHLMANN, Margreth, 59
KOKEN, Barbara, 17
Elizabeth, 17
John, 17
KOLB, Fiana, 20
George, 19
Margaret, 19
Simon, 19
KOPPENHAFFER,
Annamari, 50
Benjamin, 50
Elisabeth, 50

KOPPENHEFFER,
Benjamin, 51
Elisabeth, 51
Jacob, 51
KOPT, Catharina, 49
Conrad, 49
KOREY, Abraham, 86
KOWEL, Benj., 59
Elizabeth, 43, 59
KRABER, Anna Maria, 56
Eva, 56
Jacob, 56
Johannes, 56
Maria, 56
KRAFFT, Anna Maria, 75
Catharina, 52
Esther, 52
Feronica, 84
Fred., 78
Georg, 52
Joh. Philip, 75
Johann, 52
John, 52
Philip, 75, 83
KRAFT, Catharina, 47
Johannes, 47
Mary, 60
KRAHL, Catharina, 51
Nicolas, 51
Samuel, 51
KRAMER, Georg, 55
Jacob, 54
Johannes, 48
Magdalena, 46
Maria, 48, 49, 50, 52
Peter, 46, 48, 49, 50, 52, 55
Sara, 52
KRAUS, Anna Maria, 56
Jacob, 56
Johannes, 71
Margaretha, 71
KRAUSS, Elisabeth, 44
KREEL, Catharina, 67
Maria Catharina, 67

Nic., 67
KREISCH, Jacob, 54
KREISCHNER,
Catharina, 54
Jacob, 54
KREITZER, Adam, 22
Catharina, 22
Elisabeth, 62
Elizabeth, 22
Joh. Nicolaus, 62
Johan Nicolaus, 22
Juliana, 22
Nicolas, 22
KRESSLER,
Catharina, 54
Georg, 51
George, 54
Susanna, 51
KRESSNER,
Christina, 54
Philip, 54
KRETSCHMAN,
Godfried, 74
Sophia, 74
KRIEGER, Abraham, 66
Anna Catharina, 66
Elizabeth, 76
Jacob, 76
Maria Judith, 66
KROLL, Catharina, 46
Johannes, 46
KROP, Samuel, 116
KUBLER, Georg, 56
Johannes, 56
Maria, 56
KUHN, Benjamin, 42
Johann Georg, 50
Maria Katharin, 50
Maria Magdalena, 50
Sabina, 95
KUHUN, Catharina, 41
Johann Benjamin, 41
Maria Elisabetha, 41
KUKKEN, Johann, 50
Julianna, 50

Susanna
  Elisabetha, 50
KUNCKEL, Anne
  Maria, 73
  Johan Christoph,
    73
  Michael, 73
  Susanna, 44
KUNCKELN,
  Elisabeth, 67
KUNCKLE, Anna
  Maria, 71
  Johannes, 71
  Michael, 71
KUNETHET,
  Elisabeth, 67
KUNIG, Ester, 85
KUNTZ, Heinrich, 86
KUNTZE, Elizabeth,
    22
  Isaac, 22
  Margarita, 22
KUNTZLER, Jacob, 44
  Johann Georg, 44
KUSSER, Ann, 74
  Anna Maria, 74
  Peter, 74
KYLE, Thomas, 96

-L-
LA FERRE, ---, 57
LA FORGE, John, 71
  Mary, 71
  Mathias, 71
LACHNER, J. Mathys,
    73
  Johan Adam, 73
  Maria Eva, 73
LACKEY, John, 88
  Robert, 8
LAFERTY, John, 92
LAHMERT, Cathrina,
    66
  Jacob, 66
  Johannes, 66
LAIN, Margr., 60
LAIRD, ---, 95
  James, 30
  Jane, 8, 30
  Martha, 8
  Samuel, 89, 98
LAMB, Jane, 8
  Marg't., 96
  Mary, 8

LAMBERT, Mary
  Magd., 76
LAMBERTON, James,
    108
LAND, Elizabeth, 78
LANDI, George, 54
LANE, John, 8
LANG, Cathrina, 78
  Christina, 23, 62
  Dorothea, 83
  Elizabeth, 79
  Friedreich, 23,
    62
  J. Georg, 78
  John Adam, 78
LANGDORFFIN, Anna,
    68
LANGE, Anna
  Christina, 58
  Nic., 58
LANGSDORF, Anna
  Margred, 68
  Anna Margretha,
    65
  Anna Maria, 65
  Elisabeth, 65
  Georg, 69
  Henrich, 65
  Johan Adam, 68
  Johann Martin, 65
  Margaretha, 69
  Margretha, 68
  Marthin, 68
  Martin, 65, 68,
    69
  Michael, 68
  Phillip, 65
LANGSDORFF (See
  also
  Langdorffin,
  Adam, 66
  Anna Maria, 66
  Chatharina, 66
  Elisabeth, 66, 70
  Henrich, 66
  Margaretha, 66
LANGSDORFIN, Anna
  Margaretha, 65
LANGSTAFF, Adam, 67
  Anna Maria, 67
  Elisabeth, 67
  Henr., 70
LANSDORF, Anna, 65
  Elizabeth, 72

Joh. Heinrich, 72
Johan Michael, 65
Johan Phillipp,
  65
Maria Elisabeth,
  65
Phillipp, 65
LANWEYL, Johanes,
  84
LAOGER, Anna
  Elisabeth, 67
LAPLIN, Michael, 83
LARUE, Barbara, 75
LATCHSHA,
  Elizabeth, 8
  Peter, 8
LATIMORE, Rebecca,
  82
LATSHAW, Joseph, 8,
  116
LAUBENGEYER,
  Christoph, 83
LAUBENSCHWEILER,
  Christian, 23,
  62
  Susana, 23, 62
LAUBER, Balthasar,
  76
  Balthaser, 74
  Elizabeth, 74, 76
  Johan Adam, 74
  Johann Heinrich,
  76
  Johannes, 74
  John Frederick,
  76
LAUBSHER, Susannah,
  85
LAUDERDALE, Sarah,
  39
LAUDERMILK,
  Elizabeth, 97
LAUDRUM, Polly, 8
LAUER, David, 43
  Elias, 43
  Elisabetha, 43
  Johannes, 43
  John Philip, 84
LAUFFMAN, Anna
  Maria, 46
  Philip, 46
LAUGHLANE, James,
  Jr., 88

INDEX

LAUGHLIN,
　Alexander, 35
　Ann, 35
　Archison, 110
　Atchison, 35
　Betsy, 39
　Charity, 35
　Doctor, 27
　Easther, 96
　Elenor, 27
　Elizabeth, 36
　Hugh, 35, 36
　James, 34, 36
　Jane, 35
　John, 34, 35, 36, 99
　Margaret, 36
　Mary, 34, 35, 36
　Matthew, 27, 39
　Nancy, 39
　Paul, 27
　Robert, 36
　Susana, 35
　Thomas, 39
　William, 34, 36
LAUMAN, George, 85
　Johannes, 86
LAUTERMILCH,
　Catharina, 56
　John George, 56
LAUZENHEISER,
　Elizabeth, 78
　Jacob, 78
　Johan Jacob, 78
　Peter, 78
LAVERTY, Alex, 91
　Isaac, 91
LAWRENCE, Daniel, 74
　Mary, 74
　William, 74
LAY, Johannes, 50
LAYSON, Hannah, 88
　John, 88
　Mary, 87, 88
LEACH, Samuel, 81
LEACOCK, Jane, 39
LEAN, Nancy, 86
LEANE, Henry, 81
LEARD, Eleanor, 83
　Eliz., 83
　Samuel, 87
LECKEY, Alexander, 30

Elizabeth, 30
LEE, Caspar, 50
　Edward, 85
　Mary, 8
　Sophia, 50
LEECOCK, William, 39
LEEPER, Allen, 31
　James, 31
　Martha, 31
　Mary, 31
　Sally, 31
LEES, Mary, 95
LEFEVER, Cathrina, 85
LEFEVRE, Barbara, 8, 115
LEG, Johannes, 42
　Magdalena, 42
LEGNER, John Ludwig, 72
　Maria Eva, 72
　Mathias, 72
LEH, Eva Margaret, 17
　John, 17
LEHAR, Catharina Dorothea, 57
LEHMER, Catharina, 67
　Elisabeth, 67
　Jacob, 67
LEHNER, Eleanor, 22
　Georg, 22
LEIGHLIN, Mary, 83
LEIME, Henry, 22
　Michael, 22
　Molle, 22
LEIN, Michael, 20
LEINERT, Conrad, 54
LEIPER, John, 93
　Robert, 93
LEIPERS, Sam, 91
　Sarah, 91
LEISTER, Maria Susanna, 42
LEITNER, Elisabeth, 49
　Jacob, 49
LEMAN, Martha, 27
　Samuel, 27
　William, 27
LEMMON, Jeane, 8

LEMON, Elizabeth, 31
　Jane, 31
　John, 31
　Nancy, 31
　Polly, 31
LEMOND, Nancy, 37
LEMS, Barb. Dorothea, 79
　Christoph, 79
　Elizabeth, 79
LEONARD, Adam, 52
　Christoph, 52
　Maria, 53
　Mr., 113
LEONHARD, Adam, 54
　Christoph, 53
　Christoph Sr., 53
　Johan Adam, 53
　Maria, 54
LEOPOLD, John, 71
LEPER, Willm., 100
LEU, Johan, 51
　Maria, 51
LEVISTON, William, 8
LEWIS, Christian, 95
　David, 84
LEY, Anna Maria, 49
　George, 49
LEYBURN, James, 117
LIE, John, 52
　Margaretha, 52
LIEBERD, Elizabeth, 19
　John, 19
　Julia, 19
　William, 19
LIEH, Christian, 55
LIEHR, Anna Margaret, 53
　Anna Margaretha, 53
　Anna Maria, 53
　Catharina, 53
　Elder Johannes, 53
　Eva, 53
　Heinrich, 52, 53
　Johannes, 53
　Maria Catharina, 53
　Susanna, 53

LIGGAT, ---, 37
LIGGATE, Nancy, 38
LIGGET, James, 113
  Stephen, 8
LIGHTCAP,
  Elizabeth, 36, 39
  Godfrey, 36
  Levi, 36
  Mary, 36, 40
  Nancy, 36
  Samuel, 8, 36
  Solomom, 36
  Thomas, 36
  William, 36, 39
LIGHTEL, George, 28
  Sarah, 28
LINCH, Easker, 42
  Robert, 8
  Sophia, 42
LINCKING, Sybilla, 86
LIND, Anna Maria, 43, 53, 54
  Brother, 91
  Catharina, 45, 49, 53, 54
  Christian, 45, 52, 53
  Conrad, 49, 52, 53, 54
  Conrath, 43
  Heinrich, 45, 53, 54
  Johannes, 53
  Maria, 53
  Matthew, 91
LINDSAY, Nancy, 38
  Peggy, 100
  William, 27
LINDSEY, Samuel, 8
  William, 8
LINDSY, Jane, 29
  Jenny, 29
  Nancy, 29
  Robert, 29, 39
  Samuel, 29
  William, 29
LINN, Jane, 119
  John, 113
  Rev., 112
  William, 119
LINTER, Adam, 50

Anna Margaretha, 50
  Catharina, 50
LITTLE, Eleanor, 8
  Grisel, 73
  Jane, 73
  John, 101
  Mary, 83
  Ruth, 93
  William, 73, 82, 96, 101
LITZA, Herr, 50
LIVE, Salome, 8
LIVERICH, Nichlas, 85
LOCHBAUM, Anna Maria, 73
  Hannah, 72, 73
  Johan Martin, 72
  Joseph, 72, 73
LOCHMAN, Barbara, 75
  Elizabeth, 22
  Jacob, 75
  Mary Dorothea, 75
LOCKEY, Alex., 92
  William, 92
LOCKHART, Jane, 95
LOGAN, Alexander, 8
  John, 8, 112, 116
  Margaret, 116
  Sarah, 85
  William, 95
LOGG, Hugh, 86
LOGGENHADER,
  Benjamin, 46
  Catharina, 46
  Elisabeth, 46
LOGUE, Adam, 8, 107, 116
  Elizabeth, 8
  George, 8
  William, 8
LONG, Cookson, 83
  Elizabeth, 32
  Henry, 102
  Lodwick, 95
  Mr., 95
  Rev., 108
  Richard, 83, 101
LONGSDORFF, Adam, 68
  Elisabeth, 68
LORMAR, Margret, 83

LOSLER, Cathar., 62
  Elisabeth, 62
  Jacob, 62
LOUDERMILK,
  Elizabeth, 101
LOUDON, Archibald, 8, 112
LOUGHHEAD, James, 92
LOUGHRIDGE,
  Abraham, 112
  Nancy, 8, 112
LOVE, ---, 8
  Andrew, 100
  James, 8, 29
  John, 8, 29, 95
  Margaret, 29
  Rachel, 8
  Robert, 94
  Thomas, 29
  William, 8
LOWRY, Mary, 38
  Nancy, 31
  Samuel, 33
LUCAS, Grace, 95
  Mary, 81
LUCK, Johannes, 43
  Magdalena, 43
  Maria Susanna, 43
LUCKY, Andrew, 89
  John, 89
LUHTZ, Daniel, 50
  Elizabeth, 50
  Johannes, 50
LUKINS, Abm., 95
LUS, Elisabeth, 56
  Gottfried, 56
  Johan Georg Friedrich, 56
LUSK, Jane, 32
  Martha, 32
  Robert, 31, 32, 118
  William, 116
LUTLOW, Mary, 51
  Rachel, 51
LUTZ, Catharina, 24, 63
  Elisabeth, 57
  Georg, 24, 63
  Gottfried, 57
  Margaret, 9
  Samuel, 24, 63

LUTZIN, Susana, 24, 63
LYNE, John, 9
Susanna, 9
LYON, Belle, 9
Eleanor, 109
Peggy, 9, 108, 109
Samuel, 109
William, 108
LYTLE, John, 115

-M-
M---, Eleanor, 92
MAACK, Michael, 55
Susanna Charlotte, 55
MCADAMS, Ann, 9
John, 85
MCAFEE, Letty, 9
MCALEVY, William, 9
MCALLISTER, David, 34
MCALWAIN, Prudence, 82
MCANULTY, Hugh, 9
MCBETH, Alex, 9
Andrew, 106
Jean, 9
Peggy, 9, 114
MCBRIDE, Alexander, 9, 31, 112
David, 82
James, 89
Tabitha, 31, 112
MCBRYAR, Esther, 93
MCCA---, John, 99
MCCABE, Jane, 9
Patrick, 9
MCCALETHON, William, 82
MCCALL, Francis, 88
John, 85, 87, 88, 89
Michael, 9
William, 87, 88
MCCALLEN, John, 93
Mary, 93
MCCALLISTER, Eliz., 96
Elizabeth, 9, 97
Jean, 9
MCCALLLIN, Mary, 93
MCCANN, John, 99
Sarah, 40
MCCARDLE, Hugh, 85
MCCARDY, Charles, 85
MCCARROLL, John, 99
MCCARSLIN, Elisabeth, 69
James, 69
MCCART, Rachel, 9
MCCARTNEY, John, 9, 60
Thomas, 9
MCCASLAND, Martha, 35
MCCASSAL, Elisabeth, 69
James, 69
Nancy, 69
MCCAUL, Eliz., 96
MCCAUSLAND, Mark, 39
MCCEAN, James, 86
MCCIBBENS, Eliz., 84
MCCLAIN, James, 9
MCCLARAN, Thomas, 39
MCCLAUD, Cathrin, 60
William, 60
MCCLAY, William, 101
MCCLAYLAND, Willm., 100
MCCLEAN, James, 107
Jane, 99
Jean, 101
John, 101
Neil, 89
MCCLEARY, Elizabeth, 9
John, 39
MCCLELAND, Ann, 9
MCCLELLAN, Anne, 29
Daniel, 92
James, 93
Jenny, 29
Jo., 91
John, 86, 92
Joseph, 9, 104
Katharine, 93
Mary, 92
Matty, 9
Susanna, 101
MCCLELLAND, Hugh, 96, 102
MCCLINTOCK, Alexander, 33
Elizabeth, 34
Rachel, 9
Sarah, 33
MCCLOUD, Kitty, 9
MCCLUNG, Charles, 91
Esther, 91
Jo., 91
Mathew, 91
M'CLURE, Amelia, 107
Andrew, 30
Betsy, 30
Charles, 9, 107, 112
Jennet, 30
John, 32
Margaret, 9, 30, 40
Martha, 31
Mary, 30
Nancy, 30, 38
Robert, 30
Samuel, 82
Walter, 35
William, 96, 102
MCCOMB, Robert, 87
Thomas, 87
MCCOMMON, Jenny, 9
MCCONEL, Agnes, 92
Charles, 30
Elizabeth, 30
Isabel, 30
Jenny, 30
John, 30
Martha, 30
Mary, 30
MCCONNAL, William, 85
MCCONNEL, ---, 39
James, 102
Rev., 117
Robert, 89
William, 88
MCCONNELL, Isabella, 95
William, 100
MCCORD, John, 85
Mary, 9

MCCORMICK, Amelia, 9
Ann, 33
Cathrina, 77
Charles, 77
Elizabeth, 33, 82
Esther, 35
Hugh, 9
Jane, 33, 96
Jo., 92
Joseph, 33, 39
Martha, 93
Mary, 77
Robert, 9, 35, 39
Samuel, 32
Sarah, 100
Thomas, 33
MCCOSKEY, William, 101
MCCOSKRY, Samuel, 95
Samuel A., 107
Susan, 107
M'COUMB, Mrs., 113
MCCOVERN, Mary, 28
MCCOWAN, James, 83
MCCOY, James, 80
Johannes, 80
John, 101
Margreth, 80
MCCRACKEN,
Elizabeth, 27
Jane, 113
Jenny, 27
Martha, 27
William, 27, 133
MCCRACKON,
Margreth, 86
MCCREA, W.H., 32
MCCRORY, John, 101
MCCRUE, Samuel, 82
MCCULLOCH,
Alexander, 91
Elizabeth, 30
James, 30
Robert, 30
MCCULLOGH,
Archibald, 9
Francis, 10
George, 10
Hugh, 10
James, 10
MCCULLOUGH,
Alexander, 98

Elizabeth, 39
John, 10
MCCULLUM, Francis, 9
MCCULLY, George, 96
Nancy, 86
MCCUNE, Eleanor, 99
Hugh, 40
Isabel, 27
Isabella, 38
John, 10, 27, 40
Mary, 40, 99
Peggy, 27
Polley, 10
Robert, 27, 40
Roseanna, 10
Samuel, 27, 39, 40
MCCURDY, Agnes, 37
David, 31, 39
Eleanor, 113
Elizabeth, 31
James, 31
Janet, 31
John, 31, 113
Mrs., 31
MCCUTCHEON,
Susannah, 86
MCDANIEL, Daniel, 10
John, 99
M'DANNEL, John, 117
MCDONALD, Edward, 99
Ellse, 81
Jannet, 71
Jean, 10
John, 71, 83
Martin, 10
Mr., 34
Neal, 71
Sarah, 110
MCDOWEL, Elizabeth, 10
John, 120
Lydia, 10
Mary, 120
Nancy, 10
MCDOWELL, Alexr., 97
Ann, 96
Lydia, 103
Mary, 37, 96
Nancy, 38

MCDUEL, Edward, 83
MCELHATHON, John, 83
MCELHENNY, Hugh, 35
Margaret, 35
Mary, 35
Rebecca, 35
Samuel, 35
MCELLWAY, James, 86
MCELRAVY, Mary, 10
MCELWAIN/MACELWAIN
Andrew, 31, 32, 39
Elizabeth, 10, 32
George, 88
James, 32
Jane, 32
John, 32
Margaret, 38
Mary, 32, 39
R., 39
Robert, 32
Ruth, 32
MCENTEKERD, Jane, 83
MCENTIRE,
Elizabeth, 35, 39
MCEWEN, Francis, 10
Rossana, 113
MCFADEN, John, 39
MCFALL, Jane, 81
MCFARLAN, James, 98
MCFARLAND,
Margaret, 102
MCFARLANE,
Alexander, 33
Andrew, 29
Ann, 28, 33
Elizabeth, 28, 29, 33
James, 29, 33
Jean, 10
John, 29, 33
Margaret, 28, 33, 96
Mary, 28, 33, 40
Mrs., 113
Robert, 28, 29
Sarah, 29
William, 29, 32, 33, 113
MCFARLIN, Margreth, 82

MCFEE, Polly, 10
MCFERLAN, Patrik, 60
MCGAFFY, Elizabeth, 84
MCGEARY, Clemence, 84
MCGEE, Roger, 10
  William, 85
MCGILL, Elizabeth, 84
  Ester, 82
MCGLAUGHLIN, ---, 39
  Daniel, 39
  Sarah, 35
MCGOFFINE, ---, 39
  Agnes, 36
  James, 36
  John, 36
MCGOLDRICK, Margaret, 10
MCGONAGLE, Edward, 10
MCGOVERN, Ann, 28
  Catharine, 10
  James, 28
MCGOWAN, David, 10
MCGRANAHAN, William, 10
MCGREW, Ann, 85
  Archibald, 10
  Elizabeth, 10
  Isabella, 95
MCGRUE, Alexander, 86
MCGUFFIN, Mary, 35
MCGUFFINE, Jane, 27
  John, 35
  Joseph, 27
  Mary, 27
  Robert, 27
  William, 27, 35, 39
MCGUIRE, Elizabeth, 22
MCHAFFEY, John, 10
MACHAN, Archibald, 88
MCINTIRE, John, 27
  Joseph, 27
  Sally, 27
MCINTOSH, John, 71
  Margreth, 71

Nancy, 71
MCINTYRE,
  Elizabeth, 10
  William, 10
MCJUNKINS, John, 10
MACK, Cathrina
  Elisabeth, 72
  Michael, 72
  Susanna
  Charlotta, 72
MCKAY, Archibald, 10
  John, 55
  Mary, 10
MCKEAN, Ann, 96, 102
  Joseph, 99
  Robert, 96
  Sarah, 59
  William, 39
MCKEE, Daniel, 10
  Elizabeth, 100
  George, 10
  Isabell, 88
  John, 99
MCKEEHAN,
  Alexander, 37, 113
  Benjamin, 37
  Betsy, 37, 39
  Elizabeth, 37
  George, 37
  James, 37
  Jannet, 113
  Jenny, 37
  John, 36, 37, 39
  Margaret, 37, 39
  Mary, 37
  Mary Ann, 37, 39
  Nancy, 37, 38
  Peggy, 37
  Samuel, 37
MCKEHAN, Alexander, 98
  John, 98
MCKEIN, Elizabeth, 35
  Margaret, 35
  Mary, 35
  William, 35
MCKELLHENNY, ---, 82
MCKENNEY, Joseph, 96

MCKENNIS, Charles, 82
MCKENNY, Joseph, 82
MCKERBES, Anthony, 59
MCKERR, Robert, 99
MCKESLiN, Martha, 60
MCKEWN, Jane, 89
MCKIBBEN, Hannah, 100
  Jeremiah, 36
  Mary, 36
MCKIBBERN, Hugh, 100
  John, 100
MCKIMMON, Michael, 10
MCKINLEY, Daniel, 10
  Henry, 10
  James, 10
  John, 86
  Margaret, 101
  Martha, 10
MCKINNEY, Grizelda, 39
  Isabella, 97
  Jean, 10
  Marg't., 95
  Mordecai, 10, 110
  Nancy, 99
  Polley, 10
MCKINSTRE, Susanna, 38
MCKNAPP, Matte, 66
MCKNIGHT (See also
  McKt.), John, 10
  Martha, 82
  Polly, 99
MCKT., Agnes, 93
  David, 93
  James, 93
MCKUN, John, 101
  Samuel, 101
MCLANDBURG, John, 39
MCLAUGHLIN, Unity, 10
MACLAY, William, 101
MCMAGHAN, Andrew, 84

MCMAHAN, Margaret, 99
MCMAHON, John, 76
  Mary, 76
  Thomas, 76
MCMEEN, William, 84
MCMICHAEL, Daniel, 10
MCMULLAN, Catherin, 96
  Elizabeth, 32
  Marg't., 96
MCMULLEN, ---, 100
  Margaret, 99
  Mary, 100
  William, 10
MCMULLIN, Rebecca, 35
M'MURRAY, William, 103
MCNAUGHT, John, 88
M'NAUGHTON, Jesse, 115
  Patrick, 115
MCNEALANS, William, 10
MCNETT, Alexander, 85
MCNICKLE, ---, 95
MCNIGHT, Rebecca, 83
MCNUT, Allexander, 90
MCPHERRAN, Samuel, 96
M'PHERSON, Robert, 104
MCQUEON, Mary, 10
  Rosanna, 10
MCQUISTEN, Jane, 81
MCRORY, Samuel, 39
MCSWEAN, Mary, 96
MCTEER, Agnes, 28
  John, 28
MCWEVER, John, 84
MCWHINIE, Isabella, 96
MCWHINNY, Robard, 101
MAGAFOGE, John, 96
MAGAW, Sarah, 9
  William, 97
MAGEE, Elizabeth, 95
George, 9
Polly, 9
MAGHAN, John, 82
MAGWIRE, Archd., 96
MAHAN, Lettie, 101
MAHON, Jane, 99
  Samuel, 9, 107
  Sarah, 99
MAILEN, Elisabeth, 50
  Sophia, 50
  Wendel, 50
MAIR, Charles, 86
MAJOIRS, Elizabeth, 33
  Isaac, 33
  Nancy, 34
  Sarah, 33
MAN, A. Maria, 24, 63
  Georg, 24, 63
  Johannes, 24, 63
MANNESCHMIDT, Eva, 62
  Henrich S., 62
  Susana, 62
MANNESSCHMIDT, Eva, 23
  Henrich S., 23
  Susana, 23
MANZ, Andreas, 79
  Christoph, 79
  Margreth, 79
MAPPIN, James, 84
MARCHBANKS, James, 9
MARIEL, Anna Mar. Rosina, 58
  Christian Gottfried, 58
  Margreth, 58
MARK, Margaretha, 51
  Micha, 52
  Michael, 51
  Sus. Charlot., 52
  Susanna Charlotta, 51
  Susanna Scharlotta, 51
MARSH, William, 101
MARSHALL, John, 39, 84
  Michael, 9
MARSHBANK, James, 28
MARTE, Barbara, 52
  Elisabeth, 52
  Wendel, 52
MARTEN, Agnes, 40
MARTIN, ---, 38
  Ann, 81
  Catharina, 46
  Elisabeth, 55
  Elisabetha, 46
  Elizabeth, 81, 96
  Elizabetha, 46
  James, 9
  Jane, 32
  Jesse, 81
  John, 32, 39
  Martha, 82
  Mary, 32
  Nancy, 40
  Paul, 99
  Rosanna, 9, 32
  Sarah, 96
  Thomas, 32, 35, 39
  Wendel, 46, 55
  William, 84
MARZZALL, Leah, 19
  Martin, 19
  Susanna, 19
MASH, Grafener, 82
MASON, Elizabeth, 32
  Isaac, 39
MASS, Cathrina, 74
  Johan Peter, 74
  Johan Philip, 74
  Johan Wilhelm, 74
  Margaretha, 74
  Wilhelm, 74
MATEER, Polly, 118
MATER, Jannet, 71
MATHERS, Eleanor, 34
  Isabella, 34
  Jane, 33
  Jennet, 34
  John, 34
  Joseph, 34
  Margaret, 33
  Mary, 33
  Robert, 36, 39
  Samuel, 34
  Thomas, 33, 34

William, 33
MATHESON, Thomas, 9
MATHIS, Margaret, 9
MATTHEWS, Polley, 9
MAUCK, Elisabeth,
  52
  Margareth, 52
  Michael, 52
MAULSBY, William,
  95
MAURER, Eva, 55
MAUSON, Polly, 9
MAXSELL, James, 83
MAXWELL, James, 112
  Jane, 112
  John, 96
  Nancy, 9
MAYER, Adam, 55
  Catherine, 55
  Margareth, 55
  Michael, 55
MAYES, Samuel, 39
MEANS, Allen, 10,
  36
  Grezil, 82
  Joseph, 29
  Nancy, 29
MEAS, Joh. Nicklas,
  85
MEEK, Katharine, 93
  Samuel, 85
  William, 93
MEEKEY, Margt., 95
MEHAFFY, Bridget,
  10
  Thomas, 10
MEHLHORN, Andrew,
  83
MEHONIG, Jean, 59
MEIER, Catharina,
  50
  Johann, 50
  Magdalena, 50
MEISER, Christian,
  48, 54
  Samuel, 48
  Susanna, 48, 54
MEISSER, Christian,
  52
  Susanna, 52
MEISTER, Susannah,
  86
MEJER, Adam Henr.,
  59

Pastor Ad.
  Hinrich, 57
MELL, Adam, 19
  Betsey, 113
  Magdalena, 19
MENG, Charlotta, 49
  Michael, 49
MERCER, Margaret,
  11
MERET, Absolom, 84
MERTEN, Elisabeth,
  57
  Stephen, 57
METZGAR, Anna
  Maria, 75
  John, 75
MEYER, Adam, 75
  Adam Henry, 22
  Anna Maria, 75
  Catharina, 70
  Cathr., 85
  Henrich, 70
  Johanes, 85
  Margaretha, 70
  Margreth, 86
  Maria Elisabetha,
  75
  Rev., 106
MEYL, Andreas, 49
  Henrich, 49
  Magdalena, 49
MEYLER, Elias, 44
  Joseph, 44
  Margaretha, 44
MICHAEL, Wendel,
  110
MICHAL, John, 39
MICHELLTREE, Jane,
  83
MICKEY, Agnes, 40
  Hannah, 39
  James, 40
MICKIE, Agnes, 27
  Andrew, 27
  David, 27
  Eleanor, 38
  Elenor, 27
  Hannah, 27
  Isamiah, 27
  Mary, 27
  Robert, 27
  Thomas, 27
MIES, Margreth, 67
MIESCH, Hannos, 62

Joh. Georg., 62
  Magdalena, 62
MIHESON, Nathaniel,
  99
MIL., Sarah, 93
  Y., 93
MILD, Anna
  Catharina, 21
  Johan Georg, 21
MILLER, Andrew, 11
  Anna, 78
  Anna Maria, 78
  Barbara, 43
  Catharina, 54
  Christian, 42,
  46, 79
  Conrad, 78
  Daniel, 78
  Dorothea, 85
  Eleonora, 79
  Elisabeth, 52, 57
  Elizabeth, 11,
  83, 116
  Feronica, 42
  Georg, 78
  Heinrich, 76
  Henry, 11, 97,
  111
  Isaac, 89
  Jacob, 51, 57
  Jean, 11, 59
  Jeremiah, 103
  Jeremias, 57
  Johannes, 42, 46,
  78
  John, 11, 37,
  105, 109
  John Heinrich, 79
  Juliana, 111
  Ludwig, 43
  Magdalena, 76
  Maria, 57
  Martha, 120
  Mary, 57, 120
  Matthew, 115
  Micha, 52
  Michael, 41, 51
  Mr., 34
  Nathaniel, 86
  Peter, 54
  Robert, 110
  Ruth, 11
  Samuel, 30, 52
  Susanna, 57

Veronica, 46
Wilhelm, 43
William, 11, 37, 86, 120
MILLIGAN, Jane, 11
Margaret, 11
William, 11
MILLS, Rachel, 28
MINSCH, Joh.
  Georg., 23
  Joh: Georg, 23
  Magdalena, 23
  Thomas, 23
MIPHIN, Elisabeth, 21
MIT., D., 93
MITCH, Mary, 92
MITCHEL, Andrew, 39
  David, 92, 93
  Elizabeth, 35
  Eve, 35
  Ezekiel, 34
  James, 34, 35, 93
  John, 30, 34, 92, 96
  Lacy, 34
  Margaret, 34
  Mary, 34, 35, 92
  Rebecca, 35
  Samuel, 34
MITCHELL,
  Alexander, 86
  Cathr., 83
  John, 11
  Margreth, 83
MITZ, John, 20
MOFFATT, Sidney, 116
MOKHEL, Salome, 23
  Susanna, 23
  Wilhelm, 23
MOLD, John, 81
MOLL, Ephraim, 47
  Joh. Heinrich, 73
  Johannes, 46, 47
  Maria, 46, 47
MOLLAN, Lancelot, 11
MOLLEN, Jumuk, 60
MOMSHER, Bernhard, 50
  Maria Katharin, 50
MONEMY, ---, 38

MONEY, Elizabeth, 85
MONTGOMERY,
  Elizabeth, 97
  Hetty, 11
  James, 87, 88, 89
  Jenny, 11, 105
  John, 89, 105
  Robert, 88
  Sally, 11, 115
  Samuel, 11, 88
  Thomas, 35
  William, 35, 88, 102
MONTROE, John, 33
  Margaret, 33
  Mary Ann, 33
  Reuben, 33
  William, 33
MOOR, Elizabeth, 28, 37
  Isabel, 35
  Isabella, 35
  Jacob, 54
  Johannes, 76
  John, 84
  Margaret, 28
  Margretha, 76
  Mary, 99
  Patrick, 76
  Samuel, 39
  Thomas, 100
MOORE, Alexander, 11, 68
  Agness, 110
  Jane, 11
  John, 97
  Mary, 68
  Mose, 89
  Nancy, 11
  Samuel, 34
  Thomas, 34
MOOREHEAD, Robert, 11
MOORHEAD, Edward, 11
  Fergus, 83
  Jenny, 86
  Mr., 34
MOPHET, Jane, 33
  Phoebe, 33
  Rebecca, 33
  William, 33
MORAIN, John, 36

Sarah, 36
MORE, Eliz., 84
MORGAN, Anna
  Henrica, 57
  Elisabeth, 57
  Elizabeth, 84
  Louis, 57
MORISON, Widow, 93
MORRIS, Francis, 35
  Mary, 31
MORRISON, Daniel, 11
  Eleanor, 83
  Hance, 110
  Hans, 11
  James, 84
  John, 11, 85, 101
  Margaret, 113
  Mary, 35
  Rev., 105
  Robert, 35, 39
  William, 35, 83
MORROW, ---, 40
  Charles, 89
  Elizabeth, 82
  George, 114
  Hannah, 32
  Jane, 35
  John, 32
  Mary, 32, 82
  Richard, 83
  Samuel, 35
MORRPHE, Andrew, 60
MUHLEISEN,
  Cristoff, 42
  Jacob, 42
  Maria Sarah, 42
  Susanna, 42
MUHLEYSEN,
  Christoph, 73
  Jacob, 44
  Johan Heinrich, 73
  Maria Sarah, 73
  Samuel Fullsen, 44
  Susanna, 44, 55
MUKERSPACH, Anna
  Maria, 44
  Elisabeth, 44
  Peter, 44
MULATTO, Jack, 31
MULIN, Marcus, 83

INDEX 153

MULLER, Anna Mar.,
  26
  Anna Maria, 44
  Benjamin, 24, 63
  Catharina, 51, 56
  Christian, 45, 53
  David, 45
  Elisabeth, 44,
    52, 55
  Elisabetha, 49
  Georg, 56
  Johann Georg, 49
  John, 51
  Maria, 21, 55
  Maria
    Machthalena, 21
  Maria Magdalena,
    42
  Martin, 24, 63
  Michael, 44, 49,
    52, 53, 55
  Mrs. Jacob, 57
  Sally, 24, 63
  Thomas, 21
  Veronica, 45, 53
MURDACK, Matthew,
  11
MURDOCK, Robert, 39
MURPHY, Andrew, 87
  Hercules, 11
  Nancy, 81
  Philip, 39
MURRAI, Elisabeth,
  58
  Maria, 58
  Thomas, 58
MURRAN, John, 99
MURRAY, Anna Maria,
  79
  David, 11, 29
  Elizabeth, 85
  Jacob, 79
  James, 79
  William, 11
MUTTERSPRACH,
  Elisabetha, 48
  Johannes, 48
  Peter, 48
MYLER, Elizabeth,
  38

-N-
NAAS, Barbara, 60

N.H., 60
NAGL, Elisabeth, 49
  Joseph, 49
  Maria Magdalena,
    49
NAVIN, John, 92
NEAL, Jenny, 39
NEELY, James, 11,
  114
  Samuel, 96
NEES, Jane, 86
NEGRO, Bill, 37
  Eve, 35
  Fan, 36
  George, 40
  Grant, 34
  Hall, 35
  Jack, 35
  Jonathan, 27
  Mat, 30
  Ned, 32
  Pomp, 35
  Rachel, 34
  Sal, 29, 35, 36
  Tom, 36
  Walter, 34
NEIDIG, Adam, 17
  Magdelena, 17
  Sophia, 17
NEIL, Andrew, 88
  Betsey, 109
  Elizabeth, 88
  John, 93
  Mary, 100, 108
  Polley, 11
  Thomas, 89
  William, 108, 109
NEILSON, Joseph,
  102
  Polley, 11
NEILY, Joseph, 11
NESBET, Elizabeth,
  99
NESBIT, Charles,
  104
  Rev. Dr., 111,
    118
NESLER, Christian,
  86
NEUSTAEDTER,
  Catharine, 17
  Conrad, 17
NEW, Anna Dorothea,
  77

Johannes, 77
NEWER, Cathrina, 85
NEWLAND, Elijah, 85
NEWLON, James, 85
NICHOLDSON, James,
  35
  John, 39
  Mary, 35
  Richard, 35
NICKLSON, John, 101
NICOLSON, Anna, 70
  Maria, 70
  Thomas, 70
NIMMON, Sarah, 11
NIMMONS, Agness, 11
NISBET, Charles,
  106
  John, 87
  Maria, 106
  Rev., 103
  William, 99
NISBIT, Esther, 35
  William, 35
NIXON, William, 11
NOLAND, William,
  111
NOLLER, Maria, 71
  Philip, 71
NORTON, Betsy, 30
  Elizabeth, 11
  Sarah, 30
  Thomas, 30
NUGENT, Mary, 83

-O-
OBERLIN, ---, 52
  Adam, 52
  Friedrich, 54
  Margaretha, 52
  Maria, 52
OBERMEYER, Barbara,
  76
  Georg, 76
  Magdalena, 76
OBREYAN, Nicklas,
  86
O'BRIEN Family, 115
O'DONNELL, Edward,
  112
  Margery, 112
OFFICER, Alexander,
  30
  David, 11
  James, 30

John, 11, 111
Margaret, 11
Mary, 30
Mrs., 111
Sally, 40
OFFLEY, Lieut.
 David, 11
OFLEY, Lieut., 117
OHLWEYLER, Anna, 80
 Jacob, 80
OLIVER, Elizabeth,
 11
 James, 103
 John, 118
 Thomas, 11
O'NEAL, John, 103
O'NEIL, John, 30
ONG, Pheby, 82
OOSTER, Johannes,
 43
OPACH, Cathrina, 66
ORAM, Willm.
 Robert, 100
ORR, ---, 11
 David, 11
 Isabella, 40
 James, 11
 Mary, 95
ORVAN, Jean, 11
OTTENBERGER,
 Cathrina, 57
 George, 57
 Susanna, 57
OVERN, John, 80
 Mary, 80
 William, 80

-P-
PADON., Eliza, 93
 John, 93
PAFF, Elisabeth, 57
 George, 57
PALM, Elizabeth, 33
PALMER, Johannes,
 49
 Magdalena, 47
 Peter, 47
PANNESTACHE, Johann
 Georg, 21
PARK, Elizabeth, 97
 Johannes, 48
 Magdalena, 48
 Thomas, 101
PARKER, Andrew, 108

James, 11, 97,
 108, 116
 John, 98
 Major Alexander,
 98
 Margaret, 98
 Mrs., 34
 Rebecca, 11, 96,
 112
 Rebeckah, 116
 Thomas, 11, 103
 William, 11
PARKIESON,
 Benjamin, 93
 David, 92
 Katharine, 93
 William, 92
PARKISON, Cathr.,
 85
PARKS, Anna, 40
 David, 27
 John C., 40
 Joseph, 40
 Rebecca, 27, 40
 Thomas, 40
 William, 27
PASSEL, John, 11
 Mary, 12
 Sarah, 12
PATEN, Fanny, 32
 Francis, 32
 James, 32
 John, 32
 Joseph, 32
 Mary, 32
 Robert, 32
 Thomas, 32
 William, 32
PATER, Joh., 26
PATERSON, James, 91
 John, 93
 Thomas, 93
 William, 91
PATRICK, William,
 83
PATTAN, Agnas, 87
PATTEN, Hugh, 108
PATTERSON, Andrew,
 32
 Ann, 31
 Anne, 39
 Deborah, 30, 38
 Eliz., 84
 Elizabeth, 31

Esther, 31, 38
 George, 12
 James, 32, 33
 Jane, 32
 Jean, 12
 John, 39
 Mary, 31, 32, 33,
 100
 Nancy, 33
 Nathan, 32, 39
 Obediah, 30, 39
 Robert, 30, 33,
 39, 100
 Samuel, 32
 Sarah, 30, 31, 32
 Thomas, 31, 33
 William, 12
 Zacheus, 30
PATTISON, Charles,
 118
 Elizabeth, 109
 Rob., 93
 William, 93
PATTON, Andrew, 39
 Janet, 28
 John, 28, 39
 Margaret, 28
 Mary, 12, 28, 35,
 39
 Robert, 28
 William, 12, 28
PAUHE, Elisabeth,
 58
PAXTON, James, 90
PEARIS, Peter, 81
PECK, Johannes, 45
PEDI, Johannes, 41
 Magdalene, 41
PEEBLES, Elizabeth,
 38, 109
 Margrate, 90
 Mary, 105
 Nathaniel, 88
 Robert, 39, 105
PEELING, Elizabeth,
 12
PEEPBLES, Robert,
 99
PEG, Johannes, 43
 Maria Magdalena,
 43
PEHST, Johannes, 41
PEHT, Johannes, 42

PENDERGRASS,
  Philip, 113
PENN, Elisabeth, 61
  Philip, 61
PENNEL, Thomas, 33
PENNWELL, Thomas, 39
PENSE, Eva, 12
PENWELL, Prudence, 29
  Sarah, 12
PEOPLES, Betsy, 27
  Margreth, 82
  Robert, 27
PETER, Anna, 67
  Catharina, 67
  Ludolph Sr., 67
PETERS, Indian, 81
  John, 81
  Joseph, 81
  Mary, 81
  Peter, 81
  Robert, 81
  William, 81
PETERSON,
  Elizabeth, 112
  Henry, 112
PETITE, Catherine, 88
PETRI, Sorer, 75
PFANENKUCHEN,
  Cathrina, 76
  Peter, 76
  Rosina Cathrina, 76
PFANNEKUCH,
  Charlotta, 84
PHEFFER, Anna
  Maria, 56
  Johannes, 56
  Philip, 56
PHILIP, Anna Maria, 71, 72, 73
  Cathrina, 72
  Jacob, 71, 72, 73
  Johannes, 71
  John Michael, 73
PHILIPS, A. Marg., 68
  Catharina, 47
  Elisabeth, 60
  Jacob, 47
  Joseph, 47

PHILLIPPIN, Anna
  Maria, 69
PICKIN, Robert, 85
PIERCE, Joseph, 12
PIERSON, Jane, 86
  Sarah, 86
PIPER, Jenny, 85
  Nancy, 39
  Phebe, 39
  Widow, 89
PIRCKINS, John, 81
PLUNKETT, Isaac, 39
POBBENMEYER,
  Christina, 19
  Gabriel, 19
POEPLES, Elizabeth, 81
  William, 86
POLAINE, Ephraim, 12
POLLOCK, Eleanor, 12
  James, 101, 104, 118
  Jared, 12
  Jeared, 83
  Jereat, 117
  John, 95, 101, 110
  Joseph, 28
  Margaret, 110, 115
  Mary, 28, 104
  Oliver, 109, 115, 116
  Peggy, 12
  Polly, 116
POPE, George, 70
  Joh., 69
POPP, Andreas, 66, 67
  Catharina, 67
  Elisabeth, 67
  Nicolaus, 67
  Susanna, 66, 67
POPPENMEYER, Adam, 19
PORTER, Elizabeth, 39
  Jane, 40
  Widow, 100
PORTERFIELD,
  William, 39

POSTLETHWAIT,
  James, 115
POSTLETHWAITE,
  Amelia, 12
  James, 12
  Joseph, 12
  Sarah, 96
POTTS, Hugh H., 12
  Lieut., 118
POWER, Sarah, 12
POWERS, William, 12
PRAGUNIER,
  Dorothea, 86
PRATZ, Abraham, 23
  Johannes, 23
  Maria, 23
PRAUN, Prudentia, 57
PREISS, Catarina, 46
  Jacob, 46
PRETZ, Abraham, 24, 62, 63
  Anna Maria, 24, 63
  Catharina, 24, 63
  Johannes, 62
  Maria, 62
  Simon, 24, 63
PRICE, Richard, 12
PROBST, Andreas, 45
  Susanna, 45
PROCTOR, Ann, 86
PROVENS, Charles, 12
  Mary Ann, 12
PUELLA, Mater, 73
PUMERY, Thomas, 85
PURDIE, James, 33
  John, 33
  Margaret, 33
  Mary, 33
  Rachel, 33
  Thomas, 33
PURMANN, Johann, 54
PUTMAN, Edwin, 12

-Q-
QUA, John, 88
QUICKLE, Elizabeth, 79
  Ferena, 79
  Michael, 79

156 CUMBERLAND COUNTY CHURCH RECORDS OF THE 18TH CENTURY

QUIGLEY, Christoph, 82
James, 39
QUIN, Charles, 110
Margaret, 110
QUIREY, Eliz., 86

-R-
R---, William, 100
RABENS, Elisabeth, 67
Jean, 67
William, 67
RAHM, Barbara, 47, 49
Jacob, 47
Jakob, 49
RAINEY, Charles, 12
James, 39
RALSTON, Agnes, 34
Amy, 34
Andrew, 34, 91
Ann, 12, 34
David, 34
Elenor, 34
Elizabeth, 34
James, 34
Jane, 34
Margaret, 34
Mary, 34
Nancy, 34
Sally, 34
Sarah, 34
RALZ, Maria Elisabeth, 51
Peter, 51
RAM, Cathrina, 77
Johannes, 76
Melchior, 75, 76
Rebecca, 75, 76
RAMAGE, Rebecca, 81
RAMBACH, Rosina, 85
RAMBERGER, Ann Dorothea, 83
RAMSAY, Agnes, 12, 31
Elizabeth, 31
James, 91, 109, 118
Mary, 12, 31
Peggy, 109
RAMSEY, Anne, 32
David, 32
Hugh, 34

James, 112
Janet, 30
Margaret, 12, 31, 32, 34
Mary, 32
Nathan, 30
Oliver, 12
Polley, 12
Sarah, 32
RANDLES, Margaret, 38
RANDOLPH, Fanny, 5, 108
Paul, 12, 112
Tanny, 12
RANKIN, Mary, 102
William, 89
RAY, Eleonora, 84
Samuel, 100
RAYL, Mary, 101
READ, George, 103
Robert, 12
REAGH, Elizabeth, 97
REAM, Henry, 112
REAUGH, Polley, 12
REBBERT, Bernhard, 52
Elisabeth, 52
REDDET, Johann, 53, 54
REDETT, Catharina, 49
John, 49
Susanna Catharina, 54
REDID, John, 47
REDMAN, Sarah, 12
REED, ---, 38
Eleanor, 34
George, 12
John, 32, 34, 83
Joseph, 86
Louisa, 96
Mary, 83
Sally, 34
Samuel, 12
Sarah, 32
Susannah, 85
REELY, Martha, 96
REES, Mary, 83
REEZEN, Sarah, 95
REFERBERRY, Mary, 99

REGNAS, Susannah, 86
REHMER, Adam, 47
Jacob, 47
Maria, 47
REHNER, Adam, 46
Catharina, 46
Maria, 46
REHRER, Adam, 47
Catharina, 47
Sara, 47
REICHWEIN, Christoph, 75, 76
Christopher, 60
Dorothea, 75, 76
Eva Christina, 75
Maria Elisabeth, 60
Susan. Margretha, 76
REID, Aud, 93
Elisa., 100
John, 100
Margaret, 91
REIDER, Maria, 42
REIDINGER, Anna Maria, 42
Christian, 42
Joh. Peter, 42
REIGH, Elenor, 31
Mary, 31
Samuel, 31
REIN, Anna Maria, 20
Henry, 20
REINBECK, Barbara, 73
John, 73
Maria, 73
REINECK, Johannes, 68
REINECKIN, Barbara, 68
REINECKS, Joh., 68
REINER, Georg, 42
Margaret, 42
Schnurat, 42
REINERS, Conrad, 43
Margaretha, 43
REINHARD, Johannes, 42
Salome, 42
REINICK, Joh., 67

Johannes, 65
REISINGER, Adam, 61
REITH, Adam, 49
　Elisabeth, 48
　George, 48, 49
　Greta, 48
　Maria Catharina, 49
RELLSING, Dewald, 59
RENNELS, John, 83
RENNINGER, Anna Mar., 26
　Conr., 26
RENTZHEIMER, Maria, 57
REUTER, Ephraim, 61
REYANTH, Sarah, 82
REYNOLDS, Hanah, 100
　John, 89
　Samuel, 89
RHEINS, Esther, 84
RHEYNECK, Mary, 72
　Peter, 72
RHEYNOLDS, Mary, 101
RHIGTON, Ann, 79
　Sophia, 79
　Stephen, 79
RHINEHART, John, 12
RHODDO, Josua, 84
RHODDOW, Josua, 79
　Polly, 79
RI---, James, 100
RICHARD, Cathrina, 79
　Charles, 79
RICHARDSON, Unis, 95
RICHERT, Herman, 54
RICHIE, John, 99
　Margaret, 92
　Matthew, 92
RICHTER, Catharina, 58
　George Christle, 59
　Jo., 59
　Johannes, 58
　Magdalena, 58
RICHTSON, Magdalena, 57
RIDDLE, Elizabeth, 114
　James, 114
　John, 114
　Mary, 12
　Polly, 116
RIDSBAUGH, Barbara, 38
RIED, James R., 104
　Wilhelm, 44
RIEGER, Peter, 54
RIELY, Martha, 96
RIGGEL, Georg, 47
　Ludwig, 47
　Margaretha, 47
RIGHT, Elizabeth, 12
RIPPEL, Elisabet, 48
　John, 55
　Ludwig, 48
　Margareth, 55
　Margaretha, 48
RIPPET, Elizabeth, 37
　John, 37
　Mary, 37
　Rebecca, 37, 38
RIPPETH, John, 117
RIPPEY, Isabella, 108
　Ruth, 106
　William, 106, 108
RIPPLE, Johannes, 77
　Ludwig David, 71, 77
　Maria Sybilla, 77
　Sybilla Maria, 71
RIPPY, John, 89
　Margery, 86
　Samuel, 89
RISNER, Jacob, 80
　Maria, 80
　Peter, 80
RITCHWINE, Elizabeth, 106
RITTENHOUSE, David, 111
RITTER, Anna Maria, 48
　Elias, 48
　Margaretha, 48
ROACH, Mary, 12
ROADS, Isabel, 84
ROATH, Lydia, 12
ROBERTS, John, 40
ROBERTSON, James, 93
　John, 113
　Sarah, 86
ROBESON, Abigail, 12
　Alexander, 12
　Margaret, 12
　Mary, 12
ROBIESON, Alexander, 93
ROBINSON, Cathrina, 81
　Ester, 99
　Esther, 36
　Jane, 85, 95
　John, 36
　Mary, 36
　Ruth, 40
　Samuel, 116
　William, 82
ROBISON, James, 99
　Margaret, 37
RODGERS, John, 106
RODMAN, Rachel, 39
ROGERS, James, 104
　Rev. Dr., 115
ROGLIFF, William, 59
ROLLER, Georg, 83
ROLLETER, Peter, 79, 82
ROLLSTIEG, Dewalt, 58
　Jean, 58
　Ruffi, 58
ROMER, Adam, 53, 54
　Eva, 45
　Rosina, 45, 54
ROMERIN, Rosina, 53
ROSE, Agnes, 92
　John, 82
　Mary, 83
　Rachel, 92
　Ruth, 92
　William, 92
ROSEBURY, John, 12
ROSENMILLER, Ludwig, 56
ROSS, James, 13, 84, 104

Mary, 101
Rebecca, 84
Rosanna, 104
ROTCH, James, 84
ROTH, Catharina, 66
  Christian, 74
  Jacob, 66
  Maria Elisabeth, 66
  Ursula, 74
ROTHAKER,
  Christoph, 67
ROTHAKERN, Anna
  Doroth., 66
ROTHREFT, Henrich, 21
ROTHROCK, John, 84
ROTTSCHEL, Mrs., 57
ROWAN, David, 101
  Margaret, 13
  Mary, 93
  Peggy, 13
  Rebecca, 13
  Stewart, 13
ROWEN, Mary, 13
ROYL, James, 82
RU---, Fredr., 57
RUBBLE, Elizabeth, 23
RUBLE, Jacob, 21
  Michael, 21
RUBLY, A. Maria, 24
  Anna Maria, 24, 63
  Barbara, 25, 63
  Conrad, 24, 63
  Georg, 25, 63
  Henrich, 24, 63
  Jacob, 24, 25, 63
  Joh., 25
  Johannes, 25, 63
  Maria, 25
  Veronica, 24, 63
RUCKER, Veronica, 45
RUDISELLER,
  Barbara, 74
  Jacob, 74
  Johan Godfried, 74
RUFNER, Conrad, 19
  Elizabeth, 19
  Eva, 19
RUGER, Peter, 51

RUGGLES, Thomas, 13
RUMBLE, Henry, 13
RUPLE, Anna, 23
  Anna Maria, 23
  Jac. junior, 23
  Sophia, 23
RUPP, Catharina, 23, 62
  Jonas, 23, 62
RUPPLE, Anna, 26
  Barbara, 22
  Conrad, 22, 62
  Elisabeth, 26
  Jacob, 22
  Magdalena, 22
  Margaret, 22
  Maria, 22
  Veronica, 22
RUPPLY, Jacob, 23, 24, 62, 63
  Maria, 23, 24, 62, 63
RUSSEL, Sarah, 13
RUSSELL, William, 101
RUTH, Maria
  Margreth, 86
RYAN, Agnus, 120
  Alister, 120
  Elizabeth, 120

-S-
SADDORIUS, Josefu, 20
  Josefus, 20
SADLER, Jane, 101
  John, 101
  Richard, 101
SAILER, Catharina, 43
  Johannes, 43
ST. CLAIR, Arthur, 104
SALER, Catharina, 46
  Johannes, 46
  Samuel, 46
SALLATHE, Daniel, 66
  Johannes, 66
  Maria, 66
SALTZGEBER, Caspar, 43
  Catharine, 43

Friedrich, 43
SALZGEBER, Caspar, 41, 51
  Peter, 55
SAMPLE, Joseph, 82
SAMUELS, William, 84
SANDERSON, Grifey, 13
  Jane, 13
  Jean, 118
  Margaret, 13
  Patty, 13, 107
  Robert, 107, 118
  William, 13, 81
SANGER, Eliz., 86
SANNO, F.D., 64
SANSEBEY, Daniel, 50
SARON, James, 101
SAUER, Barbara, 43, 54
  Berhard, 54
  Bernhard, 43
SAUNDERS,
  Christina, 71
  Edward, 71
  Samuel, 71
SAUR, Cathar., 54
  Dorothea, 85
  Maria Elisabeth, 54
SAYE, James, 83
SAYERS, Margaret, 28
SAYLER, John, 71
SAYLOR, Catharina, 44
  Johannes, 44
SCHAAF, Anna
  Dorothea, 44
  Anna Gertraut, 44
  Catharina, 42
  Elisabeth, 44, 45, 48, 53, 54
  Elisabetha, 49
  Jacobus, 49
  Jakob, 49
  Jakobus, 48
  James, 42, 44, 45, 52, 53, 54
  Johann Peter, 53
  Peter, 42, 43, 54

INDEX 159

SCHAAST, Maria
  Elisabeth, 42
  Peter, 42
SCHADE, Maria, 57
SCHADOW, Rahel, 86
SCHAEFER, Daniel,
    68
  Elisabeth, 58, 68
  Jacob, 57
  Samuel, 68
SCHAEFFER, F.D., 21
SCHAEFTER,
  Nicolaus, 23
  Susana, 23
SCHAF, Elisabeth,
    45
  Jacobus, 45
SCHAFER, Abraham,
    60
  Anna Maria, 25,
    64
  Catharina, 57
  Cathrina, 67
  Christina, 25, 64
  Elis., 25, 64
  Elisabeth, 68, 69
  Friedrich David,
    56
  Hanna, 67
  Jacob, 69
  Joh., 25, 64
  Johann Adam, 66
  Johannes, 67
  Peter, 66
  Rosina, 56
  Rudolph, 69
  Samuel, 60, 68
  Susanna, 66
SCHAFERN, Cathrina,
    67
  Susanna, 67
SCHAFERS,
  Elisabeth, 58
SCHAFF, Elisabet,
    46
  Jacobus, 46
SCHAFFER, Anna
  Ferena, 75
  Christina
    Barbara, 76
  Elisabeth, 68
  George Michael,
    76
  Heinrich, 75

Henry, 75
Johannes, 68
Michael, 76
Nicolaus, 62
Samuel, 68
Susana, 62
SCHALLE, Adam, 67
  Catharina
    Elisabeth, 66
  Lucas, 66
SCHALLER, Georg, 46
SCHAMBURG, Barbara,
    25, 64
  Johannes, 25, 64
  Nicolaus, 25, 64
SCHANK, Georg, 86
SCHATTO, Henry, 83
SCHATZ, Jacob, 83
SCHEBEL, Johannes,
    42
SCHELLE, ---, 59
SCHELLI, ---, 59
SCHELPS, ---, 57
SCHIEBEL,
  Friederich, 49
  Margaretha, 49
  Samuel, 49
SCHIELE,
  Elisabetha, 70
  Magdalena, 70
  Michael, 70
SCHINDEL,
  Friedrich, 47
  Johannes, 47
  Margaretha, 47
SCHLEIFFER, Samuel,
    60
SCHLICHTER,
  Cathar., 26
  Catharin
    Elizabet, 22
  Catharina, 22
  Nicolaus, 22
SCHLOSSER, Peter,
    86
SCHMID, Conrad, 21
  Johan Jacob, 21
  Margaretha, 21
  Philip, 20
SCHMIDD, Anna
  Maria, 66
  Dorothea, 66
  Henrich, 66

SCHMIDT, Anna
  Margaretha, 68
  Anna Margreth, 66
  Anna Maria, 58
  David, 67
  Davis, 66
  Dorothea, 68
  Elisabeth, 45,
    53, 58
  Heinrich, 68
  Joh. Wilhelm, 69
  Magdalena, 43
  Marg., 69
  Peter, 69
  Salome, 66
  William, 58
SCHMITH, Anna
  Barbara, 66
  Catharina, 66
  Elisabeth, 66
  Henrich, 66
  Johan, 66
SCHNEBLY, Jacob, 81
  Sarah, 81
SCHNEIDER, Andrew,
    81
  Anna Barbara, 77
  Annamaria, 68
  Balthaser, 65
  Barbara, 42, 65,
    68, 69
  Catharina, 49
  Cathrina, 78
  Elisabeth, 69
  Eliz., 85
  Elizabeth, 77
  Johann Jacob, 78
  Johannes, 42, 49,
    65, 68
  Margretha, 65
  Maria Elisabetha,
    78
  Maria Magdalena,
    65
  Nicklas, 78
  Peter, 77
  Philip, 67, 68,
    69
  Phillipp, 65
  Samuel, 49
  Susanna, 42
SCHNEIDERN,
  Susanna, 65

SCHNEYDER,
    Cathrina, 78
    Elizabth, 77
    Johannes, 77
    Maria Elisab., 72
    Nicklas, 78, 83
    Nicklaus, 77
    Peter, 77
    Philip, 20
    Susanna, 20
SCHNEYER, Anna
    Maria, 77
    Antony, 77
    Nicklaus, 77
SCHNIERLE,
    Margaretha, 55
SCHOCK, Philip, 86
SCHOENBERGER,
    Jacob, 17
    Mary, 17
    Regina, 17
SCHOEPFLE, Susanna, 54
SCHOEPFLEIN, John
    Friedrich, 43
    Susanna, 43
SCHOEPS, Rattschen, 57
SCHOFFEREN,
    Elisabeth, 66
SCHOOP, Catharina, 44
    Margaretha, 44
SCHOOST, Jacob, 41
SCHOPFLE, Susanna, 53
SCHOPFLER,
    Friedrich, 45
    Susanna, 45
SCHOPP, Catharina, 44
    Joh. Nicolaus, 44
SCHRAMM, Anna
    Maria, 56
    Barbara, 56
    Joseph, 56
SCHUCK, Maria
    Margretha, 73
    Mary Margareth, 77
    Mary Margreth, 77
    Peter, 73, 77, 86
SCHUESS, Elizabeth, 77

Peter, 77
Susanna, 77
SCHUEZ, Elizabeth, 78
    Johannes, 78
SCHUK, Johannes, 78
    Mary Margreth, 78
    Peter, 78
SCHULPE, Rottschen, 59
SCHULTEYS,
    Benjamin, 79
    Cathrina, 79
    David, 80
    John, 79
SCHULTZ, A. Maria, 24, 63
    Catharina, 51
    Frid., 24, 63
SCHUMACHER,
    Magdalena, 53
    Margaretha, 53, 54
SCHUMPBER, Conrad, 56
    Iva, 56
SCHUZ, Maria
    Elisabetha, 85
SCHWANFELD,
    Barbara, 22
    Jean, 22
    Susanna, 22
SCHWARDT, Nicolaus, 70
    Sarah, 70
SCHWARTZ,
    Elizabeth, 22
    Johan, 22
    Margarita, 22
    Sophia
    Margaretha, 59
SCHWEITZER,
    Andreas, 69
    Catharina, 69
    Elisabeth, 69
    Maria, 69
SCHWEYGER, Anna
    Christina, 76
    Jonas, 76
    Peter, 76
SCITMORE, Benjamin, 82
SCOT, David, 89
    Margreth, 84

SCOTT, Alexander, 13
    Isabella, 99
    John, 13, 40
    Margt., 100
    Mathew, 114
    Miss, 34
SCROGGS, Allan, 40, 91
    James, 91
    Miriam, 13
SCROGS, Eleanor, 91
    Jean, 91
SCWERT, George, 95
SEARIGHT, Ann, 13
SEELLY, William, 40
SEETIN, Robert, 13
SEHNER, Georg, 21
    Madlena, 21
SEIB, Anna, 19
    Henry, 19
    Jacob, 19
    Magdalena, 19
    Margaret, 19
    Michael, 19
    Peter, 19
SEILER, A. Maria, 68
    Joh., 68
SELANDER,
    Christian, 59
    Johannes, 59
SELL, Dorothea, 79
    George, 79
    Magdalena, 79
SEMPLE, Catharine, 117
    Jean, 109
    John, 96
    Robert, 102, 109
    Sarah, 13
    Steel, 117
SENSEBACH,
    Elisabeth, 56
    Johannes, 58
    John, 56
    Regina, 56, 58
SENSENBACH,
    Elizabeth, 72
    J. Christian, 72
    Mary Margreth, 72
SENZER, Anna
    Apollonia, 72

INDEX 161

Ludwig, 71, 72, 73
Margareth, 72
Margaretha, 71, 72
Margreth, 73
SETTING, Alexander, 85
SEUFER, Elisabeth, 58
SEXTON, Eleanor, 120
Elizabeth, 120
Luke, 120
Margaret, 13
SEYLER, Cathrina, 71, 72
Elizabeth, 74
Ferena, 74
Frederick, 74
Jacob, 74, 84
Johann, 45
Johannes, 53
John Ulrich, 74, 83
Mar. Margr., 72
Margreth, 74
Maria Margareth, 71
Maria Margreth, 72
Mathias, 71, 72
SHADO, Anna Margareth, 73
Heinrich, 73
Maria Cathrina, 73
SHAFER, Elisabeth, 68
Samuel, 68
SHAFERS, Elisabeth, 61
SHAFFER, Anna Cathrina, 85
SHAFT, Elisabetha, 43
Shims, 43
SHALLY, Christian, 85
SHANNON, Agnes, 33
Andrew, 33
Ann, 33
David, 27
Isaac, 35, 40

James, 40
Jane, 35
John, 33, 35
Joseph, 32, 35
Lenard, 27
Leonard, 40
Marg't., 96
Mary, 32, 33, 35, 39
Robert, 35
Samuel, 27
Sarah, 27, 33, 35, 39
Thomas, 99
SHAP, Christoph, 75
Margreth, 75
SHARON, Elizabeth, 13
Isabella, 13
SHARP, David, 40
Elizabeth, 13, 37
Joseph, 101
Mary, 99
SHAVER, Samuel, 106
SHAW, Elizabeth, 101
Jane, 83
Nancy, 13
Philip, 13
SHEEDT, Christina, 43
Jacob, 43
Robert, 43
SHEFFIELD, Miss, 104
SHELDON, Richard, 106
SHEPFLEY, Fredrich, 45
Johann Peter, 43
John Friedrich, 43
Magdalena, 45
Susanna, 43, 45
SHERANG, Elizabeth, 84
Hugh, 83
SHERP, Ferena, 84
SHIELDS, William, 13
SHIPPEN, Elizabeth, 116
Joseph, 116

SHNEBEL, Susannah, 86
SHOAPF, Christian, 45
Elisabetha, 45
James, 45
SHOFE, Jacobus, 47
SHORAH, Abraham, 80
Cathrina, 80
Mary, 84
SHORTIE, Mary, 13
SIBBET, Agnes, 13
Jane, 13
SIEBER, Adam, 44
Elisabeth, 44
Johannes, 44
SIEBERT, Adam, 43
Elisabetha, 43
Johann Adam, 43
SIESS, Sophia, 53, 54
SIEVERT, Adam, 53
Elisabeth, 53
SILLICK, Nancy, 85
SILVERS, Margaret, 13
SIMISON, Samuel, 13, 108
SIMMERAL, Margt., 100
SIMMONDS, William, 110
SIMON, Cathrina, 86
SIMONDS, Jean, 13
SIMONTON, Adam, 13
SIMPSON, Mary, 87
Samuel, 82
Thomas, 83
SIMSON, Jane, 81
Robert, 88
SIMUND, Elizabeth, 13
SISNEY, Margaret, 120
Stephen, 120
Thomas, 120
SKIPTON, Mary, 85
SLEGELL, Susaana, 95
SLOAN, George, 100
Mary, 91, 92
Rachel, 94
SLOANE, James, 13
SLOANS, Jo., 92

SMALL, Eliz., 86
John Adam, 78
SMIELIE, Arch, 92
Mary, 92
Thomas, 92
William, 92
SMILEY, Rachel, 84
Samuel, 13
Thomas, 13
SMITH, Abraham, 119
Ann, 95
Archibald, 40
Betsy, 115
Brice, 13
Cathrina, 81
Christ., 101
Daniel, 87, 88
Dorothy, 13
Elizabeth, 13,
34, 71, 79, 82,
105, 118
Eva, 78
Georg, 78, 83
George, 13, 77,
97
Hannah, 115
Isabella, 13
James, 13, 78,
105, 110, 115
Joh. Jacob, 78
John, 13, 27, 34,
88, 115, 118
Joseph, 101
Josiah, 96
Margaret, 13, 96
Martha, 84
Mary, 34, 79, 83
Maurice, 79
Nancy, 96
Nathaniel, 105
Peggy, 13
Robert, 13, 34,
105
Ruth, 95
Samuel, 88, 89
Sarah, 14, 34, 78
Susanna, 77, 78
Thomas, 14, 95
William, 14, 34
SNIDER, John, 95
SNOTGRASS, James,
82

SNOWDEN, Nathaniel
(Nathanael), 14,
106, 113
Rev., 116
SNYDER, Anna
Barbara, 77
SOMERVILLE, David,
110
SPANGLER,
Elizabeth, 95
SPARR, George, 14
SPATH, Cathrina, 75
Christian, 75
Christine, 75
SPECK, Bernhard, 19
Magdalena, 19
SPEER, Rachel, 99
SPEERS, Sarah, 96
SPENCE, Anne, 39
SPENGLER, Anne
Mar., 57
Magdalena, 57
Peter, 57
SPICKER, Regina, 85
SPIELMAN, Anna
Maria, 41
Elisabeth, 50
Eva, 51, 54
Georg, 41
Jacob, 51, 54
Johann, 51
Wilhelm, 50
SPIES, Elisabeth,
67
Eva, 67
Jo., 67
SPILLMAN, Anna
Maria, 79
George, 79
SPILMAN, Anna
Maria, 54
SPOEDY, Martha, 92
William, 92
SPOTSWOOD,
Catharine, 116
SPOTTSWOOD, Rachel,
14
SPRAY, Susannah, 84
STAHELIN, Abraham,
77
Anna Barbara, 76
Barbara, 77
Cathrina, 75
Eva, 75

Jacob, 77
Martin, 76
Mary Margareth,
76
Melchior, 75
STAHL, Andreas, 47
Anna Margaretha,
47
Anna Maria, 45
Elisabet, 47
Elisabeth, 50,
52, 54
George, 59
Gottfried, 59
Jacob, 54
Jacobus, 52
James, 45
Joseph, 47, 50,
52
Magdalena, 47
Mary Cath., 83
STAIR, Elizabeth,
14
STAMBACH, Anna
Elisabetha, 42
Barbara, 55
Catharina, 41,
43, 46
Elisabeth, 43,
46, 47
Elisabetha, 49
Elizabeth, 79
Friederich, 49
Gertraut, 43
Jacob, 42, 43
James, 42
Johannes, 43
Lorentz, 42
Magdalene, 42
Margaretha, 42
Maria Catharina,
42
Peter, 41, 42,
43, 46, 47, 49
Phillip, 43
Susanna, 42
STAMBACHER,
Catharina, 55
STAMBAUGH,
Catharina, 42
Peter, 42
STAMPACH, Anna
Gertraut, 44
Anna Gertrud, 53

Anna Margaretha, 44
Catharina, 44
Elisabeth, 44, 45, 53, 54
Friedrich, 52, 53
Jacob, 44
Johann Friedrich, 53
Magdalena, 44
Peter, 44, 52, 53, 54
STARK, Carl, 74
Dorothea, 71, 73
Isaac, 99
Johannes, 71, 73
Ludwig, 71
Maria Dorothea, 73
STARS, John, 33
STATSKOCH, John, 71
Theo. A. Isabel, 71
STAUFFER, Magd., 85
STECK, Anna Maria, 55
STECT, Anna Catharina, 66
STEEL, Frances, 82
Jean, 14, 84
John, 119
Joseph, 106, 111
Margaret, 106
Mary, 40, 101
Omelia, 14
Robert, 40
William, 14
STEEN, James, 35
STEERN, Maria Magdalena, 65
STEGMULLER, A.
Elisabeth, 25, 64
Elis., 64
Polly, 64
Valentine, 25, 64
Willh., 64
STEIFESOHN, Anna Maria, 57
STEIFFESON, Cathrina, 57
STEIN, Anna Maria, 73
John Adam, 73

STEINBERGER, Johann Adam, 67
Margreth, 67
Peter, 67
STEINBRINDT,
Eleonora, 21
Henrich, 21
Johannes, 21
STEINBRING,
Eleanor, 22
Johan Wilhelm, 22
John Henrich, 22
STEITZ, John, 19
STENZ, Anna Cathrina, 77
Cathrina, 77
John Heinrich, 78
Leonhard, 77
Mar. Elizabeth, 77
STEPHENS, Hugh, 60
STEPHENSON,
Elizabeth, 32, 38
Isabella, 14
James, 40
Jane, 32
Jean, 14
Nancy, 14
Polley, 14
Rebecca, 14
William, 32
STERRAT, John, 100
STERRET, Bryce T., 32
David, 32, 100
Elizabeth, 32
John, 32
Mary, 31
Rachel, 32
Robert, 32
William, 32
STERRETT, Benjamin, 40
David, 105
Elizabeth, 40
Genny, 14
James, 40
John, 14
Nancy, 14, 107
Ralph, 107, 110
STEUART, Margaret, 101

STEVENS, Eleanor, 14
Isabella, 14, 97
Thomas, 110
STEVENSON,
Catherin, 96
George, 104
James, 32, 84
Mary, 106
STEWART, Eleanor, 35
Elijah, 93
James, 35
John, 14
Marjory, 93
Martha, 14
Mary, 14
Robert, 14, 93
Samuel, 93
Sarah, 14
Widow, 39
William, 95
STHORMINGER,
Barbara, 50
Jacob, 50
Susanna, 50
STIMMECKIE,
Charles, 118
STOFER, Hinrich, 57
Mar. Magdalena, 57
STOFFELMAN, Marg.
Barbara, 85
STONE, Ann, 14
John, 14
STOPELSE, Sarah, 57
STORY, Mary, 100
STRAHN, Margt., 99
STRAINE, James, 97
William, 95
STRATTLE, Edward, 99
STREHON, Mary, 92
STREITH, Eliz., 81
STRICKER, An.
Marg., 83
Barbara, 76
Cathrina, 76
Jacob, 76, 85
Lorenz, 76
STRIGLEDER,
Elisabetha, 42
Georg, 42
Henrich, 42

STRIKER, Barbara,
    76
  Lorenz, 76
STRONG, Francis,
    24, 63
  Jenny, 24, 63
  Joseph, 24, 63
STRUBELIN,
  Elisabeth, 57
STUART, Charles, 23
  Henry, 23, 62
  Isabella, 23, 62
  Jacob, 97, 101
  James, 104
  Margaret, 91
  Mary, 87
  Patty, 106
  William, 23, 62
STUARTH, Charles,
    85
STUCKE, Martin, 68
STUCKI, Fridrich,
    58
STUKKI, Anna, 59
  Friedrich, 59
STUM, Adam, 77
  Elizabeth, 77
STUMM, Apollonia,
    58
  Catarina, 58
  Jacob, 58
STUMP, Adam, 77
  Elizabeth, 77, 78
  Joh. Adam, 78
  Johan Adam, 78
  Maria Magdalena,
    78
  Maria Margretha,
    78
  Philip, 78
  Susanna, 77
STURT, Maria, 20
  William, 20
STYLES, Eleanor, 14
SULLY, George, 35
SWANSIE, Henry, 91
  Jean, 91
  Martha, 92
SWEENEY, Margaret,
    14
SWEINER, Barbara,
    14
SWEIZER, George, 86
  Jacob, 86

SWENEY, Charles, 14
  Hugh, 14
SWILEHAN, Andrew,
    120
  John, 120
  Mary, 120
SWINGEL, George, 14
SWINGLER, George,
    97
SWOPE, Gilbert
    Ernest, 27
  Kitty, 117
SYLER, Ferena, 73
  Jacob, 73
SYMENTON, Robert,
    89

-T-
TALBART, John, 29
TATE, James, 87
  Marg't., 95
TAYLOR, Andrew, 40
  Barbara, 93
  Elenor, 33
  Elizabeth, 82
  George, 33, 93
  John, 91, 93
  Martha, 93
  Mr., 34
  Nancy, 33
  Sam, 93
  Thomas, 82
TEMPLE, Jean, 14
TEMPLETON,
  Elizabeth, 14
  James, 101
THIEL, George, 53
THOMAH, Durst, 85
  Elis., 85
THOMAS, Adam, 25,
    64
  Anna Maria, 21
  Cath., 25, 64
  Cathrina, 86
  Elisabet, 25, 64
  Marthin, 21
  Ursula, 21
THOMPSON
  ---, 14
  Alexander, 36
  Andrew, 33
  Ann, 36
  Ann Elizabeth, 73
  Betsy, 103

David, 116
Elizabeth, 14,
    84, 117
Ellenor, 36
General, 103
George, 103
Gitty, 117
Hannah, 33, 39
Hugh, 33, 36
James, 14, 83, 86
James W., 33
Jane, 36
Janet, 98
Jean, 111
Leacy, 36, 39
Margaret, 14
Maria, 14, 103
Mary, 33
Mary Ann, 33
Matthew, 36, 40
Moses, 97, 101
Parson, 107
Peggy, 36
Rev., 103, 111,
    117
Robert, 96
Sally, 73
Samuel, 33, 83,
    98, 103
Susanna, 36, 107
Susannah, 112
William, 14, 36,
    73, 117, 101
THOMSON, W., 92
  William, 89
THORN, Esther, 91
  James, 91, 93
  Margaret, 93
THORNBURGH, Cath.,
    95
THORPS, Elizabeth,
    101
THOUGHLY, Georg, 84
TIWITTE, Barbara,
    22
  Elizabeth, 22
  Jacob, 22
  Maj., 22
TOMLINSON, John, 81
  Joseph, 81
  Mary, 81
  Rebecca, 81
TONGUE, John, 14

TRABINGER, Eva, 25, 64
  Henr., 25, 64
  Johannes, 25, 64
TRECKSLER, Fronica, 54
TREES, Andrew, 78
  Elizabeth, 78
  Rosina, 78
TREIBER, Anna Elisabeth, 23, 62
  Casper, 23, 62
  Elisabeth, 23, 62
TREISCH, Anna Maria, 48
  Catharina, 48, 49
  David, 52
  Elisabeth, 48
  Jacob, 48
  Jakob, 49
  Johannes, 49
  Maria, 52
  Nelle, 54
  Peter, 48, 49
  Reichert, 54
  Susanna, 52
TREISCHT, Jacob, 54
TREISER, John, 51
  Maria, 51
TREMBLE, Rebecca, 14
TREWER, Jacob, 86
TREXLER, Anna Margaretha, 47
  Elisabet, 46
  Elisabeth, 43, 45, 47
  Jacob, 43
  Magdalena, 46
  Michael, 43, 45, 46, 47
  Peter, 48
  Susanna, 45
TREYSCH, Susanna, 55
TRIMBLE, George, 14
TRINDLE, Alexander, 14, 106
  John, 14
  Sarah, 106
  William, 106

TRISSLER,
  Catharina, 48, 49
  Elisabeth, 49
  Georg, 48
  George, 49
  Susanna, 48
TROUT, Harold K., 41
TRUUNG, Philip, 50
  Samuel, 50
TSCHAN, Christina, 62
  Maria, 62
  Smick, 62
TUMMLER, Maria Catharina, 56
TURNBULL, William, 106
TURNER, Adam, 89
  James, 37, 84
  John, 34
  Joseph, 34
  Martha, 84
  Mary, 34, 37
  Sally, 14, 34

-U-
ULTCH, Andrew, 79
  Ann, 79
UMBERGER, Adam, 86
  Johannes, 53
UMBERGERIN,
  Susanna, 53
UNGER, Anna Maria, 51
  George, 51
URIE, John, 15
  Thomas, 15, 107
UROTH, Robert Mason, 15
URY, Frantz, 78
  Franz, 78

-V-
VAN HORN, Annie, 31
  Joseph, 31
VANCE, Mary, 99
VANDERBELT,
  Cornelius, 40
VANHORN, Joseph, 40
VATTEN, Johni, 52
  Julianna, 52
  Margareth, 52

VELDE, Catharina, 22
  Jacob Freidrich, 22, 23
  Maria Elizabeth, 22
VELDER, Catarine, 23
VERDIER, James, 71, 80
  Jaques, 71
  Paul, 80
  Susanna, 80
  Susannah, 71, 80
VERNON, Christian, 95
VIHMAN, Conrad, 78
  Margretha, 78
VOGELGESANG,
  Catharina, 50
  Elisabeth, 55
  Jacob, 50, 55
  Maria Margar., 55
VOGELGESANGER,
  Elisabeth, 54
  Jacob, 54
VOGELSANG, Jacob, 50
  Johannes, 50
  Magdalena, 50
VOGELSGESANG,
  Jacob, 61
VOGHT, Eva, 76
  Jonas, 76
VOGT, Elisabeth, 54
  Heinrich, 54
  Magdal., 54
  Veronica, 48
VOLTZ, Christian, 48
  Jacob, 48
  Stina, 48

-W-
WABER, Elisabetha, 43
Wandel, 43
WADDEL, Margaret, 15
  William, 101
WADE, Gilbert, 15
WAGENER, Anna Dorothee, 66

Anna Maria, 57, 66
David, 67
Maria, 66
Michael, 57
Philip, 66
WAGNER, Anna Margr., 67
Anna Mary, 18
Elisabeth, 57
Henry, 18
John, 18
Maria, 67
Mich., 60, 67
Michel, 67
WAGNERN, Maria, 60
WAGONER, Adam, 74
Rosina, 74
WAGSTAS, Charity, 30
William, 30
WAIT, Andrew, 82
WAL..., Mary, 92
W., 92
WALD, Cath., 70
Catharina, 69
David, 70
Henrich, 69, 70
Joh. Georg, 69
WALKER, ---, 38
Andrew, 28, 86
Betsey, 15
Betsy, 28
Elizabeth, 15, 27, 28
Hannah, 15, 28, 93
Isabel, 28
James, 15, 27, 28, 33, 37
Jane, 27, 28, 33, 40
John, 15, 28, 92, 95
John Jr., 93
Jonathan, 93
Joseph, 28, 93
Margaret, 15, 28
Mary, 28, 38
Rachel, 27, 28, 38
Robert, 28
Samuel, 28, 99

William, 27, 82, 91, 92
WALKERS, David, 92
W., 92
WALKTER, Groyn, 92
William, 92
WALL, Elizabeth, 75
John, 75
Mary, 75
William, 75
WALLACE, Agnes, 38
Elizabeth, 33
Hannah, 15, 82, 90
Hugh, 40
James, 89
John, 33, 114
Patrick, 40
Rachel, 15
William, 102, 106
WALLICK, Magdalena, 60
WALSH, John, 120
Joseph, 120
Margaret, 120
WALTE, Anna Maria, 67
Casp., 59
Catharina, 67
Hinr., 67
Hinrich, 59
WALTER, Abraham, 74
Andreas, 50
Jacob, 49, 50, 74
Johannes, 49
Juliana, 74
Magdalena, 49, 50
WALTERS, Jacob, 15, 106
WALTON, Roger, 120
Sarah, 120
WARD, Eleonora, 86
James, 89
WARDEN, Mary, 96
WARMS, Cathar., 57
WARNER, George, 15
WARRINGTON, William, 27
WATSON, Jenny, 82
Joseph, 15
Rebecca, 15
WATTMAN, Elizabeth, 85
WATTS, David, 111

WAUGH, Martha, 15
Rev., 115, 116, 118
Samuel, 15, 108, 113, 118
WAYER, John, 80
Mary, 80
WEAKLEY, Hetty, 98
James, 98, 111
Jane, 15, 98
Jean, 111
Margaret, 118
Nat., 118
Rebecca, 15, 112
Samuel, 98
WEARAH, Anna, 79
Georg, 79
WEARY, Anna, 50
WEBBER, John, 110
WEBER, Benjamin, 43
Catharina, 56
Catharina, 23, 62
Christina, 44
Conrath, 23, 62
Elisabeth, 17, 44
Elizabeth, 43, 44
Jacob, 17, 56
Joh. Georg, 23, 62
Johann, 44
Joseph, 56
Philip, 17
Wendel, 43, 44
WEBSTER, William, 15
WEGELIN, Philip, 84
WEIR, Ruth, 100
WEIRICH, Fallentin, 42
WEISE, Catharine, 110
George, 110
WEISER, Anna Catharina, 44
Anna Maria, 23, 51
Christian, 43, 44, 45
Jacob, 83
Johann, 51
Johannes, 23
John, 52
Justina, 23
Maria, 52

INDEX

Susanna, 43, 44, 45, 52
WEISMAN, Elisabeth, 81
  Eva, 81
  Johanes, 81
  Molly, 81
WEISS, Catharine, 17
  Cathrina, 80
  Christina, 17
  Eva, 69
  Felix, 17
  Fred., 80
  Jacob, 42, 80, 116
  Joh. Adam, 69
  Mrs., 116
WEISSEN, Cath., 57
  Magdalena, 57
WELSCH, Dan, 60
  Sarah, 60
WELSH, Georg, 84
  Sarah, 84
WENRICH, Susanna, 66
WERFELL, Benjamin, 64
  George, 64
  Maria, 64
WERFTEL, Benjamin, 25
  George, 25
  Maria, 25
WERN, Conrad, 53
WERNAN, Mary Gertraut, 86
  Mary Gertrud, 78
WERNER, Barbara, 76
  Conrad, 53
  Elizabeth, 76
  Heinrich, 53
  Jacob, 76
  Matte, 66
  Phil., 66
  Philip, 66
WERNS, Catharine, 19, 20
  George, 19, 20
  Julyeriel, 20
WEST, Dorothy, 120
  Edward, 15, 120
  Francis, 120
  Maria, 66

WESTON, Richard, 15
WETHERHOLD,
  Charles, 76
  Susannah, 76
WEYERMANN, Gertrut, 59
  Henry, 59
  William, 60
WEYGAND, Magdalena, 24, 63
WEYTH, Alexander, 24, 63
  Greth, 24, 63
WHARTON, Susanna, 25, 64
  Thomas, 25, 64
WHIGHAM, Robert, 93
  Thomas, 93
  William, 93
WHITE, Francis, 15
  Jane, 83
  Mary, 15
  Nancy, 15
  Saln., 83
  Sarah, 15
  Thomas, 15
WHITEHILL, Polly, 97
  Rachel, 15
WHITELOCK, Eliza, 38
WICKEY, Fried., 59
WIDDAIN, Polle, 59
WIDMER, Jacob, 46
  Margaretha, 46
  Maria, 54
WIDTRINGER,
  Christina, 41
  Michael, 41
  William, 41
WIER, ---, 95
  Alexander, 36
WILD, Catharina, 21, 24, 63
  Georg, 24, 63
  George, 21
  Sara, 24, 63
WILEY, John, 88
  Robert, 87
WILKINS, John, 96, 108
  Mary, 15
  Nancy, 108

WILLCOCK,
  Elizabeth, 83
WILLIAMS, Edward, 15
  Eva, 81
  Isaac, 15
  John, 83, 101, 108
  Joseph, 95
  Margaret, 108
  Matthew, 81
  William, 81
WILLIAMSON, David, 35
  Polly, 15
  Prudence, 83
  Samuel, 35
WILLS, John, 15
WILLSON, Ennis, 84
  Mary, 82
  Nathaniel, 87
  William, 81, 84
WILMSEN, Elisabeth, 57
WILSON, James, 119
  James Armstrong, 104
  Margaret, 119
  Rev., 115
WILSON, Ann, 36
  Elizabeth, 15, 29
  Georg, 61
  Henry, 15
  James, 28, 91, 119
  James Armstrong, 104
  Jenny, 15
  John, 95
  Joseph, 36
  Lathie, 28
  Margaret, 28, 119
  Martha, 15
  Mary, 28, 36
  Matthew, 29
  Nancy, 60
  Peter, 91
  Rev., 115
  Robert, 60
  Samuel, 15, 28, 29, 37, 40, 99
  Thomas, 99
  William, 15, 28, 36

WILT, Anna Maria,
  43
  Johannes, 43
  John, 36
  Maria Elisabetha,
  43
WILZ, Anna Maria,
  21
  Emmerich, 21
WIMP, John, 96
WINDT, Margaretha,
  47
  Michael, 47
WINT, Jacob, 42
  Margaretha, 42
  Michael, 42
  Nicholas, 42
WINTERBALD,
  Bernhart, 51
  Elisabeth, 49, 51
  Jacob, 49, 51
  Lenhart, 51
WIRBEL, Elizabeth,
  80
  Johannes, 80
WIRTH, Eva
  Elizabeth, 79
  Joh. Adam, 79
  Johan Peter, 79
WISE, George, 112
WITHEREW, ---, 100
WITHEROW, Richard,
  100
WITHERSPOON,
  Thomas, 98
WITMAIER, Catarina,
  68
  Catharina, 68
  Johan Georg, 68
  Johannes, 68
  Stophel, 68
WITMEIER,
  Catharina, 68
  Stophel, 68
WITMER, Anna Maria,
  43
  Jacob, 43
  Johannes, 43
  Maria, 51
WITMEYER,
  Catharina, 68
  Elisabeth, 68
  Stophel, 68

WITTMAIER,
  Christoph, 67
WITTMAYR, Catarina,
  68
  Christopel, 68
WITTMEIER, Stoffel,
  59
WITTMEIJER,
  Cathrina, 59
WITTMER, Elisabeth,
  54
  Maria, 54
  Veronica, 22
WOLF, Abraham, 24,
  63
  Daniel, 18
  Elisabeth, 25, 64
  Elizabeth, 83
  George, 25, 64
  Henry, 17
  John, 17
  John Jacob, 19
  Molly, 17
WOLFF, Elizabeth,
  19, 75
  George Michael,
  59
  Hannah, 75, 76
  Jacob, 20
  John George, 19
  John Jacob, 19
  John Martin, 20
  Magdalena, 58
  Margaret
  Elizabeth, 19
  Margr., 26
  Peter, 75, 76
WOLFFEN, Christina,
  66
WOLFFLY, Anna
  Maria, 75
  Cathrina, 74
  Conrad, 74
  Ludwig, 74
WOLSSNER, Adam, 54
  Eva, 54
WOOD, Jane, 96
WOODART, John, 109
WOODBURN, James, 40
  Matthew, 40
WOODFINE, John, 86
WOODRUFF, Anthony,
  40

WOODS, Elizabeth,
  85
  Isabel, 29
  Jane, 29, 30
  Jenny, 30
  John, 29, 30
  Joseph, 29
  Mary, 30, 38
  Mary Ann, 15
  Nathan, 15, 30,
  111
  Peggy, 15
  Polly, 29
  Richard, 29
  Robert, 29
  Samuel, 30
  William, 30, 115
WOODWARD, Jehu, 15
  Sergt. Benj., 15
WORK, Alexander,
  15, 36
  Elizabeth, 36, 39
  James, 36
  John, 36
  Letty, 40
  Mary, 36
  S., 36
  Susanna, 36, 39
  William, 15, 36,
  97
WORLE, Christofer
  David, 59
WORLEY, Francis, 84
WORMLE, Anna Maria,
  21
  Catharina, 25, 64
  Elis., 25, 64
  Elisabeth, 21,
  23, 62
  Georg, 21, 25, 64
  J. Georg, 21
  Jacob, 23, 62
  Johannes, 21
  Johannes Georg,
  21
  Maria, 25, 64
  Maria Catharina,
  21
WORMLING, Johannes,
  21
WORMLY, Abraham,
  25, 63
  Catharina, 24
  David, 25, 63

Elisabeth, 24, 25, 62, 63
Engelhard, 24, 63
Engelhardt, 24, 25, 63
Engelhart, 24
Englehardt, 24
Englehart, 62
Georg, 24, 63
Georg Elter, 24, 62
Jacob, 24, 63
Joh., 25
Joh. Georg, 24
Joh. Jacob, 24, 63
Johannes, 23, 62, 63
Johannes Georg, 24, 63
Maria, 23, 24, 25, 62, 63
Susana, 24, 63
WORRAL, Isaak, 84
WORSTIN, John, 18
Julie, 18
Samuel, 18
WOULDS, Elizabeth, 74
Peter, 74
WRIGHT, Jennet, 36
John, 36, 82
Margaret, 36
Robert, 16, 115
Susanah, 95
William, 83
WUEST, Alexander, 17
Elisabeth, 17
Jacob, 17
WULDS, Elizabeth, 74
Peter, 74
WULTZ, Jun., 75
Nanct, 75
Peter, 75
WUMMELDORF, Eva, 62
WUNDERLICH, Elizabeth, 77
John, 77
WURMLE, Engehart, 21
WURZBACHER, Anna Margreth, 73

George Fred., 71, 73
Johann Philip, 71
Johannes, 73
Margaretha, 71
WYLE, John, 84
WYLEY, Margaret, 100

-Y-
YERG, Adam, 77
Johan Adam, 77
Mary Sophia, 77
YORK, John, 82
YOUNG, Agnes, 93
Alexander, 93
Betsy, 38
Elizabeth, 103
Eva, 80
Hannah, 84
James, 95, 98, 103
Johan Christian, 80
John, 40
Joseph, 16
Margaret, 39, 93
Mary, 16
Peter, 80
Samuel, 79
Sarah, 16

-Z-
ZEAGLER, David, 104
ZETTEL, Catharina, 51, 52
Conrad, 51
Jacob, 51, 52
Wilhelm, 52
ZIEGLER, Anna Maria, 44, 73
Betsy, 17
Cathrin, 61
Elizabet, 17
Henry, 17
Jacobina, 17
Joh. Georg, 73
Johan Georg, 73
John, 17
John Philip, 17
Sabina, 17
ZIMMER, Anna Maria, 58

ZINDMEYER, Magdalena, 86
ZIRIACY, Anna Maria, 75
Elisabeth, 75
Samuel, 75
ZOLLER, Barbara, 79
ZUBBER, Andreas, 47
George, 47
Johannes, 47
Maria, 47
ZUBER, Andreas, 21
Elisabeth, 21, 46
Elisabetha, 48
Elizabeth, 47
George (Georg), 21, 46, 47, 48
Johann Jacob, 46
Johannes, 47
Johannes Wilhelm, 48
ZUFALL, John Jacob, 86
ZUMBER, Conrad, 56
Eva, 56

Other books by F. Edward Wright:

Abstracts of Bucks County, Pennsylvania Wills, 1685-1785
Abstracts of Cumberland County, Pennsylvania Wills, 1750-1785
Abstracts of Cumberland County, Pennsylvania Wills, 1785-1825
Abstracts of Philadelphia County Wills, 1726-1747
Abstracts of Philadelphia County Wills, 1748-1763
Abstracts of Philadelphia County Wills, 1763-1784
Abstracts of Philadelphia County Wills, 1777-1790
Abstracts of Philadelphia County Wills, 1790-1802
Abstracts of Philadelphia County Wills, 1802-1809
Abstracts of Philadelphia County Wills, 1810-1815
Abstracts of Philadelphia County Wills, 1815-1819
Abstracts of Philadelphia County Wills, 1820-1825
Abstracts of Philadelphia County, Pennsylvania Wills, 1682-1726
Abstracts of South Central Pennsylvania Newspapers, Volume 1, 1785-1790
Abstracts of South Central Pennsylvania Newspapers, Volume 3, 1796-1800
Abstracts of the Newspapers of Georgetown and the Federal City, 1789-99
Abstracts of York County, Pennsylvania Wills, 1749-1819
Bucks County, Pennsylvania Church Records of the 17th and 18th Centuries Volume 2: Quaker Records: Falls and Middletown Monthly Meetings
Anna Miller Watring and F. Edward Wright
Caroline County, Maryland Marriages, Births and Deaths, 1850-1880
Citizens of the Eastern Shore of Maryland, 1659-1750
Cumberland County, Pennsylvania Church Records of the 18th Century
Delaware Newspaper Abstracts, Volume 1: 1786-1795
Early Charles County, Maryland Settlers, 1658-1745
Marlene Strawser Bates and F. Edward Wright
Early Church Records of Alexandria City and Fairfax County, Virginia
F. Edward Wright and Wesley E. Pippenger
Early Church Records of New Castle County, Delaware, Volume 1, 1701-1800
Frederick County Militia in the War of 1812
Sallie A. Mallick and F. Edward Wright
Inhabitants of Baltimore County, 1692-1763
Land Records of Sussex County, Delaware, 1769-1782
Land Records of Sussex County, Delaware, 1782-1789
Elaine Hastings Mason and F. Edward Wright
Marriage Licenses of Washington, District of Columbia, 1811-1830
Marriages and Deaths from the Newspapers of Allegany and Washington Counties, Maryland, 1820-1830
Marriages and Deaths from The York Recorder, 1821-1830
Marriages and Deaths in the Newspapers of Frederick and Montgomery Counties, Maryland, 1820-1830

Marriages and Deaths in the Newspapers of Lancaster County, Pennsylvania, 1821-1830
Marriages and Deaths in the Newspapers of Lancaster County, Pennsylvania, 1831-1840
Marriages and Deaths of Cumberland County, [Pennsylvania], 1821-1830
Maryland Calendar of Wills Volume 9: 1744-1749
Maryland Calendar of Wills Volume 10: 1748-1753
Maryland Calendar of Wills Volume 11: 1753-1760
Maryland Calendar of Wills Volume 12: 1759-1764
Maryland Calendar of Wills Volume 13: 1764-1767
Maryland Calendar of Wills Volume 14: 1767-1772
Maryland Calendar of Wills Volume 15: 1772-1774
Maryland Calendar of Wills Volume 16: 1774-1777
Maryland Eastern Shore Newspaper Abstracts, Volume 1: 1790-1805
Maryland Eastern Shore Newspaper Abstracts, Volume 2: 1806-1812
Maryland Eastern Shore Newspaper Abstracts, Volume 3: 1813-1818
Maryland Eastern Shore Newspaper Abstracts, Volume 4: 1819-1824
Maryland Eastern Shore Newspaper Abstracts, Volume 5: Northern Counties, 1825-1829
F. Edward Wright and Irma Harper
Maryland Eastern Shore Newspaper Abstracts, Volume 6: Southern Counties, 1825-1829
Maryland Eastern Shore Newspaper Abstracts, Volume 7: Northern Counties, 1830-1834
Irma Harper and F. Edward Wright
Maryland Eastern Shore Newspaper Abstracts, Volume 8: Southern Counties, 1830-1834
Maryland Militia in the Revolutionary War
S. Eugene Clements and F. Edward Wright
Newspaper Abstracts of Allegany and Washington Counties, Maryland, 1811-1815
Newspaper Abstracts of Cecil and Harford Counties, Maryland, 1822-1830
Newspaper Abstracts of Frederick County, Maryland, 1816-1819
Newspaper Abstracts of Frederick County, Maryland, 1811-1815
Sketches of Maryland Eastern Shoremen
Tax List of Chester County, Pennsylvania 1768
Tax List of York County, Pennsylvania 1779
Washington County Church Records of the 18th Century, 1768-1800
Western Maryland Newspaper Abstracts, Volume 1: 1786-1798
Western Maryland Newspaper Abstracts, Volume 2: 1799-1805
Western Maryland Newspaper Abstracts, Volume 3: 1806-1810
Wills of Chester County, Pennsylvania, 1766-1778

www.ingramcontent.com/pod-product-compliance
Lightning Source LLC
Chambersburg PA
CBHW060656100426
42734CB00047B/1946